Handbook of
Group Therapy

Handbook of
Group Therapy

Edited by

Martin Grotjahn, M.D.
Frank M. Kline, M.D.
Claude T.H. Friedmann, M.D.

 VAN NOSTRAND REINHOLD COMPANY
NEW YORK   CINCINNATI   TORONTO   LONDON   MELBOURNE

Manufactured in the United States of America

Published by Van Nostrand Reinhold Company Inc.
135 West 50th Street, New York, N.Y. 10020

Van Nostrand Reinhold Publishing
1410 Birchmount Road
Scarborough, Ontario M1P 2E7, Canada

Van Nostrand Reinhold Australia Pty. Ltd.
17 Queen Street
Mitcham, Victoria 3132, Australia

Van Nostrand Reinhold Company Limited
Molly Millars Lane
Wokingham, Berkshire, England

15 14 13 12 11 10 9 8 7 6 5 4 3 2

Library of Congress Cataloging in Publication Data

Grotjahn, Martin.
    A handbook of group therapy.

    Includes index.
    1. Group psychotherapy. I. Kline, Frank M.
II. Friedmann, Claude T.H. III. Title.
RC488.G667   616.89′152   81-21865
ISBN 0-442-21939-3   AACR2

Contributors

Martin Grotjahn, M.D.
Professor Emeritus of Psychiatry
University of Southern California
Los Angeles, California

Frank M. Kline, M.D.
Clinical Professor of Psychiatry
University of California at Irvine
Irvine, California

Claude T.H. Friedmann, M.D.
Assistant Professor of Psychiatry
University of California at Irvine
Irvine, California

GUEST CONTRIBUTORS
(In Alphabetical Order)

Marion V. Anker, Ph.D.
Research Associate in Psychiatry
University of California at Los Angeles
Los Angeles, California

Rodney Burgoyne, M.D.
Professor of Clinical Psychiatry
University of Southern California
Los Angeles, California

Carlene Copelan, M.D.
Clinical Instructor of Psychiatry
University of Southern California
Los Angeles, California

Stuart Fine, M.B., F.R.C.P. (C)
Associate Professor of Psychiatry
University of British Columbia
Vancouver, British Columbia

Charles V. Ford, M.D.
Professor of Psychiatry
Vanderbilt University
Nashville, Tennesee

Walter Heuler, M.D.
Clinical Instructor of Psychiatry
University of California at Irvine
Irvine, California

Edward Kaufman, M.D.
Associate Professor of Psychiatry
University of California at Irvine
Irvine, California

Ira Lesser, M.D.
Assistant Professor of Psychiatry
University of California at Los Angeles
Los Angeles, California

Zhong-Yi Liu, M.D.
Visiting Professor of Psychiatry and
  Neurology
University of California at Irvine
Irvine, California

Tracey McCarley, M.D.
Associate Clinical Professor of
  Psychiatry
Univeristy of California at Los Angeles
Los Angeles, California

Samuel Miles, M.D.
Assistant Clincical Professor of
  Psychiatry
University of California at Los Angeles
Los Angeles, California

Fred Staples, Ph.D.
Associate Professor of Psychiatry
University of Southern California
Los Angeles, California

Alan Steinberg, Ph.D.
Research Associate in Psychiatry
University of California at Los Angeles
Los Angeles, California

George Wolkon, Ph.D.
Associate Professor of Psychiatry
University of Southern California
Los Angeles, California

Joe Yamamoto, M.D.
Professor of Psychiatry
University of California at Los Angeles
Los Angeles, California

Preface

Group psychotherapy has developed into a major psychiatric treatment modality, often replacing individual therapy as the treatment of choice. This is especially so in psychiatric institutions and general medical hospitals. Indications and contraindications for group treatment have also clearly changed: Many therapists no longer ask which treatment, individual or group, may be indicated for a patient. They now ask: What kind of group treatment?

The history of group therapy begins during World War II, when the treatment proved its merits in military psychiatric hospitals. Group therapy then developed into a treatment used in the office practice of psychotherapy and is now a major therapeutic tool in hospitals and outpatient clinics. New group treatment modalities continue to develop according to the different and emerging needs of hospitals and patients, since group therapy has proven useful with patients in all age groups and diagnostic categories.

While previous books on groups have mainly emphasized theory and technique in relation to small, slow-moving groups with a very select population of psychoneurotic patients, our book provides the clinician and student with a broader and deeper perspective of group treatment. The book is divided into six parts. In Part I, we summarize the key literature, theory, and techniques that underlie all group therapies. Part II explores, from detailed historical, theoretical, and clinical viewpoints, the essentials of group therapy for both children and adults on psychiatric wards. Part III, in addition to a discussion of the "insight" group, discusses group therapy for patients in acute crisis and special groups for chronic, long-term patients. In Part IV, we look at the growing area of liaison psychiatry, stressing techniques applicable to medical and surgical patients, special types of patients such as the aged, and the staff who treat them. Part V is rather unique: It describes how one actually teaches group therapy and uses groups to allow for growth and development among staff and students. Part VI explores the question of group versus individual therapy and examines the role of the group therapist as a person. It also contains a chapter about group therapy in the People's Republic of China.

The authors have a collective clinical experience with group therapies of over 70 years, and all three have written extensively in this area. Dr. Grotjahn is Professor Emeritus of Psychiatry at the University of Southern California; Dr. Kline is Professor of Psychiatry at the University of California at Irvine and Chief of Psychiatry at the Long Beach Veterans Administration Medical Center. Dr. Friedmann was Director of the Crisis and Outpatient Clinic and Assistant Professor of Psychiatry at the Harbor-UCLA Medical Center. He is currently Assistant Professor and Director of Psychiatric Education at the University of California at Irvine. In addition to these writers, the authors have selected several "guest contributors" with special areas of expertise.

Martin Grotjahn, M.D.
Frank M. Kline, M.D.
Claude T.H. Friedmann, M.D.

Contents

Part I:
Basic Concepts

1
Basic Concepts of Group Therapy

Martin Grotjahn, M.D.

Group therapy started with small, slow, open groups of six to eight people, often conducted by analytically trained therapists and based on concepts originally formed in the field of individual psychoanalysis.

It is assumed that dynamic group therapy constitutes the basic model of group therapy and its concepts help us understand the therapeutic process in groups as they are conducted in hospitals and outpatient clinics—in which they often are developed, by necessity, far away from the original analytic model.

The basic analytic concepts are transference, resistance, and interpretation with the aim of mastery of outer and inner reality, which includes free communication with the unconscious.

TRANSFERENCE

There is a principal difference between the transference neurosis in the dual relationships of standard psychoanalysis and transference phenomena in groups. Three trends of transference in groups can be differentiated: One transference relationship is to the central figure, the therapist, which is similar to the transference neurosis in psychoanalysis; the second transference relationship is extended to the peers in the group, and forms an important therapeutic agent; the third transference develops in later stages of the therapeutic group process and that is the transference to the whole group as an early, preoedipal mother.

Analysis of the transference neurosis has become the center of standard analysis (a term preferable to "classical" or "orthodox" analysis). It seems as if a fully developed transference neurosis tends to become unmanageable and often unanalyzable. Attempts to dissolve such regressive transference neurosis become more and more time consuming, prolonging the duration of analysis. The transference neurosis has a magic power, almost like hypnosis; it is modeled after the early mother-infant symbiosis and is often more tenacious than the original infantile neurosis.

Anna Freud,[1] in a dialogue with S. H. Foulkes, considered such development a technical mistake, probably due to an unconscious need in some analysts who want to be mothers and invite their patients to develop an intense infantile dependency. According to S. H. Foulkes's[2] observations, such transference neurosis is not just a mistake but an inherent danger of standard analysis. This has been recognized by analysts such as Lawrence Kubie,[3] who after a long life in analytic work suggested routinely a second analysis with another analyst, which should provide the chance to analyze the residuals of the original transference neurosis. Franz Alexander[4] suggested a realistic contact with the patient in order to release him from the residual regressive transference. In the opinion of this author,[5] the analytic group experience is the best solution for analyzing transference residuals. The term "transference neurosis" does not apply to group therapy, and the term (and concept of) "transference trends" or "transference situations" is preferred here.

Group therapy offers a built-in correction of transference distortions through the peer relationship. An analyst is trained to let the transference neurosis develop to full bloom, as it were. The members of a group are neither trained nor willing to accept such transference distortions for long and will correct them. This is the basis for the corrective therapeutic family experience.

The analyst is more or less a screen for the projection of the transference neurosis. The group is more like a "theatre-in-the-round"[6] for the projection of the individual and group mind, conscious and unconscious. The mind is not a thing; it is a collection of personal images, of father and mother, brother and sister, friend and enemy. The group, therefore, gives a therapeutic opportunity for the part to be projected into the reality of today.

INTERPRETATION

There are some group-specific forms of interpretations. The most effective interpretation in groups takes the form of spontaneous and responsive interaction. One does not need, for example, to call somebody "hostile." The group's responsive confrontation to the hostile person is the best initial interpretation, which then may be deepened by more formal or verbal insight.

There is another form of group-specific interpretation, which may be called "triangular interpretation." For instance, a patient complains about something and somebody in the group responds to this. An understanding interpretation of such interaction may be offered by a third person, who watches the two antagonists. This third person may or may not be the therapist.

The third group-specific interpretation may be called the "comparative interpretation." The therapist may compare two or more individuals of the group in their similarities, differences, and dynamics.

Interpretation of "the group as a whole" is a controversial issue in therapy. The idea is especially vigorously defended by group therapists who apply the theoretical systems of Klein[7] and Bion[8] to the group process. I consider group interpretation in sophisticated groups as conducted in private practice as almost totally ineffective. Most individuals react with the feeling: What the therapist says is for everybody else but not intended for me. It is the *individual* interpretation that is felt.

In the much less sophisticated and frequently more regressive hospital groups, such general interpretations are somewhat more effective. A group therapist should never berate a group—which is so tempting to do. He may, however, start an initially silent group with the words: "Well, everybody seems to be sad today—or angry? Or still sleepy?" Hospital patients are inclined to feel the collective more deeply than the much more loosely structured groups in private practice. After all, when the small groups of the private therapist are terminated, everybody goes home and is an individual person again, while the group in the hospital ward remains together and forms an more closely knit structure—even if only for short periods of time.

FORMS OF RESISTANCE

Resistance in analytic therapy is directed against insight into the unconscious. Resistance in the group—and especially in the hospital group—is directed against free communication. This becomes most obvious in the analysis of dreams by the group. Everybody in a well-conducted group understands the meaning of dreams, except the dreamer himself. Most group analysts would agree with the correctness of this observation, which is of great importance for understanding the group process.

There is a group-specific form of resistance. For instance, many groups begin the therapeutic session slowly, and this could be called a form of resistance. When a group comes together only once weekly for a session, people have to reestablish communication with one another before they can begin to interact more freely. What happened almost automatically in individual therapy, with the greeting of the therapist to his patient at the beginning of a session, has to be actively established in the group session.

Group and individual resistance intertwine. For instance, when an individual has overcome his resistance with the help of the group and begins to speak more freely, then the entire group will come to life. This applies also to the resistance of the therapist, since group interaction is much more dependent upon the freedom, the spontaneity, and the responsiveness of the therapist than is the case in individual treatment. The group therapist must be turned toward the group. If his relationship to the group is disturbed, it will reflect immediately in the inhibited behavior and interaction of the group. If the therapist has a resistance, the group will identify with that and will slow down. In such situations, the therapist must openly and honestly turn to himself and try to analyze his resistance. Only then will the group proceed.

REGRESSION

A definite hierarchy of regression is observable in groups. In individual therapy, regression is controlled, slow, and should remain reversible. This is also the situation in the small groups of private practice. In large groups of 25 to 100 or even 200 people, an almost automatic, deeply regressive process happens virtually instantly. Any group situation is a challenge to ego autonomy. In large groups, this autonomy may be relinquished.

Hospital groups are by definition more regressive than small groups. This is due to the nature of the sickness that led to the hospitalization.

FREE ASSOCIATION

It has been said that the free association of psychoanalysis is replaced by the free dialogue or discussion in the group. This statement is not quite correct. The analytic method of free association is replaced in the group by free, spontaneous, responsive interaction. This interaction is frequently more focal than free associations are bound to be.

At this point it is often asked whether a group should be problem-solving or interaction-directed. However, these are not absolute alternatives. Any group session may, and usually will, start with attempts at problem-solving, out of which then grows interaction. In hospital groups, the session is often developed to problem-solving before one can proceed to interaction. Any other procedure would lead invariably to a blockage in the group process.

CONCLUSION

In individual therapy, the patient is, so to speak, an only child. In group psychotherapy, he is a member of a family. Franz Alexander once compared the therapeutic process to a corrective emotional experience. In his sense, group psychotherapy could be called a corrective therapeutic family experience.

REFERENCES

1. Freud, A. The ego and its mechanism of defense. *In: Writings,* Vol. 2. New York: International Universities Press (1936).
2. Foulkes, S. H. *Therapeutic Group Analysis.* New York: International Universities Press (1964).
3. Kubie, L. S. Unsolved problems in the resolution of the transference. *Psychoanal Q.* 37: 331-352 (1968).
4. Alexander, F. The principle of flexibility. *In: Psychoanalytic Therapy.* Alexander, F. and French, T. (Eds.), New York: Ronald Press (1946), pp. 25-65.
5. Grotjahn, M. *The Art and Technique of Analytic Group Therapy.* New York: Jason Aronson (1977).
6. Durkin, H. E. *The Group in Depth.* New York: International Universities Press (1964).
7. Klein, M. *Contribution to Psychoanalysis, 1921-1945.* London: Hogarth Press (1948).
8. Bion, W. R. Group dynamics: a review. *Int. J. Psychoanal.* 33: 235-247 (1952).

Part II:
Group Meetings in the Psychiatric Hospital:
A New Horizon

2
Group Therapy In Mental Institutions: A History

Martin Grotjahn, M.D.

The history of group psychotherapy is not the history of one man's work or of one man's technique or theory. The field of group therapy was always a collective enterprise.

The birth of group psychotherapy goes back not more than 50 years; it was conceived shortly after the first World War and developed in the hands of many men in many different directions during and after World War II, when it came of age.

The foundations of group psychology were given by Gustav LeBon and Sigmund Freud.[1] Neither man wrote about group psychotherapy in today's sense. Freud did not even write about "groups," and he used this word only once, when he used the English term "group mind." Both men talked mostly about masses and crowds, meaning unorganized and unstructured conglomerates of people.

Nevertheless, Freud can be called the first group analyst[2] (see the *Minutes of the Vienna Psychoanalytic Society,*[3] which were published in four volumes). The Wednesday evening Society meetings in Freud's office, while intended for learning, were actually early attempts to analyze a group of people. This group went through a kind of collective adolescence, leading the way to later organized, structured groups. Freud's group of followers tried to accomplish therapeutic goals only accidentally. The principal aim was to learn and gain insight. None of these early pioneers specialized later in group therapy as we now know it.

The most precise and definite history of group psychotherapy was written by James Anthony.[4] He first wrote a personal account of his 25 years of experience in analytic group therapy and later, in 1972,[5] he published a more general evaluation.

James Anthony belongs to that small, active, and immensely creative group of therapists who originally worked together at Northfield Hospital in England during World War II. The group consisted of Bion (who combined his observations of therapeutic groups with Kleinian theory), Anthony, Foulkes, Main, and Rickman. They are the pioneers, or founders, of analytic group psychotherapy.

Analytic group therapy is based on psychoanalytic principles. Three different analytic techniques have emerged. The first technique, under the leadership of Jacob Moreno, concentrated on the analysis *of* the group. Alexander Wolf developed a technique of analyzing the individual *in* the group. The third trend of analytic group therapy is the analysis of the group *by* the group. This trend is represented by Foulkes, Pines, DeMare, Anthony, and Grotjahn.[6]

One of the most active advocates of group psychotherapy in psychiatric facilities and in the training of therapists is Raymond Battegay.[7] He points out that some of the first groups to be conducted were quite large. Pratt, at the time of the first World War, worked with what he called a "hundred or more tuberculosis patients."

Battegay introduced his systematic group psychotherapy into the psychiatric university clinic in Basel, Switzerland, in 1957. He conducted weekly, large group sessions of the entire ward, followed by smaller groups, also meeting once weekly. This arrangement included all patients hospitalized in the clinic, who usually spent an average of two months in that hospital.

Battegay recognized the need for group therapy—or group instruction—and sensitivity training groups by the personnel, to be followed later by the need of the medical staff for such instruction-like treatment.

When Battegay later formulated his experience,[8] he concluded that group psychotherapy under certain conditions goes deeper than individual treatment, especially with addicts, who constitute high percentages of the ward population. It is possible to achieve the analytic attitudes, even if not of the unconscious in the usual meaning of the word. In a somewhat aphoristic way, he quoted Michael Balint, who once said that group therapy leads to maturation, not to the analysis of any neurosis, while individual treatment may cure neuroses, but this may not be followed by maturation.

Lionel Kreeger[9] edited the most important, detailed, and comprehensive study of large groups. It is a pioneering work of great importance even if it is not specifically aimed at the clinical description of group therapy in psychiatric hospitals.

In the introduction, Lionel Kreeger states that his experience with large groups started on a psychiatric ward of 32 beds. The large groups, which included the medical staff, were composed of 40 to 45 people, which occasionally increased to 120. This beginning gradually developed into a need for nursing and medical personnel to be trained in therapy with large groups. The program was supported by the National Health Service.

Kreeger mentioned, as pioneers of group therapy, Gustav LeBon, Sigmund Freud, Jacob Moreno (who probably has to be credited with coining the term "group therapy"), Trigant Barrow, and Paul Schilder.

Group therapy developed in Britain, especially during the second World War, and one of the most important centers was the Northfield Military Hospital. From there, Foulkes, Bion, Ezreil, and Main developed their somewhat different approaches. In 1948, Foulkes, in a chapter of his book, *Introduction to Group Analytic Psychotherapy*, mentioned the treatment of an entire hospital ward as a group.

It is Kreeger's[9] opinion that large groups cannot take the place of small groups. There is a certain lack of continuity and intimacy, which seem to be necessary for the therapeutic process. A part of every large group of over 25 people remains silent and anonymous, which under certain circumstances can be utilized as an advantage for a group regression. Because of the threat to the individual by the large group, psychotic manifestations may be observed, especially paranoid anxiety, manic flight, and similar manifestations.

Working with such groups may be exhausting for the therapist, as it is sometimes impossible to think clearly under these circumstances. A "terror" of merging with the large group may at times paralyze the therapist.

Foulkes[10] differentiates three types of groups: problem-centered groups, experience groups, and therapy-centered groups. In training, the group's aim is mostly to give a participant experience in how it feels to be a member of a group. The assignment of the large group is to establish a culture or atmosphere.

The remarks of Foulkes are followed by those of Main[11]; who had previously written on "The Therapeutic Community." He talks mostly about psychodynamics of large groups, about projective identification, which for him means the externalization of pain. He observes that after the meeting of large groups the participants often stand around and continue talking, which he considers an attempt to recover the self after having lost it in the anonymity of the large group. The outstanding factor of large groups is their lack of therapeutic alliance with the therapist or with anybody else. He also makes the clinical observation that every question conceals personal thoughts and wishes and is never "innocent."

In the small group, everybody remains an individual, while in the large group, everybody begins to think in terms of the group. In small groups, individual interpretations are indicated, while in large groups, collective interpretations may be more useful.

These threats to identity in the large groups are taken up by Pierre Tanquet, who defines the large groups as groups in which all members lose their identities.

One of the most outstanding group analysts in England is Patrick DeMaré, who contributes to Lionel Kreeger's[9] book an essay entitled "The Politics of Large Groups." According to him, psychotherapy developed from the psychobiological perspective of psychoanalysis to the sociocultural perspective of present-day group therapy. He considers the large group a powerful tool of the therapist. DeMaré made a very important contribution to the understanding of the group process by stating that the unconscious mind of the large group is represented by that which is not communicated.

Psychoanalysis has delivered us from organic psychiatry; group analysis has delivered therapy from the restrictions of psychoanalysis; and the large group is beginning to show new sociocultural perspectives.

In contrast to this theoretical contribution by Foulkes and DeMaré stands Springmann[13], who returns to practical, therapeutic experience with large groups in his clinic in Tel Aviv University. Like Battegay in Switzerland, Springmann too has experimented with large groups, consisting of all the patients and the medical staff of a hospital with more than 1,000 beds. He sees in the weekly large groups a stimulus that establishes the atmosphere of the hospital and helps the patients to feel understood. There are people who feel at home only in large groups, just because of the large group's anonymity. There is a rapid turnover of patients in Springmann's groups and this increases the feeling of anonymity, which distinguishes these groups from all other groups. Still, Springmann observes that even these groups come to develop something of a "group memory," which often continues and matures even when the entire population is replaced by new patients. Large groups offer an opportunity for the participants to abandon relationships that were adopted in order to avoid a "calamity" or feared relationships.

Springmann's conclusion is that large groups may be therapeutic and may lead to permanent changes in the group and in the individual.

Skinner discusses the large group in training. He gives perhaps the deepest interpretation of group dynamics, even if it is limited to training groups. He does not talk about the setting of a psychiatric clinic. In his courses, he gives weekly sessions over a period of three years for members of the healing profession who want to be introduced to work with large groups. Originally the courses consisted of 1½ hours of weekly lectures and seminars, followed by 1½ hours of small group sessions. This is now followed in the third semester with seven 1½-hour-long meetings with all 72 students and staff members.

On the basis of this experience, Robert Skinner concludes that a group of this size cannot be controlled by one therapist, who must spend all of his time listening and learning. Therefore, a co-therapist has to be present. Such groups have great power—for good or for evil. If uncontrolled, the primitive, disintegrative forces may break the group into fragmented small groups, all fighting with one another— until an external enemy is found who may reunite the group.

If properly handled (or "harnessed"), increased awareness of self and our relations to others, interdependency, and a sense of the wholeness of both the individual and the group is often felt—especially in moments of silence. The individual must learn how to lose his ordinary boundaries without losing himself. This, in turn, may lead to an experience of the "oceanic feeling."

Springmann adds to Skinner's observation that any specialist who intends to work with large groups must have had personal experience as a member of such a group. In the initial early phase of the large groups, the leadership should be supportive and accepting of dependency and a certain idealization of the leadership by the group (Springmann's "oral phase").

In what Springmann calls the "anal phase" of the group, the leadership should be active and provocative, while in the third phase, the genital and most mature phase, he should be a challenger of all defenses. He should stand his ground against the rebellious spirit of the large group. This can be done only by multiple leadership.

Small groups, according to Skinner, tend to become like neurotic families, while large groups place people back into the melting pot.

Kreeger's[9] work is important for many reasons, even if it does not specifically outline the approach to large groups in hospitals. He and his team show the therapeutic process in large groups and how to study such groups.

There seems to be a hierarchy of regression in groups, as Koenig points out. The development goes from the slow transference regression in analysis to the differently structured and easily reversible regression in small groups. A deep and automatic, rapid regression is typical of large groups. While the therapuetic process in small groups could be called a corrective emotional family experience, the emotions felt by the large group seem to come closer to a primal scene experience (Skinner's melting pot formulation). Some workers in the field have concluded that Klein's[12] analytic theory seems to become observable in these large groups.

The work of Kreeger[9] has the great merit that it focused the attention of group therapists on the large groups. Many therapists have recognized only recently that they have worked in their wards and in their outpatient clinics with large groups, for considerable time, often without realizing it. Kreeger and his team discuss mostly large groups outside of hospitals, mostly in training situations for therapists. It is time now to focus further investigation on work done in psychiatric hospitals and outpatient clinics to utilize material collected but not yet used or reported on.

REFERENCES

1. Freud, S. Group psychology and the analysis of the ego. *In:* Strachey, J. (Ed.), *Complete psychological works of Sigmund Freud,* Standard Ed. New York: Norton (1921), Vol. 18, pp. 69-143.
2. Kanzer, M. Freud: the first psychoanalytic group leader. *In:* Kaplan, H. and Sadock, B. (Eds.), *Comprehensive Group Psychotherapy.* Baltimore: Williams & Wilkins (1971), pp. 32-46.

3. Nunberg, H. and Federn, E. (Eds.). *Minutes of the Vienna Psychoanalytic Society, 1906-1918* (Four volumes). New York: International Universities Press (1964).
4. Anthony, E. J. Reflections on twenty-five years of group psychotherapy. *Int. J. Group Psychother.* **18**: 277-301 (1968).
5. Anthony, E. J. The history of group psychotherapy. *In:* Kaplan, H. and Sadock, B. (Eds.), *The Origin of Group Psychoanalysis.* New York: Dutton (1972).
6. Grotjahn, M. *The Art and Technique of Analytic Group Therapy.* New York: Jason Aronson (1977).
7. Battegay, R. Pharmacotherapy, individual, and group psychotherapy in the psychiatric clinic. *Schweiz. Arch. Neurol. Psychiat.* **84**: 339-340 (1959).
8. Battegay, R. Gruppenpsychotherapie versus individuelle psychotherapie. *Nervenarzt.* **41**: 429-433 (1970).
9. Kreeger, L. (Ed.). *The Large Group: Dynamics and Therapy.* Itasca, IL: Peacock Publications (1975).
10. Foulkes, S.H. *Therapeutic Group Analysis.* New York: International Universities Press (1965).
11. Main, T.F. Some psychodynamic aspects of large groups. *Archivio di Psicologia,* Neurologia e Psichiatria. **35(4)**: 446-452 (1974).
12. Klein, M. *Envy and Gratitude.* London: Tavistock Publications (1957).
13. Springmann, Rafael. *In:* Kreeger, L. (Ed.), *The Large Group: Dynamics and Therapy.* Itasca, IL: Peacock Publications (1975).

3
Basic Guidelines for the Conduct of Hospital Groups

Martin Grotjahn, M.D.

The technique of therapy with small, active, slow, open groups, as used in private practice, is suitable as a model for group therapy in hospitals. We will describe the variations of this basic technique that apply to the specific situations that exist in mental hospitals and outpatient clinics.

THE BEGINNING GROUP

Generally, most therapeutic groups accommodate six to eight (and, at the most, ten) people. The group should be heterogeneous: The patients should not all be the same sex or in the same profession, or have the same psychiatric diagnosis. In the usual "slow, open" groups of private practice, people leave the group after approximately three years and are replaced with newcomers. This is also done when space opens in the group due to premature departure of members. It is advantageous for groups to change slowly, since the reaction to newcomers stimulates the curative group process.

Hospital groups are quite different from other groups. They show change-related differences because they change daily with each new admission and discharge. Furthermore, hospital groups are not as selective as the small groups of private practice. In the admission ward, every newly admitted patient is included in the large, daily (or almost daily) "morning meetings" group. A similar lack of selection occurs with the large "follow-up" groups in the outpatient clinics. Only later does the staff assemble smaller groups of patients who may benefit from more insight-directed treatment. In private practice, the physician largely follows the "family model" in the composition of groups. Such selection is not possible in hospital groups.

GROUND RULES

It is advisable to keep all rules to a minimum—and even then one cannot always insist on them. For instance, one should "insist" on punctuality, but not exclude latecomers. Occasionally it is necessary to remind the group that only one person should talk at a time. The length of the session should be between 45 and 120 minutes.

The larger the group, the shorter the session—because the aim of support is more easily and quickly realized than the aim of the smaller, insight-directed group.

When a new group starts or a new member is admitted to the group, it should be emphasized that nothing that occurs in the group should be repeated outside of it. Nobody is permitted to reveal details, which must remain as confidential as any privileged communication. Generally only first names are used, which protects anonymity.

To allow smoking or not depends upon the inclination of the therapist. I insist on no smoking and my patients seem to have no difficulty following this rule.

The vast majority of small groups meet once weekly. Attempts at more frequent meetings have been made and there is no valid objection to that. The therapist has to watch, however, that the character of the group meetings does not move toward that of individual analytic treatment with the development of a regressive transference.

Hospital groups are quite different since the population of the admission ward—and of the open closed wards—changes rapidly and almost daily with new admissions and discharges. Daily, or almost daily, meetings are a necessity and do not result in regressive transference problems.

All groups at the outpatient clinics meet regularly and weekly. Occasionally therapists elect to have their groups meet bi- or triweekly, but usually give it up and return to weekly meetings after a few months.

BODY LANGUAGE

There is a body language in groups, often expressed in the seating arrangement. There is the therapist's "little helper" at his right hand,

and newcomers sit, as a rule, close to the door to keep the route of retreat open. Near the window sit the people who prefer seeing to being seen, and naturally the opposition to the therapist sits opposite to him. It is astonishing how much a group therapist can learn abut his patients visually, in addition to the auditory information he receives.

In large groups, there are always some patients who prefer distance from the therapist—as there are others who prefer closer contact. I often think that the therapist of large groups should stand up in order to cover, or at least to see, the whole field of operation. If the large group sits in a circle, the dead space in the middle discourages communication. If an onion-like arrangement in tiers is preferred, the therapist must try not to communicate only with the first row of people.

INTRODUCING THE INDIVIDUAL PATIENT INTO THE GROUP

A patient is ready for group treatment if he has formed a working alliance[1,2] with his therapist in the initial, individual, diagnostic-therapeutic interviews. This working alliance between therapist and patient is a good basis for group treatment. At first, the members of the group are strangers, bound mainly by their relation to the therapist. Later they form attachments to one another and become a cohesive group. To introduce a new member into an ongoing group is not always easy. If no introduction is made by the therapist, then the group will slow down and at first silently and finally loudly demand to hear what the new member expects from the group.

The large groups include by necessity everybody on the ward, be they newly admitted or veterans of the ward ready to be released later the same day. This fact gives the large group a new structure with few transference ties. This is a size-specific and turnover phenomenon. The situation in the large follow-up groups of the outpatient department is somewhat differently structured because these groups work together over long periods of time, often for many years. There the loosely structured group does form a definite group cohesion. The transference that is most obvious is the peer relationship and a dependency upon the institution as a mother symbol. This makes it possible for changes of therapists to be minimally traumatic to the patients.

The working alliance between patient and therapist is changed to an alliance with the hospital, the ward, and the other group members. The larger the group and the less motivated its members, the less the working alliance is observed.

INDIVIDUAL INTERVIEWS

Much time has been spent discussing when to give a group member an individual interview with the therapist. As a rule of thumb, a group patient may be seen individually when he is in a situation of crisis that requires more time than he can expect to have in the group. I do not interfere when a patient under special pressure occasionally monopolizes the group, but this must be the exception and not the rule. A patient who turns to the group in real distress does not waste the group's time. All members participate in the conflict as if it were their own. If more time is needed, for instance in a crisis situation, I may invite the patient for an individual interview or wait until the patient requests it.

Therapists who begin to work with groups may occasionally have need of more genetic information about the patient than can be gained when a patient is admitted to a group after only an initial interview. With growing experience in group therapy, marginal interviews for informational purposes become less and less important. Patients rarely abuse the privilege of requesting an individual hour. Resistance to work in the group rarely leads to requests for individual sessions.

Legal and medical requirements of the hospital rightfully demand personal interviews before and after the admission of the patient. This does not work against group therapy in mental institutions; neither does it complicate group process. Hospital routine is a great equalizer and eliminates some difficulties for therapist and patient as they struggle to overcome the transition from individual to group therapy.

"GIMMICKS"

All "gimmicks" interfere with spontaneous and free interaction within the group. In analytic groups, no music is played, no clothing is removed, nobody is put into a "hot seat," nobody falls in or out of anybody's arms, nobody utters a "primal scream" or reverses roles. The means of interaction is verbal or subliminal, with behavioral clues.

There is no reason why this rule should change in the hospital. Anything faintly reminiscent of a performance is a step away from the honest, spontaneous, and responsive interaction that is the aim of group therapy. In large hospital groups, the main aim is the establishment of human contact with isolated schizophrenics, and any gimmicks would endanger the patient's trust.

It is, however, true that the therapists of large groups have to deal with a high percentage of schizophrenics or at least psychotic people. Therefore, they have to be actively inviting and initiate participation with both questions and answers.

A SENSE OF CLOSURE

When a group starts slowly, the therapist should not "wait out" the silence but try to locate the reason for the resistance. The therapist must have the courage to follow his spontaneity, his intuition, and his curiosity. He has to be much more active than in individual therapy, or even in small groups. The progress of the group is dependent upon the free, spontaneous, honest responsiveness of the central figure.

In order to facilitate the flow of interaction, the therapist ought to have a "sense of closure." This means he should have a feeling for the moment when the group may get stuck at one point, or with one group member, instead of moving on to new fields of conflicts, new problems, and new approaches, or perhaps even new alternatives and new insights.

The large groups of mental institutions rarely have trouble with patients who try to monopolize the session as "co-therapists". The silent pressure of the large group, in my experience, has an automatic disciplinary effect. In situations in which one patient monopolizes the conversation, it can usually be traced back to the therapist's lack of experience in group work. Inexperienced therapists are inclined to welcome the monopolists as helpers carrying the burden of responsibility for the active progress of a group session.

A sense of closure is important for the group and the therapist in all groups but it is essential for the large groups. It may be possible to find the spokesman for a small group, but the large group needs many spokesmen to express itself and the therapist may provide the opportunity and the time for many to speak.

In small groups, a therapist may be criticized as a "hit and run therapist." In large groups, such accusation may be a compliment. The therapist of the large group has to start the therapeutic process, which, it is hoped, will continue after the group session as part of the life of the ward population. This is possible in hospital groups, where the patients live together after the group finishes its formal session.

AFTER-THE-GROUP SESSIONS

Alexander Wolf[3] recommends "alternating meetings" of the group with and without the therapist. This procedure has not become generally accepted and I do not see any special advantages to such sessions. However, I do not make rules about the group getting together after the session, going out for dinner, or meeting without me during my vacations. Groups that meet informally during the usual summer vacation find it easier to start work again than groups in which the members had no contact with one another.

Hospital groups naturally continue to live together after the morning session. The life of the ward population continues the work started in the group session. One of the merits of ward groups is that they originate and propagate the spirit, the atmosphere, and the good will of the group session. This can permeate the entire hospital population and contributes to the therapeutic community. This is one more reason for daily ward sessions.

REALITY INTERRUPTING
THE GROUP PROCESS

Occasionally the reality of the outside world breaks into the proceedings of the group and may disrupt the group process. Tragedy may happen to any member of the group-family, like sickness, hospitalization, the drama of a psychotic episode, an accident, or a criminal assault. At other times it might be a national tragedy: war, the assassination of a leading personality, a general election, or a natural disaster. When elections are held, the group members may feel impelled to get into debates and it may become necessary to protect the group from deteriorating into a political convention.

Petitions should not be circulated or money collected. On such occasions, saying, "This does not belong here," will not suffice—but a change in focus from outer to inner reality has to be executed.

It may be possible not to discuss a national catastrophe, as, for instance, an assassination, but to discuss murderous hostility and the wish to kill and the defenses against that are always legitimate topics that may develop out of the group discussing national events. It is one of the most important functions of large hospital groups to re-assure excitable catatonics that we can deal with exploding hostility here—and that we can protect raging persons and the entire ward population.

When the reality threat is overwhelming, the voices of the uncon-scious fall silent and the reaction to reality must be a realistic and rational one. Only later will there be a chance to consider uncon-scious motives.

Altogether, reality experience that concerns every member of the group may help to form group cohesion.

ACTING OUT

Group psychotherapy has something of the character of "theatre-in-round,"[4] and as such invites acting out. The unfolding interaction of all members repeats rather than remembers. This is the definition of acting out.[4] Often conflicts are reenacted in the group before they can be verbalized. They are accessible to therapy in either case. Sex-ual acting out between members of the group does happen and is not necessarily a danger to group cohesion, group process, or the in-dividuals. Men usually act out an unresolved Oedipus conflict; they consider the group therapist a father representative from whom they have to steal a woman (out of his harem, as it were). Women may start a flirtation with a member of the group because he is a substi-tute for the unobtainable father-therapist. Whenever this happens, the therapist's assignment is to point out that there should be no subgroup formation and everything that happens between group members is the psychological property of the group and must be openly discussed in the group in session.

The most tragic form of acting out is suicide. In a well-conducted and established group, suicide is rare. There are group therapists who have never experienced such tragedy. Group therapy is the treatment of choice for depression. It is possible to root a depressive patient in the benevolent indifference of the group, and when that happens the patient will most likely not commit suicide. The dangerous time is in the beginning of treatment and during vacation. (See Chapter 21 on group psychotherapy in China.)

Acting out is as much a danger in small hospital groups as it is in office practice. The hospital setting should help to diminish suicidal dangers, but the group has more power than any security measures.

MISTAKES IN THE CONDUCTING OF THERAPY

Anything that interferes with group process must be called a mistake, if it is due to the therapist. The therapist may commit an error by using wrong names for members of the group, cancelling or forgetting meetings, not being active or honest enough, or inviting people to join the group before they are ready for it or when they do not fit into the family model of the group constellation.

There are other pitfalls for therapists. Asking too many questions in a group may interfere with spontaneous unfolding of the group process. In no way should questions be asked as in a police investigation. The right of the individual to privacy should be respected. There are better ways to invite people to participate in the group interaction than to investigate. (Some questions, however, are unavoidable.)

A superior attitude by anybody in the group—including the therapist—is open to interpretation, otherwise it could inhibit free associative interaction.

The therapist who sits barricaded behind his desk will lose easy and spontaneous contact with his group. The same is true for therapists who sit in comfort but offer uncomfortable little bridge chairs for the group members.

Silence in the group has to be treated with patience and interpretation, not with commands, beratings, or attempts to "wait them out." A kind of "impatient patience" is recommended, meaning invitations without urging. For the therapist to join a group in silence, as so often is done, is of no help.

The best stimulation for the therapeutic process in groups is the therapists honest, frank, and spontaneous responsiveness. He should be a model communicator. If he takes care of the group, the individuals will take care of one another.

Most of these mistakes apply only to the conducting of therapy in small groups. In large groups, a certain number of questions are unavoidable, since spontaneity cannot be expected in any group that almost daily changes some of its members. To speak in a large group seems for many people to mean losing their feeling of membership and becoming instead an individual spokesman. This cannot be routinely expected without active encouragement.

TERMINATION OF GROUP TREATMENT

According to my observation, the average length of treatment in a small, slow, open group is more or less three years of weekly sessions. Any patient in treatment for less than one year should be considered a "drop-out," meaning somebody who terminates treatment prematurely.

There are people who need the support of the group-family for many years, but it is rare that somebody continues group treatment as long as some patients remain in psychoanalysis. A patient may religiously attend group sessions for five or eight years—but that seems to be a maximum and is an exception.

At the end of treatment, the patient should have learned how to deal with his past and should be able to master his present reality. He should know how to deal with the future even if it causes conflicts or puts him under stress. He should have learned to deal with anxiety, guilt, and hostility. He should have learned how to use his psyche to deal with new conflicts that cannot be prevented. He should be free, spontaneous, and responsive, and should have the courage to be honest and to be himself, even under stress. He should have established—and should maintain—free communication with his unconscious and with others.

It is a peculiar habit of groups to never agree when somebody wants to leave just as most groups accept only reluctantly a new member. ·People are inclined to connect termination with certain dates, as, for instance, "after New Years' Day," or "after the summer vacation."

I have found it helpful to assume that the patient took responsibility to start treatment and so he may as well take the responsibility of terminating it. The judgment of the therapist and the unwillingness of the group to let anybody leave will have to be worked out by the patient and probably will suffice to delay termination until the right moment.

The question of termination in hospital groups is made by the medical staff, which decides admission, length of stay in the hospital, date of transfer to group therapy in the outpatient clinic, or discharge.

Special attention has been given to the phenomena of the drop-out, which worries all group therapists. I have differentiated in my experience five classifications of drop-outs according to the frequency with which they happen in my groups: (1) insufficient motivation to continue; (2) contraindications for further treatment (danger of activating a psychotic episode); (3) unanalyzable fear of further confrontation (for instance, when the patient begins to realize that a marriage of long duration may be endangered); (4) external circumstances or changes in the location of domicile or employment; and (5) negative transference reactions with corresponding negative countertransference reaction by the therapist.

Whether there are people whose character makes group work impossible remains unanswered. People who have not worked well in one group may do well in a second group. The same is true with one or another therapist. However, it is possible that some people may feel so antagonized by a group, or intimidated, or provoked, that they may not fit into any group and no group can be expected to make the necessary adjustments to facilitate such a person's treatment. It changes the character of a group when a new member constitutes a restriction of free expression. This happens, for instance, when an adolescent—or an actively hallucinating schizophrenic—joins an ongoing group of people with various character disorders. It may happen that the entire group turns to this, the problem family's favorite problem child, in concern and compassion. Everybody becomes a loving father-mother. The sick child may recover miraculously, but the group pays a high price for it. It is no longer a group of people trying to express themselves freely and honestly. Instead, they all have changed to therapists and ceased to be members of a group. Such should not be asked by the therapist from the group.

The hospital group, in contrast to the smaller group of private practice, has most of its questions about composition decided automatically by the hospital's admission policy, transfers to other wards, and discharges from the institution. Rapid change in hospital groups gives these groups the character of working mainly in the here-and-now. People relate to one another differently when they know they may not see one another tomorrow than when they assume that they will work together for a long time to come.

The following three clinical examples, first of a ward group, then of a follow-up group for chronic patients, and finally of an insight group in a large public clinic, may help to illustrate the dynamics, problems, and techniques of these groups.

A CONSULTANT'S OBSERVATION ABOUT THE START AND PROGRESS IN LARGE GROUPS (OR MORNING GROUPS) OF AN ENTIRE PSYCHIATRIC WARD POPULATION

July 1971

Thirty-five patients from the closed (admission) ward were present. In addition, there were six psychiatrists, several male and female nurses, psychologists, and social workers.

Everybody was sitting in one closely packed circle, filling the entire periphery of the day room.

The physician in charge of the ward had recently changed.

The session started with compliments about the evening entertainment of the previous night. A long discussion followed about one patient who had tried to commit suicide that night. Everybody tried to talk the man out of his depression. Everybody was full of sympathy and compassion. The embarrassed patient did not say anything; he stared at his bandaged wrists. (Was he the evening's entertainment?) There were several heavily medicated psychotics, some sleeping, some with open eyes. Some men with angry faces did not participate either. Somebody described himself as a "Hollywood writer" and tried hard to play the role of an active therapist or the host of a talk show.

A middle-aged catatonic woman could not be kept in her seat and walked aimlessly and helplessly around the room in front of the chairs. After unsuccessful attempts to restrict her to her seat, the therapist suggested we let her roam around. When nobody bothered her anymore, she sat down quietly.

An enormously obese woman was afraid of going home for a weekend visit because there were "two voices" waiting for her. At this point it seemed to me that the therapist was not active enough and should have responded to the woman who was afraid to go home. I had the fantasy that the therapist should sit in a wheel chair so that he could rush without effort to the place of action; the enormity of the big circle made it physically impossible to keep the whole group simultaneously in focus. It also seemed to me that my silence was taken as a clue for the therapist to remain silent. I had limited myself to an observer's role since this was my first visit on unfamiliar ground.

When the ward physician was called out of the meeting, the group immediately came to life. I asked the remaining therapists for courage, action, and dramatization. I asked for help from everybody, therapists and patients. In a large group, everybody should feel personally responsible for the session.

My first impression was that a group of this size is unmanageable. I brought this point up for discussion in the staff conference following the large group meeting. This discussion was brief since this was the last session before my summer vacation.

Later, in the staff conference, the entire staff, and that included me, verbalized their discouragement about this difficult assignment. Perhaps we had tried the impossible? Therefore, everybody looked to the consultant, who was expected to get group communication started.

October 1971

After a long summer vacation, a regular meeting with me as visiting consultant was scheduled for every Friday morning from 9:30 to 10:30, to be followed by a half-hour staff conference. The meeting of the entire ward took place every day, with the ward physician as the main therapist.

In the Friday sessions the ward chief and I sat together in what could be called the number 12 position of the circle. There were between 25 and 35 patients and 17 staff members, some of them visiting from other wards. The meetings took place in the day room.

A painfully shy little girl asked me: "How are you? What do you do here?" I answered in detail, trying to encourage her questions by answering them and trying to introduce myself to this constantly changing group with new members at every session.

Soon after the slow beginning, a young, blond and blue-eyed schizophrenic man in a semi-military outfit and high boots stood up. He was usually referred to as "our SA man." He addressed the meeting and said: "The other night I tried to run away. I knew the door was open and I ran for it. When I almost got to it, two nurses rushed out from the office, got hold of me, and brought me back. Then I knew that I was loved here. I knew that I was accepted here. I am very grateful for that." He then asked all of us to stand up and join hands, which everybody did, with the exception of one therapist, who "just didn't feel like it."

At another meeting during this month little happened. This was interpreted by the ward physician, who said: "The group is uneasy with the problem of who we can trust." From there he asked himself loudly whether anybody had doubts about him, the doctor, the black man. His last words were: "You just cannot believe we black people, after you white people mistreated us through centuries, still love you and want to help you." There was no response, and the group dispersed silently. Some of us felt moved and everybody felt better.

The Staff Conference

In the staff meeting I asked whether I should become more active or whether I should remain a witness and only go into action during the last ten minutes, if at all. To my relief everybody opted for my active participation as a co-therapist.

Somebody discussed a friendship that had developed between a Chinese and a Caucasian girl. They reached out to each other and to watch them was a pleasure. It was a model for the spirit of support we wanted to develop in the group. When somebody mentioned lesbianism, tolerance was recommended.

One staff member mentioned that the entire ward felt terrorized by the "SA man." I thought there was no reason to fear him. One of these days he would be challenged in the group and we would see how easily he collapsed. (This actually happened at a later meeting.) It also was discussed why one of the therapists did not get up and join hands when everybody else did. The therapist answered: I didn't feel like it and I didn't think it was an honest expression of feeling." We knew that the feelings of the schizophrenic young man were shallow but we also knew that to join hands was a kind of plea and should be accepted. It turned out to be a good group experience for everybody.

I also emphasized that it was all right when one of us did not respond. It showed the man that at least one of us had some doubts about his honesty and the depth of his good feelings. It is the beauty of a group that it can be accepting and doubting at the same time. In this way it gives satisfaction yet continues a demand for further change.

After this first month of participation in the large group meetings on a closed (admission) ward, I was again discouraged. These periods of doubt were interrupted by moments of hope when the group seemed to come to life. I thought generally that it was impossible to keep track of the ever-changing population and that I would never learn how to conduct such groups if I were ever called upon to do so. I realize now that at that time I was still thinking too much in terms of the individual and not enought in terms of the group.

I soon learned to change that.

November 1971

Thirty-five patients were present and seventeen staff members.

The summary of this month's meetings can be put as a question: "How did we get here? What went wrong? How do we get out of here? And then what?"

By now I had decided to give interpretations whenever possible, and the first opportunity came when a young schizophrenic girl spoke in a most confused manner. I tried to show her how it was impossible for her to talk clearly until she had clarified her relationship to her mother: Since she did not have the courage to talk about her mother outright and clearly, she had to escape into this state of confusion. The patient started to talk about her mother in a way we could understand and soon everybody wanted to talk about mothers and about the mother we all wanted to have.

During this month I began to feel that I knew the group almost as well as if I saw them every day. I had begun to learn how to relate to the group almost as if it was one patient, regardless of individuals who arrived one week and were gone the next.

To a schizophrenic man, I said: "You look like Jesus. You behave as if you want to be crucified again." I did not expect a response and did not get one.

To a little old woman who tried to be a good mother to everybody, I said: "You feed us all with your love, but who feeds you?" Thereupon she responded: "Do you mean that symbolically?" I told her that she could take it any way she wanted to as long as it made sense to her.

The "SA man" complimented me: "It is so much better here since you came," which others confirmed. One woman added: "We always feel alive on Fridays." The entire group was awakened, electrified, and several times I had to remind the group of the rule that only one should talk so that all may hear.

There was a moment of embarrassment when I turned in the last minute to a silent and helpless young woman who I thought was a patient, but who turned out to be a new member of the staff. I asked her: "What is your name?" And she said: "My name is Legion," about which I later said in the staff meeting: "You understand the language of the symbol. Your answer was perfect."

When the group dissolved, an elderly man went from person to person and said: "Thank you, thank you!" Everybody knew how demented and confused he was and still we all felt blessed by him.

One girl asked whether one could reveal secrets in the group and my answer was: "If you feel tempted to tell them to us, then tell us. If you have doubts and if this group is too large for you to speak, then keep your secrets for the smaller group in the afternoon."

The Staff Meeting

There was a general depression engulfing everybody during this month. The work seemed hopeless. But we realized at the end of the month that the whole ward, patients and therapists, had become a cohesive group.

Once I was critical toward a therapist who annoyed me by always asking her patients many questions without revealing her own feelings or attitudes. I told her: "Don't ask so often how people feel. Say: 'You look frightened, or anxious, or depressed,' or whatever you supposed was what they expressed with their looks. These patients here do not know how to express themselves in words. You must give them your opinion, to which they then may respond. They may not know how they feel. You must offer your opinion and your feeling about them to help them to get started. Do not wait for somebody in a group as large as this is; take the lead! Don't be afraid to be wrong: They will correct you."

I was afraid—and said so aloud—that I might inhibit the therapists. They seemed to hand over the group to me on Fridays to see how I would do it. I responded in two ways to this challenge: by acting as one of the therapists in charge and by constantly asking my colleagues not to let me alone. I told them repeatedly that I needed them because I didn't know everyone and was new at this job of working with large, quickly changing groups, and with so many very sick people.

I added: "Do not berate the group for mumbling, for whispering amongst one another, for not speaking up, and for remaining silent. Change a critique into an invitation."

When one of my groups does not work well, I always look to myself first to determine whether I have a resistance or feel hostile. I have made it a rule to give credit to the group when everything goes well and to blame myself when something goes wrong. One cannot blame oneself for lack of enthusiasm about working with these groups—but one must at least recognize this resistance because the activity of the therapist is necessary to the group process.

December 1971

The group talked about death, suicide, murder, and ressurection, stimulated by a movie that had been shown on the ward the previous night.

A woman with a foghorn voice was criticized for speaking that way by somebody who claimed that her voice destroyed the group interaction. Thereupon another schizophrenic woman across the room snatched the wig from the head of the foghorn-voiced woman and ran out of the room with it, hotly pursued by the rightful owner of the wig. After a short while both returned, and the group continued. Nobody laughed and nobody made a comment about the incident, but the foghorn was not heard again in that session.

An old and senile man soiled himself and had to be helped out of the session into the bathroom.

In the staff meeting I learned that no patient was excused from attending the morning meetings; everyone was herded into the day room. I wondered why we had so few loud schizophrenics and that nobody talked about their delusions or was visibly reacting to hallucinations. It seemed as if everybody was on his best behavior during the group session (compared to Liu's observations about ward groups in China). This was partly due to, at times, heavy medication and partly due to the social setting of the meeting. Even a

schizophrenic seems to understand the group's demand that he behave appropriately and follows the requests of the group. The peer
pressure exercized by these meetings seemed to be considerable. The
staff agreed that this attitude should be maintained and should not
be endangered by provocative questions.

The Christmas season became noticeable. Many patients were leaving the ward or were preparing to leave. One man got up with visible
anxiety, declaring over and over again: "I am a man." He was reassured that we saw he was a man and asked why he had some doubts
about it. Another schizophrenic man made the rounds, shaking hands
with everybody. Nobody did anything to stop him, which I considered a good sign of the tolerant atmosphere of the therapeutic
community. It symbolized the farewell mood of the season.

January 1972

One woman sitting next to me had curlers in her hair and was generally
unpleasant to look at. I inhibited my hostility and so was inactive.

In the staff meeting I took the position that we should not wait
for the group to start the session. This would be like riding a bus and
hoping that someone will take the wheel: One of *us* should take the
wheel. I asked why some black people were such good, intuitive
therapists. Do they learn that in church? Are they better neighbors
in their communities?

By now I had developed the habit of arriving at the meeting room
ten minutes before the start of the meeting so that people could
come to talk with me. This turned out to be an informal start of the
groups. One woman with whom I exchanged some pleasantries believed that she was dead and the ward physician explained to her
that this was not so. I took it as my assignment not to show her the
contradiction between her delusion and reality but to make her feel
alive and to try to understand why she felt dead.

In the staff meeting everybody was talking about death and dying
and I remarked: "I am 30 years older and closer to death than all
of you. When my time comes I hope it will be like going to sleep
in the evening after a good day. I believe in man and I also believe
in myself, or at least in my good intentions. Death is not an acute
threat to me but I certainly prefer to live. I want to go to sleep with
peace of mind. I do not know the meaning of life but I have the

suspicion that there is no intrinsic meaning. Life has to be lived, that's about it."

I felt prompted to formulate my opinion in this way because I had seen that this question played a much more important role in the discussion between the people on the ward than is usually realized. Perhaps because the ward patients' defenses are weakened they are more in contact with universal unconscious fears than is the ward staff. The ward staff may reflexively defend against these anxieties and thus cut off the patients' attempts at communication. It was furthermore my impression that the therapists needed my stand so that they could listen with less anxiety to the group, and then perhaps form and later show their own point of view and offer it to the patients as something to deal with.

There are times when the therapist must show that he understands the group's problems—and that these problems are also his own. He then may—occasionally—show his answers to these universal problems.

February 1972

The staff, including me, was again occupied with the question of whether we were trying to do the impossible and whether it would be better to abandon the large groups in favor of small ones.

In one meeting the center of the stage was taken by a woman who had tried to commit suicide by jumping out of a speeding car her father was driving.

She had broken arms and legs and attended the session in her bed, which was wheeled into the room. Another patient told her: "You should have pushed your dad onto the freeway, not yourself. "Nobody challenged this statement—but everybody heard it.

A large black woman quietly said that she had killed her baby. To this I responded that I would like to talk with her later, after the group. (As I hoped, her confession turned out to be a delusion).

A young schizophrenic claimed that he was the son of President Nixon and he too was heard and remained unchallenged. He was asking to be killed.

The attitude of the group, and this included the therapists, was: "Well, so you think you are the son of the President? What else is new?" No real interaction developed, as so often is the case when psychotics dominate the session.

In the staff meeting concern was expressed that we might have too many visitors. We decided to limit their number.

My doubts were of a different nature: Should I have reacted differently to the severely wounded woman or to the two loudly schizophrenic patients? In the first place, when I did not know what to say, I found it preferable to remain silent—and, secondly, there is no doubt that the group situation was quietly accepting, and that this, for the time being, was all that could be done. The group showed that marvelous "benevolent indifference" that is a part of tolerant acceptance and as such is helpful.

During this month the original ward physician was replaced by a colleague. The group had no special reaction to this change and one of the therapists felt inclined to stimulate an expression of opinion about it. But the group had learned to accept the departure and arrival of new patients as well as new therapists. Everybody accepted changes as unavoidable in a hospital. The transference was nonspecific but more generally directed to the hospital and the ward.

Once I thought of the worship of silence by Quakers. They had taught me to be more tolerant toward periods of silence. Quite generally, silence is not productive and should be interrupted by the therapist. The former therapist was an educator; the present one tried to be an interpreter; and I saw my assignment as a communicator.

During one of the meetings in this month a young man complained about his depression and that he felt at rock bottom. An elderly woman answered him: "In here you are not alone. We care for you. Many of us have been where you are and some of us begin to see the light again. To be here helped me and will help you."

Another woman said that she felt more depressed in the small group than in the large one. Other people noticed that they too spoke more easily in the large group than in the smaller one. It was as if they wanted to say: "Here you always can go underground and disappear in the anonymity of many people, while there in the small group there is no hiding place."

In the staff meeting someone asked why a remark in the group was helpful but the same remark in an individual session remained totally ineffective. It was speculated that such remarks in the group symbolized acceptance ("It is all right to be depressed"), while the same remark from the therapist implies demand ("You'd better get out of it fast").

April 1972

On Good Friday before Easter Sunday the group talked about death and dying. It was quite obvious that it was easier to talk in a group about that than to think about it alone or to talk about it with only one other person. The topic changed to ressurection.

No reassurance was asked, offered, or sermonized about. It was felt as sufficiently helpful to talk openly about death.

May 1972

By now, even deeply depressed people who sat there in utter isolation could be interested in the group. In spite of the quick changes in the membership, the meetings became much more active and interactive. Some sessions started with a conversation between one of the therapists and one patient. As a rule, the therapist then turned to as many people as possible until almost everybody had been reached, even if only for a moment. Volunteers who wanted to talk spontaneously and without prodding were always preferred.

The group was most tolerant toward schizophrenic production and behavior—and such behavior became rare. When an agitated, depressive patient would restlessly pace around the room, nobody was especially bothered or tried to discipline him.

In the middle of May I took over the Friday sessions at the request of the staff. I asked for assistance but nobody volunteered. I felt in need of help because at that time I still thought I needed more information about the individual patients. I learned this was not necessary. I tried from then on to relate to the group in the here and now. I changed the seating arrangement. I tried in this way to overcome the inhibiting interspace between 35, 50, or occasionally 75 people in one big unmanageable circle. I chose to arrange the chairs in rows of semi-circles with the ward physician in front, facing the "onion rings."

In the staff conferences we most often discussed individual patients. Only later did we become aware of the ward population as a whole. The mood was angry, rebellious, questioning, depressed; but also loud and active, and once even joyful.

The large ward group made steady therapeutic progress and the group process evolved and matured in spite of staff pessimism and discouragement. The group led to the development of a genuinely therapeutic milieu on the ward. I can recommend it for psychiatric inpatient wards.

THE SMALL WARD GROUP

Most psychiatric institutions have replaced the daily morning rounds with the large group of all ward patients. They meet in the morning; frequently, they divide these groups into small groups of six to eight patients, who meet in the afternoon. The composition of these groups changes quickly, as does the ward population, which changes with the daily admissions and discharges. This generates a different, more fluid therapeutic atmosphere.

The work in these large and small daily groups is often of greater benefit than may appear at the beginning. It is amazing to see how an isolated, almost catatonic schizophrenic patient may begin to relate to the group or to someone in the group. This may be a patient who, alone with his psychiatrist, will not say a word.

The benefits of the large and small groups together cannot be over-estimated. First, the therapeutic atmosphere of the ward changes; this sometimes influences the entire hospital and produces a therapeutic community spirit. Finally, the individual patient participates, and may form a relationship. Such improvement may, at times, have the flavor of dissimulation until that which seems to start as pretense leads to more solid changes.

When a schizophrenic in a group learns "how to behave" he may be dissimulating; however, he is not lost to further therapy. He is showing good intention, his relatedness to his environment, and his desire to change. Such behavior is not forced but is at first hidden.

For the psychotic patient, the hospitalization and the group therapy in the large and the smaller and more intimate groups offers help toward beginning integration, claification, orientation, and object-relatedness. Reemergence out of an acute psychotic episode starts with clarification of the chaos, followed up by reintegration of the ego. The group offers a relationship and in turn invites a better relationship of the patient to himself. The group experience is an ego-strengthening experience.

Experienced therapists will try to take every utterance, no matter how bizarre or absurd, as a communication, and will respond to it as such. It is certainly not always possible to translate such communication into everyday language, but in any case the therapist tries to respond to it insofar as he understands it. Even if the interpretation is only tangentially correct, it establishes a fragile relationship between patient, therapist, and group. On this relationship, further progress can be built. The chance that this may happen is about equal in the small group and in the large morning groups. Some patients respond better to the protective anonymity of large groups, while others need the intimacy of the small afternoon groups. Ward groups have the advantage that the hospital can conduct them daily, or almost daily. This is not possible in outpatient clinics.

Good will is not enough to help a paranoid schizophrenic. Understanding, even when it is rudimentary or fragmented, is more easily accepted by him, and more helpful. Such interpretations are more important than transference interpretation, which in groups of this kind can, with good conscience, be neglected by the therapist.

When the patient is discharged after the hospitalization and after participating in large and small groups, he and his family will be better prepared to accept referral to an outpatient group. Such a referral is essential for most of these patients.

Clinical Illustration Number One

On the way to the waiting room, where the meeting was supposed to take place, the ward physician told me that he was busy and preoccupied with a promised research project. His mind was not quite with us, but he would do his best. It turned out that he gave a lecture to perhaps 12 ward patients. I was so shocked when I realized that I would have to listen to a popular lecture about anxiety and tranquilizers that I dropped my cup of coffee. This was the only excitement in the session.

The doctor talked about the common medication on the ward; he was asked about "water pills," meaning diuretics. To my surprise I began to realize that the group was intensely interested. While they frequently asked unrelated questions about cancer, diabetes, alcoholism, and family problems, they remained interested. Most of the time was spent on a lecture about tranquilizers, illustrated by diagrams on a blackboard.

At the end of 45 minutes I realized, to my surprise, that a group had actually formed: There was general good feeling. The group members seemed to feel that the doctor took them seriously. He listened to their questions, which he answered in a way that was difficult to understand, but he gave answers nevertheless. When the doctor left, the group remained in the room in animated discussion. It was as if everybody felt: "We have a doctor, we get medical care, we have things explained on a blackboard; we have hope again; let us stick together. We are all patients here and this doctor will help us."

It was a primitive approach, but it was effective and helpful.

Clinical Illustration Number Two

The meeting took place on the closed ward. The ward chief was not present because he was giving an expert opinion at a trial. The assistant chief had just returned that day after a vacation and explained that he did not know any of the patients. All the residents were absent because somewhere else in the hospital they were taking an examination. The nurses were visiting another hospital as a part of their training. There was a kind of Sunday morning quality in the room.

The group of ten patients consisted of almost all new patients. When I compared this with the meeting of the previous week, I realized that only two of patients had been there. The rest were new to the group.

The doctor was kind, warm, and gentle, and he reached out to everybody, asking: "How was your weekend?" He sounded as if he wanted to know the answer.

It turned out that most of the patients had spent the weekend at home and used this experience for reality testing. The visit home had shown them what they could expect after discharge from the hospital. They discussed the joys and difficulties of their home visit, often going into detail. Everything was discussed in a friendly way. Dynamic interpretations were hardly possible and were not attempted.

One schizophrenic reported that his mother was visited by his doctor, who flirted with her instead of attending to him. A hebephrenic young woman had to be readmitted to the hospital and explained: "I ran away from my mother for 'fresh air.' " Nobody doubted the story—but nobody seemed to believe it either. It seemed as if the group was benignly indifferent. What anybody said was all right with the group. It did not seem to matter whether it was truth or delusion that was presented.

The third person said he had no other place to go since his mother's social security check was stolen. They had absolutely no money and he was hungry and came here to eat. The man was obviously a schizophrenic who had gotten entangled in the red tape of welfare. He had to wait now in the hospital until his world could be straightened out. This too was taken matter-of-factly.

Then came a severely hypochondriacal depressive psychotic, who added his complaints to the proceedings.

It seemed to me it was not difficult to establish a relationship with everyone, even if the relationship might not necessarily be a therapeu- one—but simply human.

When it was time for the meeting to adjourn, I turned to a friendly young man who was sitting next to me and asked him what he was doing here. He said he was just out of jail, where he had served a five-year sentence for kidnapping his mother. By way of apology he explained that his father had gotten ten years ("we did it together"). He was the oldest of six children; his mother had run away; they had needed her and had brought her back against her will. He had been home again for a few days and again he'd had ideas of violence, but he did not want to get into legal difficulties—that was why he had come here. It was doubtlessly the right thing to do.

The large and small ward groups complement each other. The larger group provides selective anonymity with the opportunity for participation. The setting is structured and the safety factor is relatively high. Ego support and reality testing are its main accomplishments.

The small group offers a chance for more personal participation at a more intimate level. The result is more personal feedback and reactions, more anxiety, and more opportunity for insight. It also prepares patients for small outpatient groups.

REFERENCES

1. Greenson, R. The working alliance and the transference neurosis. *Psychoanalytic Q.* **34**: 134-165 (1965).
2. Grotjahn, M. *The Art and Technique of Analytic Group Therapy*. New York: Jason Aronson (1977).
3. Wolf, A. The psychoanalysis of groups. *American Psychotherapy*. **3**: 525-558 (1950); 4: 16-50 (1950).
4. Dirkin, H. *The Group in Depth*. New York: International Universities Press (1964).

4
Dynamics of Inpatient Groups

Frank M. Kline, M.D.

To understand group principles and develop techniques suitable for a wide variety of patients, group therapy pioneers applied general principles and techniques from other treatment modalities. These were initially (and, in some cases, blindly) used for inpatient ward groups. Some techniques proved useful; others were of questionable value. Time and experience have slowly fostered better dynamic understanding of groups, and this has led to more effective therapy.

Valuable and useful contributions came from Lindemann's[1] 1944 crisis therapy concept and Caplan's[2] ideas of tertiary prevention, the crisis model in community psychiatry—keeping the psychiatric patient in the community, and obtaining and maintaining the sanction of the formal and informal power structure. Yamamoto et al.[3] showed how countertransference problems may lead to inadequate treatment of the disadvantaged.

Yalom's[4] description of the techniques and problems of beginning groups is a valuable contribution to ward group management. The helpful idea that patients and group leaders should react to one another, not interpret, came from Arsenian and Semrad in 1967.[5] Grotjahn and others have said that the equivalent of free association in groups is open, honest reaction and expression (although this must remain more of a goal than a fact in ward groups). May's[6,7] work suggested that it was useful to combine psychotropics and psychotherapy in the treatment of schizophrenics. Other studies have demonstrated the advantage of group combined with psychotropics (Borowski and Tolwinski's[8] work is one example).

Analytic emphasis on blank screen therapists and the "T" groups on confrontation are not applicable to ward groups, and in the hands of beginning therapists, both may be destructive. Even relatively healthy patients may have difficulty with unstructured group. For example, Malan's[9] work showed that patients in Tavestock groups liked the experience and benefited from it if they had prior and extensive analytically-oriented individual therapy. This suggests that socially skilled people with strong egos, further strengthened by analytic procedure, and relatively comfortable with their unconscious, can tolerate and benefit from unstructured group therapy. Others—normals, psychotics, and adolescents, probably cannot. The "T" group's emphasis on emotional expression and sometimes harsh confrontation is not appropriate to psychotic patients with ego defects. Since inpatients are usually desperately trying to control affect, interpersonal activity alarms them and they may have trouble even with compulsively correct and polite interaction. It isn't easy for therapists to combine and maintain the levels of intimacy, warmth, honesty, structure, objectivity, and distance that permit ward groups to function. The balance that works in one session must be adjusted at each subsequent meeting.

The busy and preoccupied therapist may forget that there are other concerns besides ideal therapy. The ideas, feelings, biases, and needs of ancillary personnel, other services, other theoretical points of view, and hospital administration must be considered. The problems of cost accountability, utilization review, PSRO's, and the Joint Commission must, of necessity, influence the hospital practice of group psychotherapy. The experienced therapist understands the place and importance of these "significant others" and uses them to the patient's and the group's advantage.

The collapse of a program developed by Bion, Foulkes, and others for the British Army in World War II shows that even the most talented therapists can come to grief when they ignore the problems and sensitivities of administration.[10] Ancillary services, hospital administration, reviewing agencies, and the rest of the hospital must be regarded as members of a larger community that influences patient welfare. This larger community, left to its own devices, usually opts for restrictive solutions.[11] The therapist or his senior administrator's efforts with this larger community can significantly influence patient care.

If patients in a particular group seem to be increasingly destructive, or appear to be prolonging their hospital stays, an alert administrator will be concerned and raise questions. The wise therapist appreciates the administrator's anxiety and finds ways to resolve it. Overly sensitive, anxious, or inexperienced administrators may even become concerned about talk. Most of us assume fantasy leads to thought, thought to talk, and talk to action. Group members talking outside the group about violence, suicide, or other seemingly dangerous subjects may alarm the administration. The thoughtful group therapist is alert to these possibilities and deals with those who may be interfering with his work with the same tolerant, sensitive, and patient effort he would use in his group. Otherwise, the mistrust that greeted Bion, Foulkes, Bierer, and others will be repeated.

The group therapist has the obligation to provide sufficient leadership so the patient's behavior is kept within tolerable limits. Clearly the therapist should have resolved his own authority problems well enough so that he can deal realistically with patients, staff, and the hospital hierarchy.

It seems apparent that a leaderless group or a seemingly leaderless group is impossible in a psychiatric inpatient ward. While talk within the group should be as free as patient anxiety permits, talk and action outside the group must be kept within limits tolerable to other patients, the hospital staff, and the hospital in general. Group therapists know most talk is playful and symbolic; it does not necessarily predict action even when the speaker is psychotic. Those unfamiliar with the group experience may be unaware of this, however.

THESIS

My thesis is simple. The majority of hospitalized psychiatric patients are best treated in groups. The dynamics of inpatient and insight groups are different, and so are some of the useful therapeutic techniques. By borrowing ideas from previous workers and researchers and using our own experimentation and experience, we can develop useful dynamic understanding and practical therapeutic techniques for ward groups.

Group, more than individual, therapy allows understanding and practice of social skills. Defective social skills are the main reason for social failure and hospitalization. If patients can overcome enough social anxiety so that they can learn from others and gain the affectual and practical support that most of us routinely get, then the patient will have an excellent chance of staying out of the hospital and continuing to improve. Group peer support and interaction can break the mold of previously acquired internal objects.

Group can also help therapists tolerate the long periods of seemingly pointless interaction that most schizophrenics need before they can allow a human relationship. In individual therapy with psychotic patients, most therapists become discouraged and push too hard or give up. Neither course is suitable. Group can help the therapist maintain a reasonable balance between optimism and resignation.

Properly conducted group allows patients to participate at their own rate and permits regulation of transference intensity. Transference can be divided between patients, and patients can talk or remain silent. The borderline, the depressed, and the psychotic usually do not need transference activation. It should be noted that the therapist shouldn't dwell on transference interpretation and genetic reconstructions, since these patients are already living out the transference. If the group leader tends to the group process, he will have a full-time occupation. If, in addition to monitoring group process, the therapist is able, within the limits of a patient's anxiety, to encourage warm, friendly, honest reaction and interaction, he will have done all that any ward psychotherapist can do.

I am deliberately ignoring the fact that inpatients consist of a wide variety of diagnoses and that there are many conflicting explanations of the causes of mental illness. Whatever the diagnosis, whatever the genetics, and whatever the immediate cause, the patient's hospitalization is the result of social failure. Group offers him the best chance to reconstitute or learn necessary social skills. Inpatient groups can begin this effort. The concept that schizophrenia and serious depression may be biochemical, genetic, or the result of subtle brain damage is irrelevant to my thesis. Even the idea that schizophrenia is a miscellaneous collection of related diseases with a common final pathway can be ignored. Whatever the origin of the disease, group psychotherapy, in my opinion and experience, is helpful. Obviously, not every inpatient can tolerate or be tolerated by groups. Most can, but the techniques used for inpatient groups are not identical to those used for outpatient insight groups.

LITERATURE

Lindemann[1] studied the surviving relatives of victims of the Cocoanut Grove fire in Boston. He found that therapy aimed specifically at expressing and resolving the loss was helpful. Later, Caplan[2] thought that during emotional crisis, individuals could utilize adaptive or maladaptive coping mechanisms. At the point of crisis and with relatively little effort, the therapist can encourage previously untried adaptive solutions. A patient recently admitted to the hospital is in crisis and perhaps prepared to try new solutions. He is mourning his social failure and the partial death of his internal objects. This and other important and significant losses make it possible for the patient to seriously consider new ways of adapting.

Caplan[2] used the crisis model of Lindemann as one of the basic principles of community psychiatry. He emphasized that patient crisis comes from recent loss. This may be loss of self-esteem, of important objects, of nonhuman environment, or even loss of goals through apparently insurmountable obstacles. In crisis therapy, you focus your mind and the patient's on why the patient is there but allow the patient, not the therapist, to define needs. The therapist should be active, spontaneous, and flexible, as well as quiet and reflective. He should willingly accept his role as transference object without necessarily interpreting it and be willing to terminate therapy when the patient wishes and not wait until the therapist is comfortable with separation. Caplan underlined the importance of keeping severely disabled psychiatric patients as close to their original physical and psychological community as possible. He stressed the importance, often overlooked by psychotherapists, of maintaining the sanction of both official and unofficial power structure. In a way that anticipates Whitaker and Lieberman, Caplan thought changes in the human condition result in temporary disorganization and anxiety but eventual adaptation. During disorganization, there may be conflictual regression expressed as unusual anxiety, symptoms, or acting out.

Whitaker and Lieberman[11] in 1967 said groups have disturbing and reactive motives (wishes and fears secondary to the wish), and that compromise solutions between the two may be restrictive or enabling. A restrictive solution has more reactive motive and more boredom but less anxiety. An enabling solution expresses more of the disturbing motive or wish but results in increased anxiety. In less traditional solutions, creativeness, originality, and anxiety go hand in hand. As a group works, it tries one solution after another until one is viable. Viable simply means a consensus by the group that this solution is tolerable. Solutions may be changed but are most easily changed as they form and when the group is young. A series of viable solutions become the group constitution or climate. Solutions are not ideal but entirely rational.

In ward groups, the collection of solutions remains sparse. Instead, we see the dynamics of a constantly beginning group. Nonetheless, Whitaker and Lieberman's emphasis on understanding the group process, not individual dynamics, as well as their understanding of group solutions, are vital contributions to our work with ward groups.

Yalom[4] outlined the principles of beginning group in 1975. He conceptualized the goal of group as analysis of interpersonal style and experimentation with behavior. He divided the evolutionary stages of group into orientation, conflict, and work. All stages are present at all times but new groups are occupied mainly with orientation. In the orientation phase, there is a search for structure, dependence on the leader, concern about boundaries, and doubt about whether others can be trusted.

In the conflict phase, there is a struggle for dominance, balanced by a desire for harmony and affection. There also is a gradual increase in cohesiveness.

When work begins in earnest, there is marked cohesiveness and few absences, with considerable inter- and intrapersonal investigation and a serious commitment to the group.

The ward group, with its rapid turnover, most resembles a constantly beginning group. There is a trend toward formal introduction, silence, monologues, talk of social discomfort, and conflict between therapeutic and social needs. Members search for rationales, size up other members, and are preoccupied with liking and being liked. They often appear puzzled, dependent, and overly eager to build structure. There is a search for common ground, a tendency to give and seek advice, plus a fair amount of lateness, absence, and other evidence of resistance. During this stage, the therapist should be active and set the group style.

Yalom thinks the leader should consciously or unconsciously fill social gaps and provide structure by action and example. The group leader should protect patients with loud, interpersonal pathology from social suicide. The therapist's example helps establish trust, allows a focus on interpersonal behavior and reactions to it, and encourages speculation on reasons for behavior. The therapist must deal actively with the addition of new members and their anxiety, as well as with the tendency of old group members to express their anxiety by closing ranks and attacking new members. The new members may express their fear by silence or defiance. Old and new members may move toward one another, against one another, or away from one another. With the addition of new members, old issues of trust, cohesiveness, and structure resurrect. Since loss and separation are vital issues to the hospitalized patient, the ward group offers continuing exposure to, as well as an opportunity to work on these problems.

Kalibat et al.[12] described a follow-up group psychotherapy program designed for 1,000 chronic, severly disabled psychiatric patients. One-half were schizophrenic, more than 90% took medication, 70% were on phenothiazines and 7% on antidepressants. The patients were chronic, had not responded to the usual verbal therapies, but could stay out of the hospital if they received medication and support. Care had to be available as needed.

Kalibat concluded that he and his workers had found "the follow-up group to be an effective and useful vehicle for providing service to large numbers of severely troubled psychiatric patients at comparatively low cost. We feel our operation may be useful as a partial solution to the major public health problems of schizophrenia in the community." Kalibat emphasized the necessity for flexible patient attendance, the value of group solutions, and how group solutions reduce anxiety when therapists leave.

Informal social groups, which developed spontaneously, met one to four hours before the formal group. These were helpful in the opinion of patients and staff. All parts of the program—medication, formal and informal groups, and an individual brief meeting with the physician at the end of group—were at the patient's discretion. There was encouragement but no pressure to attend. Kalibat's program suggests schizophrenics can benefit and will voluntarily attend appropriately conducted groups. Lesser[13] amplified, confirmed, and added additional data and theoretical underpinning to Kalibat's work.

Maxmen[14] believes ward groups produce rapid decreases in symptoms and increase the patient's ability to think clearly and clinically. Thinking clinically is the ability to step outside intense transference reaction, observe oneself, then correlate and integrate new solutions. This enables patients to respond effectively to their illness and permits therapeutic behavior toward others.

Gunn[15] made videotapes of inpatient therapy groups. He showed these to patients and thought this increased cohesiveness and shortened the early phases of therapy.

Fleischl[16] said therapists should be supportive to discharged hospital patients. This blocks rehospitalization. He notes that outpatient groups serve as testing grounds, develop social skills, and provide for potential human contact. In short, they do some of the same things as an inpatient ward group.

Fried[17] believed chronic patients have trouble expressing direct feelings and needs because their hope for help from others has been repeatedly and severely disappointed. The result is an introjection of a cruel, punitive superego, secondary splitting, and projection. Group can begin to modify these introjects.

Steiner[18] addressed the problem of decreased ego function and decreased autonomy. Schizophrenics seem unable to organize and maintain intrapsychic objects. Group is especially helpful to patients who avoid external object relations. Group can provide corrective emotional experience for patients who feel others are of no help. It can increase ego function and help patients acquire organized and consistent intrapsychic objects, thus increasing autonomy. The group does this, in part, by becoming a "good enough mother." The therapist should have limited expectations and remember that patients can learn to imitate or conform to the role expected of them. This outward conformity can lead to internalization of social norms. The group can also serve as a transitional family for patients with poor experiences in their own family.

Grotjahn and Kline[19] observed that a ward group's preoccupation with the seemingly mundane can serve as a valuable entree to the patient's and the group's unconscious, and inform the therapist of group and individual dynamics as well as providing clues for treatment. The mundane is, for these patients, a tolerable and safe medium of communication. The careful therapist respects this necessary oblique contact.

A summary of the literature suggests that patients in ward groups suffer from unreliable introjects and unhappy, frustrating, destructive social experiences. They are in crisis, show defective ego function and are prone to be excessively cautious in interpersonal contact. The "introjects" are predominantly chaotic, inconsistent, critical, punitive, and cruel. Inpatients often have difficulty expressing themselves directly and will use stories or metaphor to describe their feelings and concerns. Displacement, denial, splitting, and projection are their common individual mental mechanisms. These defenses are present in the group process but usually less so.

The therapist needs to be active, human, and honest. He must be patient with the slow progress of the group and not ambitious about improvement. There is no reason why the patients should not imitate or role play appropriate social behavior since this can later be internalized.

The group dynamics are those of a collection of individuals in crisis with high levels of anxiety and depression and defenses against these affects. There also are defenses against cognition that may lead to affect. The group will be preoccupied with issues of trust, concerns about loss and separation, and feelings of personal worthlessness based on repeated social defeats. It will be difficult to establish a cohesive inpatient group.

The therapist must be alert to countertransference problems that develop when working with the disadvantaged. Different, but equally troublesome, countertransference problems can develop from the therapist's interaction with the hospital community. Inappropriate role models, inherited from training, may interfere with the active, open, and honest stance required of ward group leaders.

DYNAMICS OF A WARD GROUP

Patients in ward groups are in crisis and have been socially defeated. They have underlying anxiety and depression but usually show only secondary defenses against these painful affects. Acting out, psychotic preoccupation and production, isolation, hopelessness, and resignation are some of these defenses. There is a tendency to use denial, splitting, and projection as primary defenses. Perception and integration of information may be repressed because it will lead to painful affect. Inpatients have been subject to severe loss and separation anxiety as a result of the failure of their introjects. A useless introject must be killed, buried, and mourned. This process may be more painful than mourning a dead intimate. If outside social contact is available, new introjects can be developed. Unfortunately, inpatients have been chronically and acutely deprived of (as well as disappointed in) social contact. Introjects need constant tolerable social contact to survive, thrive, and change.

Ward patients have also suffered severe losses in self-esteem and a decrease in internal and external structure. They may have passed through denial and anger to resignation and hopelessness. As a result, they often feel they have no power to help themselves and are so worthless no one else will help them. They may, based on their experience, see others as hostile and destructive. Yet every patient retains a core of hope, a desire for social contact, and a longing for good objects. This is so even when the primary defenses are denial, splitting, and projection, and even when internal objects are punitive and destructive. Transference and much of the patient's behavior in group is clearly related to the quality of the internal objects.

Group dynamics are those of the beginning group so eloquently described by Yalom. In addition, the ward group prefers to talk of mundane things and will discuss personal concerns indirectly and in the metaphor. These patients need structure, in and out of group. They desperately need role models. Sometimes the therapist is the only one who can provide this. The group, as a whole, needs to learn that other people can be helpful. Later, group members will introject the helpful aspects of others either as new internal objects or as modifications of old ones. The group, as well as the individual members, struggles with crises of both external and internal loss, and separation accompanied by depression, anxiety, and mourning. Old introjects must be decathected or modified. New ones may be acquired. Even in brief inpatient groups, new, partial introjects are organized. The new introjects are often a distillation of the best qualities of each group member, since, given unencumbered choice, most people prefer good things to bad. If introjects can be softened or changed enough to permit the patient to continue in a post-hospital group, then the therapist has been successful.

Countertransference problems may be considerable. Therapeutic ambition may result in pressing patients beyond their means and thus increasing the patient's self-perception as unlovable and unworthy of love. The same therapeutic ambition may lead to an intolerant attitude toward the group's indirect communication and a tendency to push more than necessary for direct, honest confrontation and premature transference interpretation.

On the other hand, the therapist may struggle with a tendency to regard his patients as unsocial, deviant, alien, and hopeless. It is important that psychiatric inpatients be seen as part of human society, kept in the community, and in contact with normal society. The group's behavioral standards should be as socially realistic as possible.

For some therapists, the most difficult countertransference problem is their conviction that they must be blank screens, immune to affect, and nonreactive to the patients. Unfortunately, this only convinces inpatients that they are subhumans being observed by a detached, superior, and disinterested scientist.

The therapist must beware of tendencies to scapegoat parents, society, the government, and the immediate bureaucracy. This does not mean he should turn a blind eye to the defects or problems in any of these areas—but he must block attempts to focus group affect on outsiders. The therapist does not need to totally block such conversation but must be alert to underlying dynamics, keep his comments therapeutic, and not join in the witch hunt.

All institutions, hospitals more than most, worry about change. Administrative structure is unconsciously, but carefully, designed to get the job done with a minimum of pain and anxiety. An organization demands control of individual eccentricity. Tampering with organizational structure stirs fear that egocentric emotional chaos will be released. We must respect the formal and informal power structure and its concern with the maintenance of reasonable order, just as we respect any group's restrictive solutions. We respect its structure even while we work to change it. The dedicated group therapist must keep in mind that the hospital, as a whole, functions as a group and a series of subgroups. It shares the therapy group's struggles between disturbing and reactive motives resolved by enabling or restrictive solutions.

Since propinquity overcomes paranoia, the careful group therapist will directly, or through his senior administrator, keep the hospital director informed. Regular contact with the hospital administration and the ancillary personnel who can make or break a group is essential. The administrator is willing to deal with realistic problems that lead to improved service but deeply appreciates the time and information needed to prepare for the change. He may have trouble being entirely fair to those who deliver unpleasant surprises.

In those cases where the administrative hierarchy or ancillary personnel are excessively worried about group psychotherapy, it may be the result of lack of knowledge, an unfortunate past experience, or a current unrealistic fantasy. These can all be worked with. However, when a hospital normally tolerant of group therapy becomes critical, it may indicate that the group is in some way being mismanaged. A well-run group should not increase destructive acting-out nor should it increase the length of stay. It certainly should not stir up a hornet's nest of opposition. If it does, the therapist must slow down, temporarily tolerate restrictive solutions, and slowly work toward enabling compromises. Above all, he must look to his countertransference. If, at any point, the group is, or becomes, unacceptable to the institution, the group therapist needs to examine his countertransference to the group and to the institutional structure.

Running an inpatient group is hard and frustrating work. You rarely see much in the way of results but it can prepare patients for the ongoing group and social experiences that will lead to real, and even permanent, improvement in mental health.

REFERENCES

1. Lindemann, E. Symptomatology and management of acute grief. *Am. J. Psychiatry* **101**: 141-148 (1944).
2. Caplan, G. *Principles of Preventive Psychiatry*. New York: Basic Books (1964).
3. Yamamoto, J., James, Q., Bloombaum, M., and Hattem, J. Racial factors in patient selection. *Am. J. Psychiatry* **124**: 630-636 (1967).
4. Yalom, D. *The Theory and Practice of Group Psychotherapy*, 2nd Ed. New York: Basic Books (1975).
5. Arsenian, J. and Semrad, E. V. Individual and group manifestations. *Int. J. Group Psychother.* **17**: 82-98 (1967).
6. May, P. R. and Tuma, A. H. Treatment of schizophrenia. An experimental study of five treatment methods. *Br. J. Psychiatry* **111**: 503-510 (1965).
7. May, P. *The Treatment of Schizophrenia*. New York: Science House (1968).
8. Borowski, T. and Tolwinski, T. Treatment of paranoid schizophrenics with chlorpromazine and group therapy. *Dis. Nerv. Syst.* **30**: 201-202 (1969).
9. Malan, D. H., Balfour, F. H., Hood, V. G., and Shooter, A. Group psychotherapy. A long term follow-up study. *Arch. Gen. Psychiatry* **33**: 1303-1315 (1976).
10. Kaplan, H. I. and Sadock, B. J. *Comprehensive Group Psychotherapy*. Baltimore: Williams & Wilkins (1971).
11. Whitaker, D. and Lieberman, M. A. *Psychotherapy through the Group Process*. New York: Atherton (1964).

12. Kalibat, F., Kotin, J., and Kline F. For chronic patients: the follow-up group. *Transnational Mental Health Research Newsletter* **18**: 2, 9-10 (1967).
13. Lesser, I. M. and Friedman, C. T. Beyond medications: group therapy for the chronic psychiatric patient. *Int. J. Group Psychother.* **30**: 187-199 (1980).
14. Maxmen, J. S. An educative model for inpatient group therapy. *Int. J. Group Psychother.* **28**: 321-338 (1978).
15. Gunn, R. C. A use of videotape with inpatient therapy groups. *Int. J. Group Psychother.* **28**: 365-370 (1978).
16. Fleischl, M. Techniques of psychotherapy with chronic patients. *In:* Wolberg, L. R. and Aronson, M. L. (Eds.), *Group Psychotherapy 1979: An Overview.* New York: Stratton Intercontinental Medical Book Corp. (1979).
17. Fried, K. W. Within and without: the examination of a ubiquitous resistance in group therapy. *In:* Wolberg, L. R. and Aronson, M. L. (Eds.), *Group Psychotherapy 1979: An Overview.* New York: Stratton Intercontinental Medical Book Corp. (1979).
18. Steiner, J. Holistic group therapy with schizophrenic patients. *Int. J. Group Psychother.* **29**: 195-210 (1979).
19. Grotjahn, M. and Kline, F. Group therapy in psychiatric hospitals and outpatient clinics. *In:* Wolberg, L. R. and Aronson, M. L. (Eds.), *Group Psychotherapy 1979: An Overview.* New York: Stratton Intercontinental Medical Book Corp. (1979).

5
Group Therapy with Adolescents

Stuart Fine, M.B., F.R.C.P. (C)

Groups are useful assessment and therapeutic modalities for adolescents in different settings.[1,2,3] They have been used in schools,[4] recreation centers, social agencies, courts, psychiatric outpatient, day patient, and inpatient programs[5,6,7] from 1950 to the present. Group therapy can be used alone or in conjunction with individual and family therapy. Groups have been used with adolescents who, although asymptomatic, were identified as "at psychological risk."[8] Group therapy has been successful with handicapped adolescents,[9] retarded adolescents,[10,11] delinquent adolescents,[12,13] pregnant, unwed teenagers,[14] and obese adolescents.[15] Groups have been used as a way of screening adolescent patients for assignment to group or other therapy programs.

Three books have been written about adolescent group therapy in the last 12 years.[1,2,3] A review of the literature was published in 1968.[16]

The ways in which groups exert their influence are numerous.[17,18] The peer group is important to adolescents' modification of attitudes and to changing their behavior. Adolescents are trying to emancipate themselves from their parents, establish sexual role identities, decide on vocations to pursue, and settle their attitudes toward sex, drugs, work, and leisure. Peer group values and behaviors are often accepted and adopted.

All types of therapeutic groups should provide socially acceptable values, and therapists should model socially acceptable behavior.

Some group therapeutic factors are catharsis in an accepting environment, confrontation about behavior or attitudes by group leaders, or, better still, by peers, self-disclosure and the experience of being accepted, the universality of problems, self-understanding, vicarious learning, and (above all) instillation of hope.[17] The satisfaction obtained from altruism in a group, and the guidance of peers and leaders is also therapeutic.[17] Group cohesion, where members have a sense of belonging, is helpful and perhaps necessary before individual members change.

There are also special features of adolescent groups. Phelan[20] points out that adolescent groups differ from those of adults in that the therapist of adolescents needs to be a teacher and parent in addition to a therapist. Adolescent groups provide a forum where adolescents can examine their impact on others. They can discuss and examine their life experiences. They can experiment with thinking and acting and see the effects, and peer pressure can help change values and behavior.[21]

STARTING THE GROUP

When establishing a group, attention must be paid to the size of the proposed group, diagnostic categories that should be included, age range, sex, use of other psychotherapeutic modalities (concomitant individual and family therapy), the number of sessions per week, and the total number of sessions envisaged. Decisions must be made about assessment procedures, whether new members can be added after the group has begun, and how to deal with absences from the group, violent behavior, and social contacts outside group.[1]

Several adolescents need to be interviewed and assessed, as only some will be suitable for the group and not all those who are thought to be suitable will agree to come. About sixteen teenagers need to be seen to obtain a sufficient number (about eight) for the group. There are two levels of selection. One is to select a suitable mix for the particular group. Some of the reasons why adolescents might not want to come to group are shyness, fear of the psychopathology of the other members, or not understanding how group can help. Once persuaded to come, most adolescents are conscientious about attending. Much group work with adolescents has been done in closed settings with juvenile delinquents. Many of the following remarks about group have been gleaned from experience with outpatient groups, but the general principles would apply to inpatient groups.

Adolescents who are withdrawn and isolated seem to improve after a group experience.[1] Relative contraindications to inclusion in a group are the frankly psychotic, drug addicts, and delinquents who consistently show no evidence of anxiety or concern for others. Many also exclude adolescents with an I.Q. under 80, unless all members of the group are mentally retarded. Special groups can be organized for some adolescents who fall into categories of relative contraindication, but these groups require special expertise and structure from the leader. (It is surprising how different adolescents are in group, compared to an individual interview and compared to how the family describes them.) In adolescent groups aged 14 years and under, mixing sexes is not recommended.

There are advantages to having male and female co-therapists in the group. They may be from different disciplines—for example, a social worker and a child psychiatry resident.

Because most adolescents attend school, the group usually commences near the beginning of the school year and continues until early May. Attempts to hold an adolescent group over the summer months meet with limited success because of vacation or work during the summer.

New patients should be given some orientation to adolescent group therapy. The candidate for group may be seen alone and then with the parents. The co-therapists may do these interviews together. The therapists should try to establish with the adolescents which attitudes and behaviors they wish to change and what the goals are prior to the beginning of the group. The parents should be told that all matters discussed in the group are confidential and they should not expect the therapists or the teenagers to divulge any of what happened in the group. The adolescent and his family may have another therapist to help them with the individual and family problems that arise. Occasionally the individual and family therapist is also one of the group therapists. Then it is difficult to decide whether certain information obtained in these other interviews can be divulged in the group, and group members will tend to have a closer relationship with the group therapist who is also their individual or family therapist.

The ideal group size is eight to ten members, with two cotherapists. Observers may watch through a one-way screen, but the group members should be aware of these observers and should be given the option of meeting them if they so wish.

The group should meet in the same room each week. It may be better to sit on cushions on the floor, as this seems to make the setting more informal. If there are two therapists, they should not sit next to each other.

The therapists should meet with the clinical supervisor and other trainees once a week or biweekly. Written summaries of each group are useful and can be copied so that each member has a copy before the next group. This is a technique suggested by Bloch et al.[22] and it provides continuity from session to session, emphasizes certain issues, allows the group members to realize what the therapists are trying to do, and keeps the observers and supervisor informed. If videotape facilities are available, an attempt should be made to videotape an early, middle, and late session so that changes can be objectively shown.

THE GROUP IN PROCESS

Some rules should be established in the first session. Confidentiality should be stressed and a statement of the purpose of the group made (e.g., "Each person is here for different reasons but we hope that by getting to know one another you can emphasize one another's good characteristics while helping to change some of their irritating and upsetting behavior. You may also be able to help one another to look at different ways of solving problems."). Each person should state his name and given some autobiographical information.

Participants may be encouraged to tell something about their families and the family relationships, school, friends, special skills, and interests, and they may role play some of their interpersonal problems.

Beginning exercises may be useful if the therapists are comfortable with such activities as breaking into a circle and breaking out again, gently pummelling one another's backs, lying on the ground, and using progressive muscular relaxation and deep breathing techniques.

Adolescent groups go through the same phases as adult groups. First there is jockeying for acceptance by group members, then hierarchy formation where some members dominate others, and may even challenge the group leaders. Then there is struggle for the affection of group leaders. Schitz[23] has described these three phases this way: "The in or out phase (acceptance); the up or down phase (dominance); and the near and far phase (affection)." Bion[24] describes the dependence-independence phase, the flight-fight phase, and the pairing phase. Also described are: "The stages of initial politeness and good behavior; griping, testing, and acting out; dependency and demandingness; and ultimately mature problem solving and separation."[3]

Group members need some instructions on how they can help one another.[25] They should be encouraged to ask for more details, ask how a group member felt when something happened and to say how they solved similar problems in the past. They should be discouraged from being critical of how incidents were handled unless they can point out a better way. They should not simply reassure fellow members by telling them not to worry about certain problems "as they might go away." They must be discouraged from changing the subject and an optimistic attitude should be reinforced.

There are some common themes in adolescent groups that reflect the tasks of development of adolescents. These include a new relationship with parents and with peers of the same and the opposite sex, dealing with their own impulses and emotions, and deciding on goals in life and a set of values. Attitudes toward divorce are discussed in group when separations and divorce occur in the families of the participants.

Since these groups often take place only once a week for 30 sessions, because of the school year, the work of the group has to be done more rapidly than is the case with some adult groups.

COMMON GROUP RESISTANCES

The establishment of mutual trust and the gradual expression of more honest opinions and feelings help group members share concerns and suggest ways of solving problems.[25,26] The process of establishing group cohesion and belonging can be facilitated by group leaders who address statements and questions to the whole group and who talk about the group as "we." Some group ventures facilitate a sense of belonging. One group cleaned and decorated a rundown basement for its group venue. Their sense of belonging was greatly enhanced.[27]

Several attitudes and maneuvers impede group progress.[3,28] These are resistances and can be frustrating to neophyte and experienced group therapists. Group members are often *reluctant to confront one another* about maladaptive or irritating behavior. There may be *long silences,* which can be resistant but can also occur when the group members consider and absorb ideas and attitudes. The only ways therapists can determine what the silences may mean is to examine them in the context in which they occur and ask questions. Therapists may make statements about what they think are the causes for the silence, and see whether the group acquiesces or "protests too much," in which case the therapists may be correct. *Absences and lateness* are often used to attract attention, yet it is surprising how infrequently members verbally note that someone is absent or ask why someone comes late. Even when it is a group rule that when patients know they will be absent, they should call, they don't. (Perhaps this is to see whether they have been missed.) Certain topics may be raised *to test* whether the therapists are willing to discuss them. For example, sex, drugs, and "bad" language may be used to see if the therapists are tolerant and can be reasonable and critical. Group members may want to discuss general topics so that specific concerns can be avoided. They may change the subject frequently and indulge in horseplay or fidgeting. Some members try to *monopolize* the group discussion and others avoid discussing any personal problems but show intense interest in the problems of others. Somatic complaints and descriptions of delinquent exploits may obscure feelings of anxiety, guilt, sadness, or anger and discussion of these feelings.

Occasionally group members will *scapegoat* one member of the group. An example of this was when a girl with a severe speech defect was picked on by an entire group because she called one of the boys "Chrith" instead of Chris. This boy was concerned about his masculine image and was incensed at this name. The whole group insisted that the girl could pronounce the name correctly "if only she would try harder." She did try again, only to produce "Chrith" again, at which point Chris threw his sneaker at her. She began to cry. Chris was asked to leave the group until he felt he could describe rather than act out his feelings. The rest of the group then scolded the girl for the remainder of the session "for pretending to be handicapped."

It is not unusual for one group member to be placed on the "hot seat" and become the center of discussion and allow the other members temporary safety from their own anxieties. This sometimes results in "neglected" members who threaten to leave since they find the group "boring" or "unhelpful." This is probably because they cannot get the attention of the group leaders, who focus on the member in the "hot seat."

WAYS OF ENHANCING THE EFFICACY OF GROUPS

The group leader's characteristics[29] are important in fostering change. One study of adolescents in twelve different groups, each with eight members and two co-therapists, compared four therapist characteristics: caring, self-expression, confronting and clarifying, and controlling. The better leaders need a blend of caring and self-expressiveness. Therapists who are controlling, even though they provide clarification and confrontation, are less effective.

Patients do better when they are told, prior to starting group therapy, what to expect in group and how they may get the most out of group.[17] It is unlikely that free-floating discussion will be as effective as a structured, goal-oriented learning process.

One novel idea for enhancing group efficacy is the use of volunteer adolescents, who are recruited, selected, and provided with brief training.[32,33] These volunteers become models for self-disclosure and empathy, but unlike the group leaders are the same age as referred patients. When groups with volunteers (four volunteers in each of two groups of eight) were compared with a group of eight with no volunteers, the patients in the groups with volunteers had a better attendance. The volunteers were conscientious about attending and were perhaps good role models. Adolescents became less emotionally distant in groups with volunteers. The difficulty with the program was the amount of time required to recruit, select, and train volunteers. Using members who have already been in a group before may be as effective as using trained volunteers.

In a follow-up of adolescents in group, done by the author, many adolescents complained that therapists tended to take the group process too seriously and that there was not enough laughter and humor, suggesting that adolescents need more emotional distance than adults.

CO-THERAPY

Provided that co-therapists get on well together, or at least are able to discuss and resolve their differences, there are advantages to sharing group leadership. These advantages include one therapist monitoring behavior while the other makes interpretations or confrontations, modeling self-disclosure, providing male and female role models, and showing how differences of opinion can be resolved or partially resolved while remaining friends.

SPECIAL PROGRAMS

"Group behavioral training"[8] can benefit high school students with few symptoms who are judged to be at risk. These are students who have high levels of anxiety and low self-esteem; they later may become socially incompetent, develop psychological symptoms, and require help. Group behavioral training for these students consists of eight sessions with a teacher, recruited from the high school the students attend, teaching social skills. Students who have received this training have shown improvement, compared to a control group which has not.

Some special groups are activity-oriented. Camping groups[35] and sports programs[36] show how peer cooperation can be maintained independent of formal therapy or after a formal group therapy experience.

Although many groups form to convey information to adolescents (e.g., groups for diabetic teenagers and groups for teenagers on renal dialysis), such groups can cause social skills and attitude changes in the adolescent.

RESULTS OF GROUP THERAPY WITH
CHILDREN AND ADOLESCENTS

Relatively little research has been done on comparing the effectiveness of adolescent group therapy with other modalities. In 32 studies of group therapy with delinquents, most showed positive results, especially those where behavioral and modeling techniques were used. Discussion groups appeared to be the least effective.[12]

A large review of group therapy with children under the age of 14 "reveals unconvincing evidence of its effectiveness." An approximately equivalent number of studies yielded generally positive, mixed, and equivocal results.[37]

USE OF ADOLESCENT GROUPS
FOR TRAINING THERAPISTS

Adolescents in group therapy are interesting because they tend to talk freely and may change moods and behaviors rapidly. Extrapolations and conjectures from nonverbal behavior are not as necessary as in group therapy with younger children.

Several ways of teaching group have been suggested.[38] The most common is for the new therapist to receive brief instruction, then have the therapists start their own group accompanied by regular supervision, with audiotapes, videotapes, and/or written summaries of the group. These serve as memory aids and the tapes or case reports are used to teach perceptual and interpretive skills and to suggest practical group management skills. Tapes are particularly useful for identifying and correcting countertransference.

CONCLUSION

Adolescent group psychotherapy is an enjoyable psychotherapeutic endeavor for both patients and therapists. The efficacy of groups is difficult to prove. That it is effective with some adolescents seems to be accepted on anecdotal evidence, but careful controlled studies still need to be done.

It is easiest to establish an adolescent group psychotherapy program where there are several potential group leaders in an agency or clinic, but it is possible in a private office. Different theoretical frameworks of group functioning (psychoanalytic, behavioral modification, and small group theory) may be used, but whatever theory is adhered to, adolescents demand more active participation of group leaders than do adult groups. There are different conflicts to resolve and different ways that the group resists change compared to adult situations.

REFERENCES

1. Berkowitz, I. On growing a group: some thoughts on structure, process, and setting. *In:* Berkowitz, I. (Ed.), *Adolescents Grow in Groups: Experiences in Adolescent Group Therapy.* New York: Brunner/Mazel (1972), pp. 6-28.
2. Berkowitz, I. and Sugar M. Indications and contraindications for adolescent group therapy. *In:* Sugar, M. (Ed.), *The Adolescent in Group and Family Therapy.* New York: Brunner/Mazel (1975), pp. 3-26.

3. MacLennan, B. W. and Felsenfeld, N. *Group Counseling and Psychotherapy with Adolescents.* New York: Columbia University Press (1968).
4. Byles, J. A. Helping students to adapt to high school through the use of small groups. *Can. Mental Health* 27: 2-3 (1979).
5. Becker, B. J., Gusrae, R., and Berger, E. Adolescent group psychotherapy, a community mental health program. *Int. J. Group Psychother.* 6: 300-316 (1956).
6. Powles, W. Group management of emotionally ill adolescents in a Canadian mental hospital. *Can. Psychiatric Assoc. J.* 4: 77-89 (1959).
7. Chiles, J. A. and Sanger, E. The use of groups in brief inpatient treatment of adolescents. *Hosp. Community Psychiatry* 28: 443-445 (1977).
8. Kraft, I. A. An overview of group therapy with adolescents. *Int. J. Group Psychother.* 18: 461-480 (1968).
9. Hartman, L. M. The preventive reduction of psychological risk in asymptomatic adolescents. *Am. J. Orthopsychiatry* 49: 121-135 (1979).
10. Bayrakal, S. A group experience with chronically disabled adolescents. *Am. J. Psychiatry* 132: 1291-1294 (1975).
11. Fine, R. H. and Dawson, J. C. A therapy program for the mildly retarded adolescent. *Am. J. Ment. Defic.* 69: 23-30 (1964).
12. Fisher, L. A. and Wolfson, I. N. Group therapy of mental defectives. *Am. J. Ment. Defic* 57: 463-476 (1953).
13. Julian, A. and Kilmann, P. R. Group treatment of juvenile delinquents: a review of the outcome literature. *Int. J. Group Psychother.* 29: 3-37 (1979).
14. Didato, S. V. Delinquents in group therapy, some new techniques. *Adolescence* 5: 207-222 (1970).
15. Kaufmann, P. N. and Deutsch, A. L. Group therapy for pregnant unwed adolescents in the prenatal clinic of a general hospital. *Int. J. Group Psychother.* 17: 309-320 (1967).
16. Stanley, E. J., Glaster, H. H., Levin, D. G., Adams, P. A., and Coley, I. L. The treatment of adolescent obesity: is it worthwhile? *Am. J. Orthopsychiatry* 38: 207-208 (1968).
17. Hodgman, C. H. and Stewart, W. H. The adolescent screening group. *Int. J. Group Psychother.* 22: 177-185 (1972).
18. Bloch, S. Group psychotherapy. *In:* Bloch, S. (Ed.), *An Introduction to the Psychotherapies.* Oxford: Oxford University Press (1979), pp. 53-82.
19. Yalom, I. D. *The Theory and Practice of Group Psychotherapy,* 2nd Ed. New York: Basic Books (1975).
20. Phelan, J. R. Parent, teacher or analyst: the adolescent—group therapist's trilemma. *Int. J. Group Psychother.* 24: 238-244 (1974).
21. Boenheim, C. Group psychotherapy with adolescents. *Int. J. Group Psychother.* 7: 398-405 (1957).
22. Bloch, S., Brown, S., Davis, K., and Dishotsky, N. The use of a written summary in group psychotherapy supervision. *Am. J. Psychiatry* 132: 1055-1057 (1975).
23. Schitz, W. C. *FIRO: A Three Dimensional Theory of Interpersonal Behavior.* New York: Holt, Rinehart & Winston (1958).

24. Bion, W. R. *Experiences in Groups and Other Papers.* New York: Basic Books (1961).
25. Rappaport, J., Gross, T., and Lepper, C. Modeling, sensitivity training, and instruction: implications for the training of college student volunteers and for outcome research. *J. Consult. Clin. Psychol.* **40**: 99-107 (1973).
26. Friedman, R., Schlise, S., and Seligman, S. Issues involved in the treatment of an adolescent group. *Adolescence* **10**: 357-368 (1975).
27. Bruce, T. Group work with adolescents. *J. Adolescence* **1**: 47-54 (1978).
28. Duffey, M. Factors contributing to the development of a cohesive adolescent psychotherapy group. *J. Psychiatric Nurs.* **17**: 21-24 (1979).
29. Anzima, F. Transference-countertransference issues in group psychotherapy for adolescents. *Int. J. Child Psychother.* **1**: 51-70 (1972).
30. Gadpaille, W. J. Observations on the sequence of resistances in groups of adolescent delinquents. *Int. J. Group Psychother.* **9**: 275-286 (1959).
31. Hurst, A. G., Stein, K. B., Korchin, S. J., and Soskin, W. F. Leadership style determinants of cohesiveness in adolescent groups. *Int. J. Group Psychother.* **28**: 263-277 (1978).
32. Fine, S., Knight-Webb, G., and Vernon, J. Selected volunteer adolescents in adolescent group therapy. *Adolescence* **12**: 190-197 (1977).
33. Fine, S., Knight-Webb, G., and Breau, K. Volunteer adolescents in adolescent group therapy. Effects on patients and volunteers. *Br. J. Psychiatry* **129**: 407-413 (1976).
34. Cabral, R. J., Best, J., and Paton A. Patients' and observers' assessments of process and outcome in group therapy: a follow-up study. *Am. J. Psychiatry* **132**: 1052-1054 (1975).
35. Hobbs, T. R. and Shelton, G. C. Therapeutic camping for emotionally disturbed adolescents. *Hosp. Community Psychiatry* **23**: 298-301 (1972).
36. Dozier, J. E., Lewis, S., Kersey, A. G., and Charping, J. W. Sports group: an alternative treatment modality for emotionally disturbed adolescents. *Adolescence* **13**: 483-488 (1978).
37. Abramowitz, C. V. The effectiveness of group psychotherapy with children. *Arch. Gen. Psychiatry* **33**: 320-326 (1976).
38. Berkowitz, I. H. and Sugar, M. An experience in teaching adolescent group psychotherapy: observers become participants. *Int. J. Group Psychother.* **26**: 441-453 (1976).
39. Ackerman, N. Group psychotherapy with a mixed group of adolescents. *Int. J. Group Psychother.* **5**: 249-260 (1955).
40. Bardill, D. R. A behavior-contracting program of group treatment for early adolescents in a residential treatment setting. *Int. J. Group Psychother.* **27**: 389-400 (1977).
41. Tuckman, B. W. Developmental sequence in small groups. *Psychol. Bull.* **63**: 384-399 (1965).

Part III:
Group Therapy In The
Outpatient Clinic

6
Crisis Groups
Claude T.H. Friedmann, M.D.

Mary, an attractive but rather inarticulate young woman, was crying profusely. Jim, an elderly black man, limped into the room, his cane banging loudly on the floor. Tiny Marsha, looking and sounding a good ten years younger than her stated age of 25, was unburdening herself: Her sister has just suddenly died from asthma. Wilma sat stoically silent in the corner; no emotion showed on her face. Michael, who only a week ago had made a serious suicide attempt, looked sad and bewildered. Obese and childish Jane kept interrupting with trivial (to the group) but important (to her) ruminations about her recent trip to the grocery store.

It was my first crisis group, and by the end of the hour, I thought I was the toastmaster for "Queen for a Day." I was ringing wet, emotionally drained, and barely able to stand up. My partner, a psychiatric intern named David, was asking for supervision. Somehow, I wished he would ask for a drink!

Mary's husband, it turned out, had been missing for the last three days, hiding from the police. He was suspected of participating in a burglary. Mary hadn't slept since he had disappeared; money was running short; and her youngest child had the flu. Jin, who had alcohol on his breath, wanted a disability statement filled out. He was unable or unwilling to accept depression as the cause of his back pain, blaming it on his last job. Nonetheless, he threatened suicide no less than three times during the session. Marsha's sister, a chronic schizophrenic, had gone into status asthmaticus the night before. She had died suddenly a few hours later. Marsha, a borderline and dependent woman, alternated between thoughts of her sister and worries that her grandmother would throw her out of her apartment. Wilma, toward the end of the session, announced that she was "all better" and "wouldn't be back to the group." I never did learn what it was that she was "all better" from. Michael, a bright, articulate college student, was profoundly depressed. He discussed his recent decision to leave school and live with his parents. He said he loved group and wasn't suicidal today, but he said little else and refused to take anti-depressants. Jane giggled a lot, interrupted frequently, and was finally asked to "cool it" by Marsha—but was continually egged on by Mary's empathetic questions. When the intern finally interrupted her, she broke down, wailing hysterically about how "lousy she felt" and "how insecure it makes me feel to know that nobody cares."

I was presented, then, with an overwhelming array of acute situational disorders, depression of various shades, character pathology compounded by acute disorders, suicide, alcoholism, financial distress, and infidelity—life and its traumas. It was a session full of heavy emotion, constant interraction, and lack of focus—a difficult first day, and one that would be repeated over and over.

The group would vary in size—some weeks only two patients, other weeks nine or ten. Generally, though, we had four to six patients in the group. The turnover rate was very high (see Fig. 6-1), with very few patients staying for the allotted ten sessions and many staying for but one or two. "I don't feel like I'm doing anything," the intern would constantly complain. "This is a waste of time, but I'd rather do the group than see them all one at a time. Too bad there aren't enough therapists in the clinic to give all these people the individual attention they need."

"What is my role?" the intern would constantly query. "What should I be doing?"

Indeed, compared to all other types of interactional groups, the crisis group is a unique, puzzling, and difficult entity. Whereas group membership tends to be stable and long-term in most groups, crisis groups are unstable and short-term. Most interactional groups try to "uncover" emotion, but crisis patients wear their hearts on their sleeves. Insight, the use of the past to explain the present, and other standard techniques are often seen as luxuries to patients dealing with what, in their eyes, are life and death situations. Therapists trained in analytic, dynamic, Tavistock, or other standard group techniques are often lost in the sea of crisis. Moreover, such sought-after factors

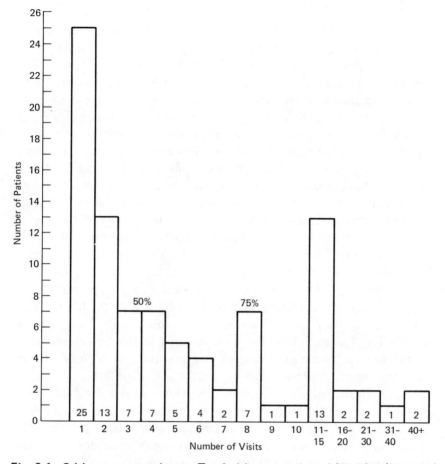

Fig. 6-1. Crisis group attendance: Total visits per patient, 3/77-9/78 (Monday/ Thursday group, N = 92.)

as group cohesion and group process often seem remote in the high-turnover, high-pitched tenor of the crisis group. And patient selection, a favorite topic of most group therapy texts, seems at times an "academic point" as regards these groups.

In addition to the above problems, most crisis literature and practice promotes individual treatment for such patients. Group therapy is often disparaged and considered a distant second choice. Therefore, it takes at least an entire chapter to answer my intern's questions.

CRISIS—DEFINITION AND COMMON
TREATMENT MODALITIES

It is not my intent to review the entire crisis treatment literature. A summary, however, of some of the basic papers[1,2,3] is in order. First, a "crisis" is defined as a life event brought about by real or perceived "hazard" that results in the individual's usual homeostasis being upset. Coping styles learned from past life experiences are inadequate to handle the hazard. The result is an acute psychiatric illness of variable proportions, ranging from situational reactions to depression to psychosis. If left untreated, most crises resolve themselves. Some, however, do not and lead to chronic illness (i.e., the true post-traumatic neurosis). Homeostasis, thus, may be achieved at a lower level than before the hazard, never achieved, or achieved at the previous level but without defense against further similar hazards. Crisis theory postulates that a therapeutic window exists for approximately two weeks, during which the patient is in the height of crisis, with turmoil being acute. If treatment is begun during this period, the patient has the opportunity, with very brief treatment (six to ten sessions or less), to learn new coping styles and establish a better homeostasis than prior to the hazard. Indeed, remarkable results have been reported. The theory is that the human being in this heightened state of emotion and with his defenses down is quite capable of making great therapeutic strides.

Treatment, usually described in the literature as individual,[4] consists of focusing on the here and now, utilization of the therapeutic relationship, and support of the ego, plus *active* therapeutic intervention on the part of the therapist, setting of concrete goals, and setting up a time limit (brief) for the treatment.

There exists, in addition, a literature regarding crisis treatment with families and a rather slim but interesting one for group therapy. The crisis group literature will be discussed later in this chapter. First, let us review the experience we had at the Adult Psychiatry Crisis and Outpatient Clinic, Harbor-UCLA Medical Center, Torrance, California.

OUR EXPERIENCE WITH CRISIS GROUPS

The Realities and Problems

Approximately 200 patients were treated over the six-month period detailed here. This amounts to about 100 per group, as we had two parallel groups. Each was led by a staff physician or psychologist plus a psychiatric intern. The staff remained stable, but the interns rotated every three months. The staff members provided supervision for the house officers, in the form of modeling plus post-session debriefings. The interns functioned as the primary therapists, did the initial evaluations, wrote prescriptions, and did the charting. About 50% of the patients received psychotropic medications, usually in the form of minor tranquilizers, antidepressants, or phenothiazines.

Patients were screened prior to entering the group. The diagnostic workups included, where appropriate, psychological testing. Psychotic patients, sex offenders, sociopaths, and patients who absolutely refused group were not admitted to the crisis groups. Most alcoholics were sent to a special group for drinkers. The resulting groups were nonetheless highly heterogeneous; they all had a high turnover rate, frequent new admissions, and an extreme admixture of racial, ethnic, age, sexual, and social groups. About 66% of the patients were white, 60% were female, and 65% were unmarried. The diagnostic spectrum covered the nonpsychotic categories, with acute adjustment reactions, character disorders, and affective disorders predominating. All patients were in some sort of crisis, with up to 25% having suicidal ideation and 15% having made an actual suicide attempt.

The groups met twice a week for one and one-half hours. A patient could stay in the group for as long as three months. Fig. 6-1 details the actual length of stay for the patients in one of the two groups. Note that 25% had dropped out after their first visit, 50% after visit three, and 75% by visit eight. Clearly, this was an extremely difficult group for the therapists to manage: The turnover was immense, attendance and size on any given day were extremely unpredictable, and therapeutic impact was difficult to assess. It was, at times, most difficult to convince the therapists that they were any more than sandbags and baby sitters.

Outcome Study

Twenty-nine consecutive patients were studied upon entry into the crisis groups and at intervals of one, two, three, six, and twelve months. Although the dropout rate during follow-up was fairly high, the data were, by in large, heartening. We utilized several measures of improvement, and will report here the results from the Global Assessment Scale (G.A.S.).[5]

Table 6-1. Clinical Status of 29 Patients in Crisis Groups, One-Year
Follow-up, as per Global Assessment Scale (G.A.S.)

MONTHS OF FOLLOW-UP	MUCH WORSE	MODERATELY WORSE	NO CHANGE	MODERATELY IMPROVED	MUCH IMPROVED
12 (N = 15)	0	0	3	3	9
6 (N = 4)	0	0	2	1	1
3 (N = 2)	0	0	0	2	0
2 (N = 1)	0	0	0	1	0
1 (N = 1)	0	0	0	1	0
None (N = 6)					
(N = 29)	0	0	5	8	10

Fifteen of the twenty-nine patients (51%) were followed the entire twelve months, four for six months, two for three months, one
for two months, and one for one month. The other six were completely lost to follow-up. Table 6-1 indicates improvement in the
G.A.S. at twelve months in twelve of the fifteen; at six months in
two of the four; at three months in two of the two; at two months in
one of the one; at one month in one of the one. In summary, eighteen
of the twenty-three patients followed (78%) were found to be improved. Although this study, like all outcome studies in psychiatry,
does not necessarily prove that crisis groups "cure" patients (i.e.,
we had no control group and a fair loss to follow-up, and we don't
know how many patients might have gotten better on their own, etc.),
our numbers are in line with the few other outcome studies in the
literature on crisis groups. Trakas and Lloyd,[6] for example, found
that 83% of the patients they could track for six months follow-up
were improved after crisis group therapy. Donovan et al.,[7] in a one
year follow-up study of middle class crisis group patients, showed significant results in the 43 patients (out of an initial 141) whom they
were able to track.

These two studies, like ours, suffer from the defects of high drop-out rates during follow-up and lack of or poor controls. Assessment work by Strickler and Algeyer[8] was also positive, but no follow-up after discharge was done. Clearly, this is an area that requires further research; the pilot studies, such as they are, are optimistic. The above-named authors, and others, all report on groups with diagnostically heterogeneous populations, high turnover, and short stay. Therefore, although our data are not on their own conclusive, they, along with these other accounts, lend credence to the hypothesis that crisis groups are indeed a viable and efficacious method of treating the non-psychotic psychiatric patient in acute disequilibrium.

THE ROLE OF THE THERAPIST

The literature[8,9,10] and our experience are congruent in regard to the role of the therapist in crisis groups. As stated above, these are high-turnover, short-stay groups with patients who are emotionally "wired." The therapist must proceed on the assumption that each meeting may be the patient's last (see Fig. 6-1), and that passivity on the part of the therapist will be seen by the patient as a sign of disinterest. The patients are desperate; they want immediate help.

The therapist, therefore, must be incisive, quick on his feet, direct, and, above all, *active*. This activity, however, should have both form and plan. First, with so many patients coming and going, the therapist must facilitate the group process. By this I mean actually form the group cohesiveness rather than let it develop. Whereas long-term, traditional groups allow people many weeks to get acquainted, crisis groups require instant socialization, so to speak. Thus, the therapist must introduce all new people, ask them to share their stories with the group, explain the group rules, etc. When elements of one patient's problems resonate with another's (i.e., depression), or when similar life situations are noted (i.e., mother with young children), the therapist should point it out. When a particular feeling, idea, or issue is voiced by several members, the therapist will point this out. Put another way, the therapist must try at all times to get the patients to interact, talk to one another, and share with one another. When people realize that their terrors, sadness, and insecurities are not unique (they are often felt to be, but seldom are), they feel less isolated and alone.

A second, and major, feature of the crisis group is the level of emotion. Unlike the more usual interpersonal groups where the therapist often attempts to bring out feelings and decrease intellectualization, the crisis group presents the opposite problem: how to modulate the emotion to foster cognition. The crisis period, being highly charged, is also a magic moment in the therapeutic sense. One need only read Frank's[11] *Persuasion and Healing* to better comprehend the role of emotion in the healing process. The therapist must skillfully identify and focus on feelings, modulating them so that they are neither too great nor too diminished (clearly, if a patient is too emotional, or the group too charged, then learning cannot occur either), and then work toward understanding. *But*—and here, in my judgment, is the tricky part—the therapist must let the group do most of the interpretation and cognitive work. As Yalom[12] has shown, patients hear other patients better than they do the therapist. They feel kinship to the peer group, and less "put down" by its advice. They report that empathy and advice from peers is more important than empathy and advice from the therapist (a fact confirmed, in regard to crisis groups, by Donovan et al.[7]). The therapist, therefore, must, in my judgment, use the skills of facilitation and modulation of emotion in such a way as to get the patients interacting with one another—not just with the therapist. The crisis group is not six or eight simultaneous individual therapies, but a group process, and thus more powerful than individual work. The therapist must be active, yes, but not overly paternalistic: He is the facilitator of process.

The therapist is also the interpreter of process. You may ask: "What? Process in a high-turnover, heterogeneous, short-term group?" Process, I suggest, like transference, is something you always have with you. Each meeting will have a theme, or a series of themes (i.e., suicide, problems at work, bad marriage, depression, etc.). Individuals will present their issues, either as new patients or as updates of previous weeks. The therapist may have to draw some reticent people out, but often group members will do the work for him. (In fact, at all levels the group members can help the therapist—as in any group.) The therapist will also identify and focus emotions and feelings. We've discussed all this already. But as this occurs, the therapist should keep a "third ear" cocked for the "group unconscious," the process.

Finally, and perhaps most important, the ultimate goal of crisis therapy is to give the patient new and stronger coping mechanisms, so that this—and any future—crisis can be mastered without continued or repeated decompensations. Clearly, the first steps toward this include emotional catharsis and discussion of the problems. Empathy from fellow patients and the therapist are important, as are the mutual experiences the group offers by allowing many patients to listen and discuss and feel together. Ultimately, this should lead to the question of "How are you handling your problems now (and in the past during similar crises)?" and "How else could you deal with them?" Here, the therapist, by both encouraging other patients to help their peers, and by his own interpretations and suggestions, can be very helpful. The therapist lends ego strength, cohesion, and direction to the group (i.e., is supportive) and, additionally, via process comments and active questioning and suggestions, tries to lead the patients toward a fuller understanding of their problems and a fuller methodology for coping with them. What is particularly important to remember here, once again, is that crisis groups do not often allow the therapist the great luxury of using the past to interpret the present and affect the future. The crisis groups are here-and-now groups, and the therapist must learn to harness the feelings, words, and processes he notices toward an active understanding and interpretation. When we again realize that the present may be only one or two sessions for a large number of our patients, the therapist's task is clearly seen as difficult—and, as noted above, is often felt to be impossible. It is the rare therapist, I believe, who can do such intense work more than a few hours a week, without "burning out." Our therapists worked with one group per week (two one and one-half-hour sessions per week) and spent the remainder of their clinical time doing other things, thus avoiding the staff burn-out syndrome.

Before moving on, we should note an additional feature—and pressure—of the crisis group: concrete life and medication issues. A high pecentage (about 50% in our groups) of crisis group patients may require medication for anxiety, depression, sleep, etc. The therapist has precious little time to establish the diagnosis and decide what medication, if any, and how much might be indicated. In addition, patients may wish to discuss such issues in group, rather than focus on their interpersonal and life problems. We have found that brief individual sessions, just before or after group, are the best way to deal with this and other such concrete issues. Often, however, considerable clinical skill is needed to move patients in group away from these concrete issues, and a group process of avoiding major issues (i.e., suicide, homicide) by focusing on such concerns must always be looked for. Similarly, these patients have a higher than average need for concrete interventions in other areas (e.g., disability forms, welfare papers). This too can tax the therapist, and it should be dealt with in ways similar to medication issues. And what, finally, should the therapist do for the patient who doesn't show or drops out? We recommend a phone call, or, if that fails, a letter. We find, however, that these methods rarely bring a patient back.

GROUP VERSUS INDIVIDUAL CRISIS WORK: ADVANTAGES?

The great challenges to the crisis group leader are outlined above. Obviously, they could be seen as disadvantages to doing this intense group work. The individual in crisis, if treated one to one, can receive the undivided attention of a therapist, present perhaps fewer difficulties in relation to diagnostic and medication issues, and offer one set of emotions and problems at a time. In short, the therapist is faced with the much easier task of caring for one acutely ill patient at a time. On the other hand, he must spend much more time doing it. In addition, a cancellation of an individual patient leaves a gap in the day for the therapist. In this high-turnover population, the group clearly minimizes such effects. Additionally, by allowing the therapist more time for other types of work, the group can help prevent burning out, clearly a problem among crisis therapists who spend large portions of their time doing individual work. In terms of education, the group also provides an advantage: The co-therapist supervisor can teach by example and be on the spot at all times. The supervisor of individual crisis work by trainees must be an observer, or, worse yet, a recipient of second-hand reports. Finally, several authors[8,9] have noted that crisis groups allow large numbers of poor people access to care that, in terms of cost and time, clinics might otherwise not be able to deliver.

But what of the patient? Here, the data are equivocal, but at least one can say that they support crisis group work as being at least as therapeutic as individual crisis therapy (see "outcome study" above). In short, the bulk of outcome studies in both regards are positive. But outcome studies in psychiatry, in general, are often difficult to interpret or "unscientific" in the more rigid sense of the word. Patients are people; they lead lives; their environment, finances, personal lives, etc., are uncontrollable in the experimental sense of the word. And follow-up, especially in the population described in this chapter, is often extremely spotty. Only about one-half of the patients in our outcome study, for example, could be located one year after they began treatment. Ultimately, I must look to common sense and some of Yalom's work to extrapolate some, albeit subjective, conclusions.

Yalom[12] has clearly shown that, in regard to interpersonal groups, patients report that emotional catharsis and the words of their peers, other patients, are two of the most important aspects of group therapy. The therapist *per se* is not seen as the key to therapeutic success—it is the group members. My common sense tells me that these features of the crisis group—peer support and peer pressure—will ultimately be proven to be immensely positive forces in crisis work. Therefore, it is quite likely that the crisis group modality is superior to the individual modality. Certainly, some of the published work cited above makes this contention. In the meantime, for the therapist like myself who clearly prefers the challenges, nuances, processes, and discussions of group work to the one-to-one therapies, it is definitely a challenge worth taking.

SUMMARY

The nonpsychotic patient in crisis may clearly benefit from group therapy, as several studies of crisis groups show. The patients are in an acute disequilibrium and are usually highly charged emotionally, and their ability to cope with their life hazards is, at best, minimal. In this state they are highly susceptible to relatively quick, and often life-lasting, therapeutic intervention. When such patients become a group, they present unique challenges to the group therapist: relatively little diagnostic time, high-turnover, brief stay in group, and extreme heterogeneity both of diagnosis and of socioeconomics. In addition, high emotion and severe problems are the rule of the day. The therapist must be facile, active, supportive, and facilitative. He must be able to get the stories told, foster group cohesion, modulate feelings, interpret process, and generate understanding. The ability to foster peer-peer interaction may be crucial. It is very tough work, but data are accumulating to support its virtues. And, draining as it is, it can be fun.

REFERENCES

1. Darbonne, A. R. Crisis: a review of theory, practice, and research. *Psychotherapy: Theory, Research and Practice* **4**: 49-53 (1967).
2. Caplan, G. *An Approach to Community Mental Health.* New York: Grune and Stratton (1961).
3. Lindemann, E. Symptomatology and management of acute grief. *Am. J. Psychiatry* **CI**: 141-148 (1944).
4. Peck, H. B. and Kaplan, S. R. Crisis theory and therapeutic change in small groups: some implications for community mental health programs. *Int. J. Group Psychother.* **16**: 135-149 (1966).
5. Endicott, J., Spitzer, R. L., Fleiss, J. L. et al. The global assessment scale. *Arch. Gen. Psychiatry* **33**: 766-771 (1976).
6. Trakas, D. A. and Lloyd, G. Emergency management in a short-term open group. *Comp. Psychiatry* **12**: 170-175 (1971).
7. Donovan, J. M., Bennett, M. J., and McElroy, C. M. The crisis group—an outcome study. *Am. J. Psychiatry* **136**: 906-910 (1979).
8. Strickler, M. and Allgeyer, J. The crisis group: a new application of crisis theory. *Social Work* **12**: 28-32 (1967).
9. Block, H. S. An open-ended crisis-oriented group for the poor who are sick. *Arch. Gen. Psychiatry* **18**: 178-185 (1968).
10. Alleyer, J. M. Using crisis groups in a crisis-oriented setting. *Int. J. Group Psychother.* **23**: 217-222 (1973).
11. Frank, J. *Persuasion and Healing.* Baltimore: Johns Hopkins Press (1961).
12. Yalom, I. D. *The Theory and Practice of Group Psychotherapy.* New York: Basic Books (1975).

7
The Follow-up Group: Outpatient Treatment

Ira Lesser, M.D. and *Claude T.H. Friedmann, M.D.*

The long-term treatment of the chronically impaired psychiatric patient has been a neglected area in American psychiatry. For years most of this treatment has been carried out in large state hospital systems, primarily involving inpatient care. Outpatient followup was not a high priority and, as a result, hospitalizations were lengthy and rehabilitation efforts meager. During the last two decades, as cutbacks in state hospital systems have been implemented, there has been an increased appreciation of the need for providing aftercare services for this underserved population.

The magnitude of the problem is reflected in the statistics regarding trends in psychiatric services in the last 20 years.[1] In 1950, readmissions to inpatient facilities accounted for approximately 40% of all inpatient admissions. By 1975 this figure has grown to 65%. The "revolving door" became well established. The average length of hospitalization decreased markedly as a result of many factors, including the advent of powerful psychotropic agents, the community mental health movement, and the recognition of the potentially adverse effect of long-term institutionalization. As a result, outpatient treatment has shown a phenomenal rise, increasing an estimated 1,000% over 25 years.

Much of the burden for this increased outpatient census is being borne by publicly financed institutions, (i.e., county facilities, community mental health centers, VA hospitals). This is not surprising since the more severe and chronic psychiatric illnesses cluster in the lower socioeconomic classes. The problem such institutions face is to provide long-term care to a wide variety of patients in an economically feasible framework. In addition, the therapeutic interventions most appropriate to this population have not been studied with rigor, so that there are no well-established guidelines for mental health planners to follow.

Reviews of the literature concerning follow-up care of discharged patients lead to dissatisfaction with both study design and results. Bachrach in 1976[2] commented on the urgent need for well-designed studies so the needs of these patients could be understood and met. The one fact that stood out as a factor in reducing rehospitalization was availability of "alternative facilities" outside the state hospitals. This chapter will focus on a program designed to offer such an "alternative" (i.e., the long-term outpatient treatment of the chronic psychiatric patient).

A serious problem that needs to be addressed is that of compliance, both for medications and aftercare services. Serban and Thomas[3] showed that for chronic schizophrenics, only 36% of a cohort of 516 took their medications and only 41% sought regular aftercare services even when this was readily available. Readmission rates for the hospital were significantly correlated with the failure to use medications and aftercare services. We need to understand these resistances to treatment and encourage people to engage in those treatments that have shown themselves to be effective.

Clearly, the discovery and use of psychotropic drugs has had a marked effect on the nature of psychiatric practice in the last 25 years. Among other things, it has promoted the early return of individuals to their community by reducing the length of hospitalization. Davis[4,5] reviewed the impact and importance of these drugs, clearly pointing out the reduced relapse rate, and psychiatric morbidity. There is the danger that medications may be regarded as the panacea for all the problems of the chronic patient, and thus withdraw or cease the human contact that these patients desperately need, and so often fear. Combining pharmacotherapy and group psychotherapy can counteract this trend.

In exploring different therapeutic modalities used for treating large numbers of chronic patients, some things become clear. The "traditional" individual psychotherapy paradigm is regarded by many as inappropriate for severely disturbed, chronic patients.[6] Various factors account for this: the patients' inability to maintain intimate contact with other individuals, their difficulty in keeping appointments, the potential for psychotic transference relations, the psychological drain on the therapist, and the expense. Despite these potential problems, there are dedicated therapists who do continue to see such patients in long-term individual treatment, even psychoanalysis. However, on a large scale, this would be a prohibitive task. As a result of some of these practical problems, and with a sound theoretical basis, group therapy has emerged as an indispensable treatment for the chronic patient.

Althought the literature on outcome studies in psychotherapy is incomplete, there are several studies that present supportive evidence for doing group therapy with chronic patients. Shattan et al. in 1966[7] reported their experience with patients recently discharged from psychiatric hospitals and treated with group versus no group therapy in addition to pharmacotherapy. They noted a significantly lowered rehospitalization rate and an absolute increase in discharges from the clinic for the group therapy patients. A controlled study of similar design by O'Brien et al.[8] showed no significant difference in the rehospitalization rate at 12 and 24 months, but scores on the Overall Gorham Brief Psychiatric Scale (BPRS) and the Social Effectiveness Scale were significantly better for the group therapy patients. In contrast, Herz et al.[9] found no significant differences in rehospitalization rates or other outcome measures between the two treatment modalities. However, they noted that the group therapy model was "better received" by staff and patients alike than individual treatment. The therapists in their study were first-year psychiatric residents who were inexperienced in dealing with this difficult patient population. Recently, Price et al.[10] reported that their experience with aftercare services in South Carolina greatly favored group therapy for the chronically impaired individual, noting a significantly reduced rehospitalization rate over individual treatment.

May[11] reviewed controlled studies of treatment for schizophrenia, noting that "the evidence in favor of the efficacy of pharmacotherapy was overwhelming," and that "there is considerable evidence to underline the value of combining pharmacotherapy and outpatient efforts to reduce residual disability after remission." May also noted that group therapy was "more effective than individual treatment."

Claghorn et al.[12] treated schizophrenics as outpatients, using individual and group treatment along with antipsychotic medications. All patients were treated with neuroleptics and all improved on a series of rating scales, and "there were subtle, but meaningful changes in emotional functioning due to concurrent group therapy."

The conclusion drawn from the experiences of the last two decades is that from a theoretical, clinical, and economic point of view, combining group psychotherapy and pharmacotherapy for the chronic patient is reasonable. Attempts to do this have been described, calling the groups "medication groups,"[13] "follow-up groups,"[14] and "aftercare groups."[10] The goals of treatment have been described as "maintaining the status quo," "to monitor and enhance the effectiveness of administration of psychotropic drugs," and "to do supportive . . . not uncovering psychotherapy."

Most of the literature describing these groups has stressed the supportive nature of the group, with either implicit or explicit warnings against attempts at fostering individual psychodynamic understanding leading to personal growth. An example of this approach is that of Masnik et al.,[15] who feels that the therapists need to accept the "regressed state of these patients, and gratify their oral-dependent strivings." Hence, they set up their group around coffee and cookies, deliberately keeping discussion at a superficial level. They feel that although this could promote passivity and perpetuate the patient's disorders in group functioning "at a higher psychosocial level," one must do this type of work with this population, or "there is no patient to treat." Perhaps as a result of this type of thinking, the pharmacotherapy group literature rarely addresses the nature of the group process, the issues dealt with in groups, and the dynamic issues raised therein.[16] In a recent report,[17] we have explored many of these issues and we will reemphasize some of these points below.

Mendel[18] addressed the long-term treatment of the chronic patient (he discusses the chronic schizophrenic as a prototype for chronic patients). He makes the point that supportive treatment never ends, that the helpers must always be available. He conceptualizes long-term treatment as dealing with recurrent crises, by intensive outpatient experiences or hospitalization, if necessary. Aftercare is seen as working with the patient after the crisis resolution, and to work toward prevention of further crises. We heartily agree with this approach to the chronic patient, but question Mendel's absolute dichotomy between "expressive" and "supportive" therapy. He states that "expressive" therapy is contraindicated for psychotic and borderline patients. We think genuine insight can be achieved by psychotic patients without severe disorganization, and this can occur in a group setting, which also provides all the elements of supportive care.

DESCRIPTION OF THE GROUPS

Our work was modeled on the follow-up groups at the University of Southern California, Los Angeles County Medical Center[14] and done at a university-affiliated county hospital in Los Angeles. As our previous report[17] states, the patient population is primarily from the lower socioeconomic strata. The adult outpatient clinic receives referrals from other services (psychiatric and medical) in the hospital, from the state hospital system, and from community agencies; in addition, many patients are self-referred. The follow-up groups are composed of patients felt by the staff to have chronic psychiatric problems, who are ambulatory and do not need constant supervision.

Over a two-year period, 200 patients were seen in the follow-up groups: 55% were schizophrenic (mostly chronic), 26% had a major affective illness, and the remaining 19% were distributed between organic brain syndromes, severe character pathology, and neurotic problems. The average age was 41 years; 57% were women. Over 85% received some type of psychotropic medication, and an equal number had at least one prolonged psychiatric hospitalization. This data is almost identical to Kalibat's,[14] which reports 1,000 patients who attended group an average of once per month. Over 40% of the patients have had at least two hospitalizations, and 25% three or more.

The groups meet for a total of one and one-half hours per week, with additional appointments available on an emergency basis. There are two therapists, a third-year psychiatric resident, and a psychiatric social worker. One hour (usually the first) is an open-ended group session dealing with whatever problems arise. The last half-hour is devoted to dispensing and discussing medications with individual patients. The resident meets individually with patients for several minutes to renew prescriptions, inquire about side effects, assess the efficacy of the current drug regimen, and to judge whether additional medical intervention is necessary. Also, during this last half-hour, the social worker is available to help with individual problems relating to practical matters such as welfare, disability, housing, etc.

Group attendance is encouraged but allowed to be flexible. Patients regulate how often and for how long they attend the group; there is no fixed time limit to treatment. Each group has a roster of about 30 to 50 patients, with about 8 to 15 patients attending any given session. The groups seem to have three distinct subgroups of patients. There is a "core group" of about 5 to 8 patients who come each week, another group of about twice that number come irregularly but attend the entire session, and a third group who come irregularly for medication refills only, but do not attend the one-hour group session. Both before the group begins, and after the formal hour is over, patients will mingle with one another, talk over coffee, and occasionally exchange phone numbers for extra-group activities.

The groups are structured to maximize several goals. Foremost is the provision of comprehensive psychiatric services to a large population of patients. Keeping people out of the hospital, maintaining and monitoring medications, increasing social skills, decreasing isolation, and providing an atmosphere for personal exploration and growth are part of the treatment program. These groups are set up without time limit (i.e., they will meet on the same day, in the same place, with at least one permanent therapist for years). This fact is of tremendous comfort to patients who can return after prolonged absences to a friendly and supportive environment.

Groups such as these fit very well into the comprehensive services offered at public institutions. Patients have easy access to the group and can benefit from adjunctive programs as needed (e.g., alcohol rehabilitation, vocational rehabilitation counseling, job training). In addition, crisis intervention and partial or full hospitalization can be readily available if the need arises.

UNDERSTANDING THE GROUP PROCESS

Because these groups do more than provide medications, we are interested in the nature of the group interaction and the twin themes of content and process. We have found that, although difficult, it is possible to identify group themes and issues, make them explicit, and interpret them without untoward results. It has become apparent

Table 7-1. Levels of Group Communications

CONCRETE PROBLEMS	INTERPERSONAL PROBLEMS
Poverty	Patient–therapist
Poor living situations	Patient–family
Inadequate welfare system	Patient–landlord
Poor nutrition	Patient–neighbors
Concurrent medical problems	Patient–employer
Inadequate health care	Patient–merchants
Political and social events	Patient–society
Psychiatric symptoms	Patient–patient
Medications	

GROUP THEMES

Separation-individuation
Dependency
Fears of abandonment
Anger (at caretakers)
Passivity
Suicide, death
Parenting
Transference

that there are different levels of communication within these groups (as in all groups), and the therapists can choose to deal with some issues and to ignore others.

As shown in Table 7-1, there are three broad categories of communication that arise from the group. Most often, members will start out with concrete problems: difficulties with welfare checks, poor housing conditions, transportation problems, etc. These are genuine problems and present real difficulties to people with few resources. The issues are dealt with as realistic ones by pointing out options, discussing how other group members handle similar problems, and supporting problem-solving efforts. As the group continues to deal with these issues, it often becomes obvious that they also are talking about not getting needs met by the group and the therapists. This becomes a more abstract issue, a "group theme." We have found that it is possible to make these themes explicit and to discuss them to some extent. The therapists need to use caution in the timing of these interventions and to gauge how far they can safely delve. But the point is that one can discuss these issues; they are not, as most of the literature suggests, "taboo." The group issues that do arise parallel many of these seen in more analytically-oriented groups. The difference lies in how they are dealt with, and not going too far too fast, or too individually.

One of the major therapeutic tasks is to create an atmosphere in which patients can comfortably share their problems. Many symptoms, such as hallucinations or delusions, are frightening to the patient and frightening to others. If group members indicate that they can tolerate discussion of these issues, a major breakthrough in the individual's isolation can be achieved. Occasionally, patients will hallucinate or be frankly delusional during group; this is especially true for new patients. The other group members often become "therapist helpers," aiding the psychotic members to become aware of their pathology. Group members also share their own experiences with medications, doctors, and their symptoms, thus helping change an autistic experience into a shared one.

Specific symptoms can be seen in the larger context of the group process and can develop into a group theme. An example occurred when a group was dealing with the suicide attempt of a member's relative. After expressing support and sharing similar experiences with this patient, the group members became silent and seemed apprehensive. Suddenly, another member began to actively hallucinate, responding out loud to "the voices." The group immediately called this behavior to his attention, assuring him that no such "voices" were present in the room; he became everyone's patient for a short while. The group members were supportive and the therapists addressed the anxiety felt by this patient. After the patient calmed down, the therapists were able to comment about the group process (that it was difficult to talk about suicide and that this topic stirred up feelings in the group). The hallucinating patient provided a distraction that was a relief for the group because the topic of suicide was effectively averted. After this was pointed out, the group was able to continue its discussion of suicide and the individual members seemed more at ease in revealing their personal experiences. This vignette highlights the importance of allowing patients the freedom of expressing themselves in a setting where they will receive emotional support. Further, it points out how a symptom can be the result of anxiety as well as an attempt to ward off further anxieties.

There are a number of recurrent themes that regularly make their appearance. Perhaps the most frequent of these is the issue of separation. Their psychopathology makes these patients particularly vulnerable to separations, and they have difficulty dealing with the related issues of dependency. Therapists' vacations can cause discomfort in the group, but this is rarely expressed directly. Instead, the group bemoans "big government," "an inadequate and unjust welfare system," "the gap between the rich and the poor" (concrete problems). These issues can be dealt with solely as reality issues, or used to point out the group's unexpressed feelings toward the therapist's upcoming absence. On one occasion when this was done, a flood of emotions sprang forth, with one 40-year-old, chronically depressed woman sobbing and calling out for her "mommy"—who had been dead for ten years. The group responded supportively and was able to deal with deaths in their own families and with their fears of being left alone. The therapist's vacation passed without any exacerbations in the patients' symptoms.

The issues of separation, termination, and abandonment are universal themes in psychotherapy and are intensely felt in these groups. Edelson[19] talks of the "narcissistic wound" that one suffers when termination, or the fear of termination takes place, and this is very apparent in these groups. Severely ill psychiatric patients are especially sensitive to perceived slights to an already shaky self-esteem. They often interpret a therapist's absence as the result of their own "badness" and consider separation as a form of punishment. Neglecting these issues because one is not supposed to do "uncovering psychotherapy" in these groups denies the patients an opportunity for growth.

There is a difference between group interpretations and individual interpretations. Perhaps some cautions about insight-oriented comments in such groups are the result of inexperienced therapists trying to point out affect, transference, and personal reactions to individual patients. The metaphor of the group process interpretation is workable. Putting one patient in the emotional hot seat is not. Obviously you neither force nor block the group process, but do gently facilitate it. If the group's anxiety becomes excessive, attendance will rapidly drop. This gives the therapist a warning that something is wrong. What is usually wrong is that transference and affect have been excessively personalized.

Despite the fact that group treatment and treatment in institutions usually decreases the intensity of transference reactions (see below), a therapist leaving the group, as residents do each year, can cause a great deal of upheaval in the group. Well-functioning group members suddenly decompensate, some members take extended "vacations," attendance decreases, requests for individual sessions increase, and psychopathology seems more evident. The focus of attention at these times should be on the feeling regarding the upcoming loss and on the various nonadaptive solutions that members have chosen to deal with these feelings. If the therapist has dealt with his own feelings about leaving the group and can encourage the verbal expression of feelings from the members (angry though they may be), the termination experience may be one from which patients emerge in a stronger position.

Another common theme revolves around the view of the therapists being all powerful, wonderful, and knowing, while the patient is passive and helpless. Although the positive aspects of the transference should not be attacked with too much vigor, the therapist must inject some reality into the patients view of the world. An example occurred with one patient who was having difficulty with his disability insurance. A state law required a specific waiting period before disability payments could be made, and the patient was upset over this. The group told the therapist to write a letter, feeling that if he wrote a letter supporting the patient, the law would be changed. The expectation was that the therapist could do this, or anything he wanted, while the patient was totally helpless. The therapists spent a great deal of time dealing with these wishes, but they had to acknowledge that they were not as powerful as they were seen, and that the patients were not as helpless as they saw themselves. The issue of the patients' perceived helplessness became an important topic for discussion.

The above themes are not an exhaustive list, but are frequent repetitive topics that emerge from group discussions. Dealing with some of these themes may arouse considerable discomfort in the therapists when they are addressed. The patients, although often quite passive, are reservoirs of primitive affect, including rage that may explode and be directed at the therapist. One needs to be aware of this and to modulate the depth with which these issues are brought up and discussed. But the denial of these feelings by the therapist can be interpreted as "proof" that the patient is a bad person who has such terrible thoughts that one cannot even talk about them.

ADVANTAGES OF GROUP THERAPY
FOR THE CHRONIC PATIENT

The merits of the group approach in psychotherapeutic work are well known and have been covered in depth by Grotjahn[20] and others. It is not our intent to reinterate these here, but to focus on the specific advantages of this approach to the chronic patient.

One of the difficulties encountered in individual treatment of the chronic patient is his reluctance or inability to keep weekly appointments. The use of an open-ended, attendance-optional framework greatly reduces potential power struggles over appointments. Our system gives the patients the responsibility for choosing when and how often they will attend group. However, the therapists do encourage attendance and insist on at least monthly contact when medications are involved.

The subject of transference reactions was alluded to earlier in this chapter. In dealing with chronically ill patients, the possibility of strong and perhaps psychotic transference reactions is ever-present. The use of a group setting, especially with two therapists, markedly attentuates but does not abolish the intensity of those transference feelings. In addition, the idea of the "institutional transference" is helpful in conceptualizing the attachment chronic patients can make.[21] Therapists can make use of and encourage this bond to the institution to help people stay in treatment for long periods of time. Utilizing transference reactions in these ways, while a modification of the traditional analysis of the transference, seems appropriate and beneficial.

Co-therapists lend continuity to the groups. Vacations or illness of one therapist does not lead to cancellation of a group. At the end of the academic year, the psychiatric resident leaves the group, but the social worker remains. This helps minimize the disruption to the group and provides a further sense of continuity, as well as a chance to work on separation attachment and the transiency of all things human.

Reducing the intense isolation with which the chronic patient lives is of paramount importance. The group setting promotes interpersonal exchanges and allows for greater socialization. Recognizing the difficulty these patients have forming interpersonal relationships, it is surprising how much contact there is between patients outside of the group. This may take place only on the day of the group as patients share coffee in the cafeteria; but the relationships are important, for they may be the only personal contacts available. We also encourage the group to plan parties around holidays and when the therapists leave. Members take responsibility for bringing in food and supplies, and a community spirit is established. It is difficult to envision these kinds of opportunities in individual treatment.

Another important advantage of group treatment is that it allows patients to work at their own pace. Since the groups are large and have flexible attendance, patients may participate to the degree that they feel comfortable. They may be silent for weeks or months and perhaps only after this time feel safe enough to verbally join the group. The group also provides the opportunity for increased self-esteem when patients become therapist-helpers.

Jerome Frank[22] said an important element in successful psychotherapy is that the therapists believe in what they are doing and transmit this to the patient. Perhaps the care given to the chronic patient has been less than optimal because therapists have perceived their treatment as a boring chore to be endured. The groups described may help change some of the negative attitudes that pervade treatment of the chronic patient.

One advantage, especially to the dynamically trained therapist, is the opportunity to do more than "maintain the status quo" therapy. As has been indicated above, issues can be dealt with in greater depth than the literature suggests, without untoward results. This is more appealing to therapists and makes for livelier and more interesting groups. Several therapists involved in the follow-up groups feel they can do as much genuine therapeutic work with these groups as they can with their "insight-oriented" groups.

Some techniques, such as seeing patients in groups, making attendance optional, using co-therapists, and stressing the attachment to the institution make severe power struggles and psychotic transferences less likely. It also makes for less wear and tear on therapists.

In institutions that teach mental health professionals, the follow-up groups are excellent training experiences. There is an ample opportunity to study serious psychopathology after a long time and without the acuteness of an inpatient setting. As universal group issues are dealt with, the similarities with less severely ill patients become more apparent than the differences. One can generalize from the experience gained to other modes of therapy with different populations.

Finally, the health care delivery system benefits from this type of group treatment. In this day and age, economic factors play an increasingly large role in the delivery of health care. The follow-up groups are a therapeutically sound and cost-effective approach to providing care for a historically undercovered population. With the expenditure of only three hours per week of therapist's time, a group of 30 to 35 chronic patients are given comprehensive psychiatric services, and opportunities for personal growth, in addition to support and pharmacotherapy. There is no loss of the therapist's time that would occur with missed individual appointments; knowing that the group is always available seems to decrease the patient's emergency clinic contacts.

POTENTIAL PROBLEMS OF FOLLOW-UP GROUPS

There are a number of problems that may arise during the course of administering and running follow-up groups. Because of the large size of such groups, they may be seen as an easy place to "dump" patients who do not fit the stereotype of the "good" patient (non-YAVIS patients[23]). Therapists who, for one reason or another, do not want to treat selected patients individually, may send them to the follow-up group. This may be inappropriate for the patient and the group alike. For example, patients with antisocial personalities tend to disrupt these groups.

Not all patients who have had one or several psychotic episodes, with or without hospitalization, necessarily belong in the follow-up group. Some of these patients may be well-functioning between episodes and would benefit from a more intensive (individual or group) psychotherapy experience. This seems especially true for individuals who are manic-depressive. When not psychotic, they function quite well and may not gain much from this type of group. Perhaps a group of patients suffering from major affective disorders would be a more appropriate treatment modality for these people.

The hostile, paranoid patient poses special problems in this group. They are a therapeutic challenge in general. These patients tend to monopolize the group time and create enough confusion and anxiety among the group members to bring therapeutic work to a standstill.

We have found it helpful if one of the therapists has made a prior alliance, however tentative, with his patient. This can be used during the group to help calm the patient and decrease his hold over the group. This may require several individual sessions before placing the patient in the group, but is well worth the extra time and effort.

Because of the large number of patients, it is difficult for the therapists to gain an in-depth understanding of each individual. One often feels at a loss when patients come irregularly and the therapist is not "up to date" on what is happening in the patient's life. Therapists need to become more secure and accept their inability to achieve the unattainable goal of total control of their patients' lives. By keeping the focus of the group on the here and now, and remembering that the group experience is a healing force in and of itself, the therapist's discomfort can be lessened.

SUMMARY

We have described a program of follow-up groups for chronically impaired psychiatric patients. The rationale for combined psychopharmacology and group psychotherapy was outlined and the reasons for this particular format discussed. We emphasized that issues commonly neglected in the treatment of disturbed patients may be addressed and worked with, without increasing morbidity. The groups offer a means of providing good quality patient care, and the potential for personal growth, at reasonable economic cost and without overburdening the time or resources of the therapists.

During the past two years, the rehospitalization rate has been about two patients per group per year. Although not a controlled, double-blind study, this figure compares favorably with those from individual treatment.[9,10] In addition, we estimate that about five patients per group have gotten jobs and are productive in the community. When this is contrasted with repetitive prior hospitalizations, and with other observations, we conclude that these groups are a safe, efficient, and therapeutic method for treating the chronic patient.

We feel that institutions faced with increasing demands for their services should consider this alternative as a means of providing comprehensive psychiatric care to very needy patients, of providing excellent training for a variety of mental health professionals, and of keeping costs at a manageable level.

REFERENCES

1. Redlich, F. and Kellert, S. R. Trends in American mental health. *Am. J. Psychiatry* **135**: 22-28 (1978).
2. Bachrach, L. L. A note on some recent studies of released mental hospital patients in the community. *Am. J. Psychiatry* **133**: 73-75 (1976).
3. Serban, G. and Thomas, A. Attitudes and behavior of acute and chronic schizophrenic patients regarding ambulatory treatment. *Am. J. Psychiatry* **131**: 991-995 (1974).
4. Davis, J. M. Overview: maintenance therapy in psychiatry. I. Schizophrenia. *Am. J. Psychiatry* **132**: 1237-1245 (1975).
5. Davis, J. M. Overview: maintenance therapy in psychiatry. II. Affective disorders. *Am. J. Psychiatry* **133**: 1-13 (1976).
6. Macleod, J. A. and Middleman, F. Wednesday afternoon clinic: a supportive care program. *Arch. Gen. Psychiatry* **6**: 72-81 (1962).
7. Shattan, S. P., Dcamp, L., Fujii, E., Fross, G. G., and Wolff, R. J. Group treatment of conditionally discharged patients in a mental health clinic. *Am. J. Psychiatry* **122**: 798-804 (1966).
8. O'Brien, C. P., Hamm, K. B., Ray, B. A., Pierce, J. F., Luborsky, L., and Mintz, J. Group vs. individual psychotherapy with schizophrenics. A controlled outcome study. *Arch. Gen. Psychiatry* **27**: 474-478 (1972).
9. Herz, M. I., Spitzer, R. L., Gibbon, M., Greenspan, K., and Reibel, S. Individual vs. group aftercare treatment. *Am. J. Psychiatry* **131**: 808-812 (1974).
10. Prince, R. M., Ackerman, R. E., Carter, N. C., and Harrison, A. Group aftercare—impact on a state wide program. *Dis. Nerv. Syst.* **38**: 793-796 (1977).
11. May, P. R. Rational treatment for an irrational disorder: what does the schizophrenic patient need? *Am. J. Psychiatry* **133**: 1008-1012 (1976).
12. Claghorn, J. L., Johnstone, E. E., Cook, T. H., and Itschner, L. Group therapy and maintenance treatment of schizophrenia. *Arch. Gen. Psychiatry* **31**: 361-365 (1974).
13. Isenberg, P.L., Mahnke, M. W., and Shields, W. E. Medication groups for continuing care. *Hosp. Community Psychiatry* **25**: 517-519 (1974).
14. Kalibat, F., Kotin, J., and Kline, F. For chronic patients: the follow-up group. *Transnational Mental Health Research Newsletter* **18**: 2, 9-10 (1976).
15. Masnik, R., Bucci, L., Isenberg, D., and Normand, W. "Coffee and . . . ": a way to treat the untreatable. *Am. J. Psychiatry* **128**: 164-167 (1971).
16. Payn, S. B. Group methods in the pharmacotherapy of chronic psychotic patients. *Psychiatric Q.* **39**: 258-263 (1965).
17. Lesser, I. M. and Friedman, C. T. Beyond medications: group therapy for the chronic psychiatric patient. *Int. J. Group Psychother.* **30**: 187-199 (1980).
18. Mendel, W. M. *Supportive Care: Theory and Technique.* Santa Monica: Mara Books (1975).
19. Edelson, M. *The Termination of Intensive Psychotherapy.* Springfield, Ill.: Charles C. Thomas (1973).

20. Grotjahn, M. *The Art and Technique of Analytic Group Therapy*. New York: Jason Aronson (1977).
21. Lamb, H. R. Treating long-term schizophrenic patients in the community. *In:* Bellak, L. and Barten, H. (Eds.), *Progress in Community Mental Health.* New York: Brunner/Mazel (1975), pp. 119-139.
22. Frank, J. *Persuasion and Healing.* Baltimore: Johns Hopkins University Press (1967).
23. Schofield, W. *Psychotherapy: The Purchase of Friendship.* Englewood Cliffs, N.J.: Prentice-Hall (1964).

8
Follow-up Group Meetings

Martin Grotjahn, M.D.

The following report uses clinical material to illustrate the observational basis of group therapy research.

THE "FOLLOW-UP" GROUP

September 1976

It was Friday afternoon, 1:30, and the group had already met in the waiting room. When the meeting room opened, the group slowly walked in and formed one large circle of 35 people. There were two therapists and I, as a consultant, sitting at approximately three, six, and nine o'clock in the circle.

While watching the group come to order, I thought: "These are really sick people." I realized in the course of the meeting that almost no one could be expected to see these patients individually for any length of time. I became convinced that any sustained treatment would have to be offered in groups.

The meeting began while several conversations that had started in the waiting room were continued. Everybody chatted with everybody else and waited for the doctor to appear.

These people seemed to me to be not only the sickest but also the poorest of the poor in the city. Still, everybody was properly dressed, the women looked as if they had visited a beauty parlor recently, almost everybody had a shiny wristwatch, and many had arrived in their cars, often with other patients. Almost everybody smoked, much to my annoyance.

There were many black men and women, Mexicans, a few Orientals, and whites, who formed the largest group but not the majority. The seating arrangements, dress, and interaction suggested that this group was truly integrated.

I was introduced as a "visiting professor" who had come to see how group work was done here. The co-therapist expressed pleasure about my presence. This succeeded in making me immediately welcome to the group. I have found it generally true that if the therapist accepts a visitor, this is followed, without exception, by the group's acceptance. The therapist's resistance is immediately reflected by doubts and resistance in the group. The resistance is expressed in a long discussion.

A woman sitting opposite me asked immediately: "Do you know Karl Menninger? How is he? He was of so much help to my family." I answered that I knew him well and that I had worked in his clinic for two years. He had been sick but is well again.

A gigantic black man asked me whether I understood dreams and told me his dream of the previous night: "I am flying in a red and white plane. A young man, and I really don't know him, was with me. That's all."

I asked who that young man was and the big black man said nonchalantly: "That's the young man who got himself murdered. He tried to murder me with my own butcher knife, which I always keep under my bed when I sleep." I managed to hide my uneasiness and asked him whether perhaps his conscience bothered him. And that he still may think about this man? I was careful not to go too far with my interpretive questions since I was a guest. I answered only because I was directly addressed. Then I waited for my chance to retreat into the background.

The discussion was taken over by two enormously fat women, one on crutches because of a fall that had broken her hip. Both were in tears. One was so depressed she said that she bought everything fattening and ate it. The other one had been nursing her dying grandfather and said that food was her only hope these days. The group felt that it would be more important for her to take care of herself than her grandfather.

Later in the session, an Oriental woman tried to tell me her dream and her therapist, who was a disciplinarian, told her she was sidetracking the group. The therapist also make a side remark that implied that I had already fallen for the "trick" of the patients who seduced me into dream interpretations instead of dealing with reality problems.

At the end of the meeting, I turned to a silent member of the group and asked him to say something. It turned out that he was not a patient but a pharmacologist who attended these meetings as part of his training.

STAFF MEETING

The supervisor handed the subsequent staff meeting over to me as authority on group therapy. I did not like leaving my place as participating observer, but accepted the invitation nevertheless. The therapist confessed how difficult it was to start her groups and I reassured her that this was generally the case. To confront these groups feels like voluntarily descending into Dante's Inferno, without Virgil as guide. One feels keenly one's therapeutic helplessness but an astounding thing happens: It seems as if little is accomplished, as if nothing helps, yet the entire group seems visibly relieved. The patients seem to feel "better" at the end of the meeting. Probably that is all we can expect from a group of such sick people.

When I was criticized and asked to explain my response to the dream, I explained that not to respond amounts to a rejection of the entire group, and that I had no choice as a newcomer who had to justify his intrusion. Not to respond would have slowed down the beginning group process. I wanted to tell the therapist that I am not a dream interpreter but use dreams to approach the dreamer's central problem. (I also suspected that my critic considered dreams resistance because she did not understand them. I did not say this at that time.)

October 1976

At the start 25 people were present, 35 were present at the end of the session. They were equally divided between men and women. There were two therapists, one of whom was a physician and the other a female social worker. I, as a consultant, completed the assembly.

Two women monopolized the beginning of the debate with stories of living alone and feeling insecure and threatened in a tough environment. The whole group joined them and discussed what could be done to prevent assault and robbery. From there the discussion went to the fear of losing control, "getting sick again," and needing renewed hospitalization. Yet everyone felt better after this discussion because of the general good will in the group.

The social worker repeated several times: "Do not worry. Nobody is going to lose control here. We will all help you to control yourself." It was quite clear that she did not intend to allow any expression of psychosis.

Both therapists tried to comment on "the group as a whole." They spoke in terms of "the group seems to fear" or "the group tries to find support," etc. Nobody reacted to these remarks. Everybody seemed to think "group" always meant "the other ones," not themselves.

In the staff meeting I tried to encourage the therapist not to be afraid of psychotic expression. The patients should feel they are accepted regardless of their condition. Violence is an exception. Acceptance by the group is the most effective reassurance for the psychotic person who is terror stricken by his hidden rage.

During the next session, the group was without a therapist because of a flu epidemic. I tried to take charge of the group. For a short time I disregarded undisciplined behavior: Several people talked simultaneously, and talked with one another, forming smaller subgroups while disregarding the rest of the people. The group behaved as if it was still in the waiting room, waiting for their therapist to arrive. They took little notice of their substitute therapist.

I called the group to order and explained once more my presence and function. A monopolist tried to take over; a "Boy Scout" type on my left entertained with feeble-minded, moralistic boasting and loud, brash advice. A black woman spoke about her two strokes. After a short moment of silence everybody wanted to talk about Las Vegas, where to stay in order to gamble cheaply, how much money to risk, how to win, and how to avoid losses.

One elderly woman told me proudly that she had been coming here for ten years; this was true of another patient as well. Both were quite outspoken and said frankly that the group saved them from loneliness, and that the "party" here was better than Bingo.

In the subsequent staff meeting I admitted how difficult it was for me to conduct such groups and how grateful I was to the monopolists for getting things started. I now understood why therapists appreciated anyone who broke the deadly silence. However, a monologue is a poor substitute for group interaction. We may not feel like silencing a monopolist with authoritarian brusqueness—but by changing actively from him to somebody else. I also began to understand why the regular therapist was more controlling than I had at first thought was necessary.

In the last meeting of the month, a woman who had called herself "helpless" complained that she did not know how to proceed with the welfare bureaucracy. The entire group came to life and gave her advice on how to find her way through the red tape. People were quite specific, giving exact names, addresses, and telephone numbers.

At this time I began to recognize individuals. For instance, the giant with the butcher knife turned out to be a good "co-therapist." He asked the right questions to get people to participate. Somebody needed an operation, and spoke about her fears. Everybody told her reassuring stories about their own experiences and the group for a while took on the character of a surgical ward where the veterans of surgery told new people how to proceed and "to fear nothing."

As is so often the case, the group caught fire in the last 15 minutes. One girl was uneasy about sex, and there was a general exchange of experiences, warnings, and advice. At the staff meeting we discussed how far one could go with interpretations, and I quoted Frieda Fromm-Reichmann as having said: "Our patients are not shy shrinking violets—and we do not need to treat them as if they were." In discussing what to say when people discuss their past transitory psychoses, I suggested what John Rosen used to say to his patients: "It is good to have had a psychosis and to have come out of it. It is a crime to remain psychotic." Rosen's technique of intervention aims, as I see it, at shifting guilt from having bad thoughts (which everybody has) to feeling guilty about being sick.

I noticed that the women were more active in groups than the men and that the physicians seemed to have more difficulty than the other therapists. The physicians seemed bent down by the heavy burden of unusable knowledge. They had to learn to combine their medical training with their humanity. I further noticed that it is a great advantage to have a large woman in the group who looks as if she were

pregnant with all the members of the group. It takes a mature therapist to accept such help, but these "mothers" are a blessing in any
group.

Finally, I assured the therapists that they did not need to begrudge
the time spent by welfare patients advising other welfare patients.
This is an important contribution to group cohesion.

One of the many lessons I learned during this month was how well
patients responded to the group and how patients often functioned as
effective co-therapists. It was a surprise to learn that they had been discharged from the closed ward of the hospital only one or two months
previously, after more or less recovering from a psychotic episode.

When I joined the group a week later, somebody discovered that
I could not easily move because of my bad back. He turned me
around and started to give me a back massage. That set the tone for
a general conversation, which included me as if I were none of the
group. This felt quite pleasant to me. There were many medical
questions, not all answered by me, but some answered by members
of the group.

One of the new members had both forearms bandaged because he
had recently slashed his wrists. He was apologetic about it but otherwise silent. A large black woman turned to him and said: "I was
more depressed than that. I was the most depressed person in the
whole world and now look at me. Soon you will be glad to be alive."

This was not given as advice or reassurance—but as a statement, a
message of hope. The woman simply compared her experience with
his. What was said was heard by everyone, even if nobody responded.

Another man said that he was "rolled" the night before. He had
come out of a bar, quite drunk, and was robbed of everything he had:
money, identification papers, and, worst of all, his driver's license. He
was peculiarly philosophical about it and told the story like someone
reporting an adventure. The group reacted by telling him how to
get new papers. Many women talked about their fear of assault,
rape, and injury. One of them vividly told the story of her big German shepherd dog who sleeps in her bed every night but had not
awakened when thieves ransacked the room. The group had a stoic
reaction that startled me: They all agreed, "When they get you, they
get you. There is nothing you can do about it." This was disquieting
for me, but reassuring for everybody else. It seemed to me that they
probably accepted their helplessness while I fought and denied mine.

Out of the silent group at the beginning of the next session, a woman complained: "I hear voices all night long." Another woman recently hospitalized for a psychotic episode turned to her and said: "Never mind. They are demons—the world is full of them. They go away and come back." The woman talked as if there was nothing to worry about. She seemed to have a reassuring influence on her fellow schizophrenics.

Other people joined in and somebody announced: "My doctors will not allow me to hear voices again." Surprisingly, she really cannot hear them any more. Then the problem was dropped.

The next topic started with a woman saying, "My mother told me never to call her again." The woman cried bitterly. Somebody else wanted to know how old the patient was. She said she was 39. Then the other patients wondered out loud how a woman of 39 still could cry about her mother not wanting to talk with her. This was not said to educate or with irony, but just stated as an astounding fact to be wondered about, as another curiosity in this curious world. A woman said, "I have three children. I am their mama and they all complain to me. They always want to know what they should do. I just let them talk. I don't like this world either, but what can we do?"

Another woman turned to the 39-year-old "baby" and said, "Forget about your mother. Look for friends." The first woman answered, "Nobody comes." A young woman volunteered: "I'll come. I'll visit you." The whole group half-kiddingly and half-seriously, but quite joyfully, said, "We all will come." It was not the promise that counted, but the expression of good will.

The group started anew with a woman saying, "I don't want to come anymore; my daddy tells me I am more upset when I come home from the group than when I leave to go to the group." This was discussed in detail with astonishing understanding.

One woman turned to one of the men and said, "Tony, you are the life of the group. You care for us and we care for you. Don't you too stop coming." The man called Tony obviously was having hallucinations and quietly answered, "I found God." One woman spoke about her fear of Tony and all the women slowly realized that they were all afraid of men. They all agreed that men were cruel, violent, and dangerous.

In the hour of consultation with the therapists, I tried to show how everybody in the group, at one time or another, was a good, understanding, affectionate therapist. We, the professionals, should recognize that and it should make us modest. We, of course, try to do something much more ambitious, perhaps impossible, and that is to understand everybody at the same time. We want to help or cure everyone. It may be enough for us to be and to endure with them, and to appreciate their effort to improve. That may be the most helpful thing we can do.

9
A Clinical Illustration of "Insight Groups"

Martin Grotjahn, M.D.

There is a second type of group therapy in the outpatient clinic, more structured in its requirements and more ambitious in its aims than the "follow-up" groups. The sessions last 90 minutes and the groups are smaller, rarely consisting of more than eight people. The therapy attempts to combine insight with emotional experience through interpretation and interaction. These "insight groups" are not much different in their dynamics from the groups any psychiatrist conducts in his private office.

Patients are more carefully selected for these groups than for the large follow-up groups. Patients are selected on the basis of their ego strength, which should allow them to gain and use insight. The words "insight group" are not too well chosen, since the group process takes place mostly in the here and now. Genetic material, genetic interpretations, and analytic constructions move into the background.

After the sessions, the therapist in charge is available for medication, other medical assistance, or any need, just as after the large groups. Here, too, all groups are conducted by two therapists. Supervision is available on a weekly basis by consultants. These supervisory meetings are also necessary for the emotional support of the therapists, who are under considerable stress since they are often new to their work and feel threatened.

I do ask in advance about the patients, since I want to react to them spontaneously, and without previous expectations. In the clinical illustrations given below, I was familiar with both the therapists who had chosen me as their consultant and invited me to join the sessions.

CLINICAL ILLUSTRATIONS

January 1977

The group was led by two therapists (a psychiatrist and a registered psychiatric nurse). I joined the group after it had been meeting for several months. The group had been told to expect me.

The members of the group sat in a semi-circle, open to the one-way screen behind which a technician operated a videotape camera. Neither therapists nor patients were aware which sessions were being taped and which were not. I was so completely involved in the group process that I was at no time aware of the taping. That seemed to be equally true for the other therapists and the patients.

The semi-circle started on the left side with the nurse and continued with me. Then came the group of three women and three men, one of whom was Mexican, with a limited understanding of English. The psychiatrist concluded the lineup. This seating arrangement varied some, but not much.

At the first meeting, 45 minutes were spent discussing my presence. The group asked: "Who are you?" "What do you want?" "How often will you be here?" "How long will you stay?" I answered all these questions. After 45 minutes, however, I objected to this procedure. I had never been greeted in this way by any group and I felt that the group was not properly prepared. I suggested that the therapists were ambivalent about my presence and that the group reacted accordingly. The two therapists remained silent; later they preferred to repeat one question to the patients: "How do you feel?" The group members imitated the behavior of the therapists and asked the same question to one another. No interpretation seemed to be offered.

After my intervention, one of the women turned away from me and wanted to know from the group what she should do when she got so very angry at her husband. The group responded: "What do you *really* feel?" The patient fell silent for the rest of the session. Later

I suggested that the woman felt rejected because we did not respond to her need. She resented that we neither cared about nor understood her trouble at home.

Another woman talked about the person sitting to her right, and complained that he did not respond to her. Suddenly she reached out and hit him. She then cried bitterly, and finally the two embraced.

At the end of the session, I compared two men with each other: One patient pretended to be much more angry than he really was and the other seemed to laugh more often than he really felt like laughing. Only when the laughing man got up to leave after the session had been terminated did I notice that he had a partial spastic paralysis of both legs, which made it difficult for him to walk.

Later, in a meeting with the therapists, I discussed their ambivalance toward me. They responded with loud denial, which I accepted as a reaction to our first meeting together.

I also did not think it was right for the therapists to withdraw, as if they were handing the group over to me. The group did not like it and it was not really my function to take the group over.

I said that I would have investigated the relationship of the woman and her rage against her husband. Even so-called insight groups have to start with outer-directed problem-solving. Insight and interaction usually will follow attempts at problem-solving.

I would have interfered with the woman hitting her neighbor and then embracing him. She should learn how to express herself verbally instead of acting out and dramatizing her feelings. Otherwise, we learn little.

At the end of a later session, I turned to a silent woman and said, "I would feel badly if we closed this session and you had said nothing." Whereupon the woman broke into tears. At first I wondered whether anyone could or would explain what had happened? Neither the group nor the therapist volunteered an answer. So I said, "It is better to cry than to sit here silently and control your depression. The time will come when you will explain your grief to us."

Somebody summarized the group topic as: "There is so little love in the world," which I took to mean: There is so little love expressed in this group. The therapists do not seem to care; they are just onlookers.

After the group session, the medical therapist startled me with a question. He wanted to know whether I am so "direct, free, and active" in my private office when I work with my own private patients? I said: "Naturally. I am as free and open here as I am in my office."

The group members walked together to the parking lot and were overheard to say: "Grotjahn really brings us together. He really makes us work. He wakes us up!"

February 1977

The group again was silent and I tried to interpret this individually by getting at the personal reasons for silence. The therapist commented on my procedure: "Grotjahn is really concerned with the group and everybody in it."

During this month, videotape recordings of two sessions were shown to all residents and staff members in order to discuss the sessions. I was shocked to see how boring the group was on a small screen. We never saw the entire group, but only one or two individuals at a time talking or interacting. The camera always focused on whoever was talking.

I had not been aware of how much seemingly unmotivated laughter was heard, probably to relieve tension. This laughter seemed to me totally pointless. I also noticed how much coffee drinking filled the times of silence. I planned to mention embarrassed laughter and coffee drinking when I had the opportunity.

I was annoyed at how much I used my hands—much more often than anybody else. I excused my pointing my index finger at people by telling myself I did not know their names. I realized later that I pointed the same way at patients whose names were quite familiar to me. There was also a haughty expression on my face at times when I waited and listened. I was totally unaware of this before I saw the tape. Sometimes I literally "held my mouth" with my hand in order to keep myself from talking too much, and being too critical or even hostile.

It was most instructive for me to step out of the isolation in which we therapists usually work and to have a videotape recording shown to a group of colleagues—and to myself.

The questions by the residents naturally showed their lack of experience, but they were able to make me look at myself and explain why I did something at that moment and why I did not do something else at another moment. My intuitive grasp of the therapeutic situation is based on experience and observations. I often respond to subliminal clues without becoming fully conscious of my perceptions or my reasons. The motivation to interpret, interact, or not to do so remained mostly, and always partly, preconscious or even unconscious.

At times my friend Frank Kline could guess the reasons for my behavior and could explain it better than I could.

In contrast to the real performance, videotape viewing is extremely boring for most people. It has to be made tolerable by frequent interruptions, playback, interpretations, and debates.

The residents remarked dryly: "Grotjahn is always on camera." Then they wanted to know the reason for every remark and every intervention. They were critical but open-minded, and eager to get acquainted with any other model of therapeutic behavior other than the passive, reflecting-mirror model that motivates the therapists to turn every question back on the group.

The residents noticed that I was turned to the group, visibly attentive. The medical therapist was leaning far back in his chair, almost lying down, with his feet outstretched, as if he wanted to tell the group: "This is your turf—not mine. I am only watching and certainly not competing with Grotjahn's charismatic personality."

One of the therapists wanted to continue with me as a consultant "forever." The physician was hesitant and finally said, "Not forever—but it is very interesting for the time being." I concluded that it was about time to change to another group with a different therapist.

In one of the last meetings of the month, and after my coming departure had been announced, the group listened to the same woman talking about her husband for 65 minutes. I finally interfered, first by offering my understanding of the woman's behavior and saying, "Your husband is an orphan, he behaves like one, and he married you to establish a kind of orphanage with you as the mother and him as the orphan. You were maneuvered to play the role of the good mother and a mother cannot divorce her son. He seems to force you to remain in a situation which has become painful as time goes on." After that I said, "We cannot spend all our time with one person, and should move on now. Everybody should have a chance to express himself during a session." The therapist asked the group: "How do you like being told what to do?" The group did not react to his question.

After the session, the physician asked me, "Have you always been so free?" We agreed that one needs time and experience to develop confidence in oneself, in others, and in the group process.

In the last hour of the month I said goodbye to the group. One patient became depressed, claiming that in these two months she had learned more than in the last two years. I assured her that I would remain in the clinic and that perhaps I could come back occasionally for a visit, if invited.

This remark to the patient in despair was criticized by the residents when they viewed the videotape recording. They felt that this would have been my chance to interpret the excessive dependency needs of this patient and her infantile transference. It was my impression, however, that this could not be done at that time and that one would have to wait a long time during which the patient should be allowed to indulge her dependency. To try to dissolve her dependent transference as I was leaving would be destructive.

In spite of criticism about my therapeutic role, no one could deny that the group had come to life. Somebody added: "Even the therapist came to life." One instructor remarked: "Grotjahn is a strong medicine for a beginning therapist."

One incident was especially criticized. My left-hand neighbor in the group was a young woman who had remained silent, obviously lost in loneliness and despair. When I asked her to speak to us, she said, with obvious hostility, "What do you want to know?" So, for shock value, I asked her: "Well, tell us whether you are still a virgin." This shocked the group of patients, the therapist, and the audience who viewed the tapes. I explained that I did not expect an answer from the patient, but I would expect her to react to the question and to my invitation to join us in the next meeting. It seemed to me more promising to shock the patient into hostility, which I suspected was the reason for her not talking with us, than to plead with her.

After the last session, every member of the group came up to me to shake hands. To my surprise, all the women hugged me and wished me well.

September 1977

I joined a group of staff members and residents to observe through a one-way screen a group of six patients with two therapists. The

observing team included the medical director, Frank Kline, and between 10 and 24 residents. The director gave a running commentary
about the group process while watching the group. In this way, two
groups were in session: The therapeutic group and the group of observers. This method made it possible to watch the group without
getting bored or sleepy. It was an advantage to see a live group and
not just the small screen of the television set. I found myself mostly
watching the therapists and neglecting the group of patients. All
of them had been carefully selected by the senior therapist himself,
and found fit for therapy in an insight group.

It was impressed by the therapist's body language. He was quite
good looking, a Jesus-like bearded man, who turned to the group by
leaning forward in his chair. He was sitting in a way that clearly expressed his intense attention, his interest and even his affectionate
devotion to his assignment. He moved little, said less, asked nothing,
and turned the procedure back into the group whenever they turned
to him. The result was that the group turned mostly upon itself and
within a short time was loudly interacting. I was amazed to see how
this extremely passive approach had results similar to my active
intervention.

Every session started slowly but there was no doubt that within
half an hour the group would begin to interact.

When the therapist expressed himself he was carefully diplomatic,
and always smiling, as if he wanted to apologize to the group for his
presence. The group obviously gave up its attempts to interact with
him and left him alone in his role of observer. When he occasionally
stepped in, the group seemed to be surprised and immediately continued on their own way again. He rarely interpreted the group's
behavior, and mostly addressed his comments to the individual, and
then in his apologetic way. This did not allow the patient to hit back
or interact with him. He seemed to avoid any form of confrontation.

I was surprised and critical when a patient came 60 minutes late
and the therapist never reacted to it. He explained later, after the
group was dismissed, that he was waiting for the group to react. He
did not feel it was up to him to make a comment. It was my opinion
that the therapist has to give an example first, before he can expect
the group to react.

Another time, the therapist, who always joined the observing group
after the therapeutic group had left, was very angry, and complained

loudly about the passivity and antagonizingly slow movement of the group. The obvious comment was that they patterned themselves after the model the therapist set. If I were annoyed to that degree, I certainly would let the group know it.

I left the group of observers before the difference in approach between the therapist in charge and me became disturbing for the group of observing residents. I am not a shepherd, as I think the therapist was. I am a challenger of the group's collective defenses.

After I left, the group slowly dwindled to a few members and then terminated. Perhaps more assertive activity by the therapist would have helped—but perhaps not.

Part IV:
Group Therapy and the Medically Ill

10
Group Therapy in Medical Illness

Samuel Miles, M.D.

Disease may be defined as psychosomatic when the origin or progress of somatic complaints is influenced by life situations.[1] Complaints may or may not be directly related to organic pathology. Crucial to the definition is that psychological factors influence the progression of the illness.

According to Engel's[2] biopsychosocial model of disease, many, if not all, illnesses can be considered psychosomatic. Even when psychological factors cannot be shown to influence pathology, the presence of organic disease influences the psyche. We should address the person, not the illness, if we want to help with the illness. We should not forget that it is a person who seeks treatment, not a disease; this may often be forgotten, even though it is a principle of "holistic health."

Group therapy, in one form or another, has been used in the treatment of medical illness since at least the turn of the century.[3] It has been used as an economical educational tool and an inspirational forum, as well as a potent therapeutic modality. Groups have been used as part of preventive, therapeutic, and rehabilitative programs. They have been organized by professionals, as well as by patients and their families, to meet a perceived need. Some groups have become national and international organizations, such as Alcoholics Anonymous, Overeaters Anonymous, and the British Diabetic Association. They have functioned politically and have been a source of informal communication, hope, advice, and contact with specialists. In many self-help groups, professionals are used only as consultants, and then only when needed. The task of running the group is left to the members.

This chapter ignores self-help groups and limits the presentation to the professionally led groups of patients with medical disorders. Since our primary focus is on disorders that respond to psychotherapeutic treatment, the terms *psychosomatic disorder* and *medical disorder* will be used interchangeably. We recognize that some disorders are "more psychosomatic" than others, and that some patients are more prone to use somatic problems in dealing with their psychological conflicts. We might define a spectrum of patient characteristics from "psychosomatic" to "psychologic," with the "psychosomatic patient" being more susceptible to somatic illness when under stress. Group therapy may provide advantages for treating these people, even though the substitution of somatic for psychic complaints adds to the problems of establishing and maintaining a therapeutic environment in a group.

Psychosomatic patients have difficulty introspecting. They may be seen as impersonal, overcontrolled, rational, and stereotyped in their relationships. They may be clinging and establish symbiotic relationships with therapists that lead to therapists feeling irritation, impatience, despondency, and dissatisfaction. Therapists may be tempted to assume the omnipotent medical roles[1] demanded by these patients. On the other hand, therapists may be overwhelmed with helplessness or exhaustion, as they try to meet the "insatiable" needs of these patients. On the whole, the individual therapy of these patients is a formidable task. Group therapy offers some distinct advantages.

The group may act as a very powerful therapeutic force. Patients sharing common problems help overcome resistances to acknowledging psychological factors. The psychosomatic patient is "forced" to talk about himself in group and may, from this, learn to be more introspective. Group members share therapeutic responsibility. Thus, they gradually rely less on the physician and become more maturely independent.

In addition, since the transference is split, its intensity is lessened and it is less frightening to the patient. There is an opportunity to identify with others who share similar circumstances; isolation is diminished, as is the threat of separation.[4] With co-therapists there is an opportunity for group members to observe that conflicts between therapists are resolved, rather than hidden. This can correct the somatizing patient's misperception. When the group is heterogeneous, the psychosomatic patients may identify with other group members as they articulate emotional conflicts and, eventually, learn to express their own.[1,6] Homogeneous groups do not offer this advantage, but they are comfortable for primitive patients who fear individuation. Homogeneous groups protect and stabilize. They are especially useful where alleviation of anxiety is a primary goal, as with patients with coronary disease, smokers, and pregnant women. If character change is necessary, as with bronchial asthmatics, heterogeneous groups are best. Homogeneity produces comfort, status quo, and boredom. Heterogeneity offers increased change and increased anxiety.

The psychosomatic patient approaches group as if it were a fixed structure with standardized rules. Many experience the entire world that way, as if they are bound to the exact rules of their primary family. They seem to want to restore what was established. Change, especially differentiation among group members, and separations are greeted with regression and somatization. Therapists find that interventions usually must be directed to the group as a whole. There is a need to feel that everyone is treated uniformly, and interventions addressed toward individuals are not tolerated well. This well-established principle of technique is particularly useful to groups of somatizing patients.

Archaic, aggressive self-destructiveness is difficult to overcome, since it is associated with object inconstancy and the operational thinking of alexithymia.[7] "Addiction" to the group or to the therapist may occur as a defensive maneuver. The symbiotic wishes aroused may be difficult to work through. What is learned in group may not be transferred to outside life and therapeutic stalemate may ensue. While direct interpretation of the dynamics and transferences of a group may not always be wise, the therapist should be aware of these issues and, occasionally, intervene in an unobtrusive way when these factors are operating against therapy.[8]

Reports of clinical experience with group psychotherapy for psychosomatic disorders between 1945 and 1970 are favorable. Between 66% and 100% of patients are reported improved,[4] including patients with severe underlying psychiatric disorders and those with a history of unsuccessful individual treatment. Patients with persistent somatic complaints, a high frequency of clinic visits, and minimal response to medication have been shown to benefit from group treatment, both by a reduction of complaints and by a decrease in clinic visits. These results were maintained at follow-up six to fifteen months later.[9]

Group therapy, like any therapy, is not for everyone. Hypertensives may show an elevation in blood pressure in groups,[10] while patients with chronic pulmonary disease may be physiologically unable to tolerate the strong emotion that is stirred up in group[11] (although group treatment has been most consistently reported with positive results in coronary artery disease and migraines[4]).

Obese patients lost little weight with up to two years of group psychotherapy, though they did improve in general adaptation and emotional well-being. Educational, inspirational programs, such as Weightwatchers, can be helpful for the motivated person, but results often depend upon continued group participation.

At this time, selection of patients for group therapy should be determined by the personality and psychopathology of the patient rather than by other factors.[4]

As noted above, groups may be homogeneous, with all members sharing the same diagnosis, or heterogeneous, with many disorders represented. They may even mix somatizing patients with the usual insight group members (although this is difficult for both the group and the somatizer.) The aims of a particular group therapy may be classified between the polarities of "analytic" and "supportive," though the old term *repressive-inspirational* evokes more vividly the differences between groups.

All groups are supportive by nature, but in the supportive repressive-inspirational group, all other tasks are put aside. The leader is a good, but autocratic, leader who constantly directs treatment and exhorts patients to do what is indicated. Treatment failures are not dicussed. In at least one version of this type of group, patients who show improvement are allowed to share the platform with the leader and present inspirational addresses.[12] Natural childbirth classes and Alcoholics Anonymous groups generally follow this format. Relaxation exercises or some other tension-reducing devices often play a prominent role in the activities of these groups.

The leader of the analytic group, on the other hand, tries to restrict his activity to the interpretation of individual or group dynamics.

His goal is to facilitate the group members' increasing understanding of themselves.

Most therapy groups today fall somewhere between these two extremes, with therapists who sometimes inspire their patients, sometimes interpret, and mostly facilitate communication. Concordance between the patients' goals and those of the therapist is crucial to successful therapy. The therapist must vary his techniques in order to help his patients achieve *their* goals. If the goal is socialization, the therapist may avoid interpreting transferences in the group unless they interfere with socialization. Modest goals, by the therapist's standards, may have a large impact on selected patient populations.[13] Other patients may require more from therapy, and a different level of activity from the therapist. To facilitate group cohesiveness, patients selected for a group should have similar goals.

ASTHMA

Psychological factors are believed to play an important role in asthma as etiologic and perpetuating factors. Even when bronchoconstriction is clearly caused by allergy, certain psychological events occur; the patient may become somewhat constricted in emotional response. Like the patient with chronic lung disease, the asthmatic sees dyspnea as a danger to avoid. Since it may occur with emotional states, such as anger or anxiety, these states are avoided.[11] The attacks may be used as substitutes for expression of hostility; they may hide emotions that have made the patient anxious, guilty, or ashamed; or they may be used to evoke sympathy, attention, or affection from a person symbolizing the depriving mother in the transference.[14] Thus, the asthmatic attacks often serve a major, but ambiguous, role in the patient's communication system.

Group therapy improves the asthmatic patient's relationships, increases confidence, and decreases anxiety. Results of studies on group treatment effectiveness for asthmatics are mixed. The best results were in a group run by internists, who also prescribed symptomatic medication and ACTH. They saw the patients twice a week and were available for individual consultation. The group patients requested less symptomatic treatment and showed more "index of improvement" than controls.[15] A concurrent group, led by a psychiatrist, was discontinued because patients stopped coming.

Sclare and Cricket,[16] on the other hand, report no change in asthmatic symptoms between patients in a therapy group and a control group after once-a-week group therapy for two years. Personality changes were apparent, however, including diminished anxiety, increased self-confidence, and improved social relationships.

Differences in results between these two controlled studies may be related to differences in frequency and quality. The Groen and Pelser[15] groups met twice as frequently, the therapists were available after the sessions and were the same physicians who prescribed for the asthma. The patients in the Sclare and Cricket group met less frequently. The therapists were less available and were not the same doctors who prescribed the other treatment. The patients chosen for groups may have been different. Sclare and Cricket chose patients from those attending asthma clinic, while Groen and Pelser selected patients who had been admitted to the hospital at least once for status asthmaticus. The latter may have been more motivated to change.

More common than these homogeneous groups, and perhaps more useful for asthmatics, are heterogeneous groups. Other patients may model emotional expression. The events of the group may evoke an asthmatic attack and allow the patient to recognize the psychological factors in his illness.

Reckless[6] noted "asthma like behavior" in asthmatics in his group. He defined this behavior as inspiratory grunting and expiratory wheezing of mounting intensity, often culminating in the use of an aerosol bronchodilator and/or temporarily withdrawing from the group.

When he, or another group member, noticed the beginning of this behavior, all activity stopped and all attention focused on the asthmatic patient. He was asked what was happening in the group just before he started wheezing. If he had trouble identifying the manifest or latent content of the group interaction, it would be done for him so that he could incorporate the events and his emotions intellectually and emotionally. At the same time, he was discouraged from taking medication. Instead, the patient was asked to select a trusted group member and make some body contact to reduce distress and anxiety. Often the patient would sit on someone's lap. This approach was found to reduce the frequency of asthmatic attacks both in and out of the group. Patients reported that they felt punished when the group focused on them. They could only escape by stopping the attacks or learning to identify internal conflicts and talk about them. Withholding the medication may allow patients to recognize that they could control the attack without drugs.

Asthma attacks that occur in group are more likely in older patients with unsupportive marriages, poor employment records, low motivation, and an inability to introspect.[3] These factors also are related to a poor prognosis.[15] A favorable prognosis accompanies youth, no hospital admissions, an accepting spouse, satisfying work, good introspective ability, and the ability and willingness to talk about emotions in group. "Robust" psychotherapy may produce symptom substitution where the asthmatic trades asthma for depression.

Asthmatics run a regular course in treatment with minor variations determined by the composition of the group and factors related to the individual asthmatic.

These patients begin the group skeptical about psychotherapy. They discuss the circumstances of their illness, focus on somatic factors, and deny emotional factors. Cautiously, the patient begins to criticize the medical profession. As criticism becomes more open, the patient may also ask for special favors. Aggressiveness alternates with placation. Gradually the aggressive outbursts focus on family members. Some asthmatics only listen silently, afraid to jeopardize the therapist's "good opinion" of them. Gradually, patients recognize a correlation between emotional stress and asthma. This discovery may repeatedly be forgotten as resistance sets in, but, gradually, some asthmatics improve. The improvement of some group members may lead to deeper exploration of the personality variables involved in the asthma and the establishment of a "group theory" of the pathogenesis of asthma. Rivalry may occur between patients who show improvement and those who do not.

Patients with supportive environments leave group therapy quickly and with good results. Those without supportive environments, who can relate their attacks to life events and use the group to reduce guilt and anxiety through "confession" and ventilation, do well. Patients who remain reluctant to reveal themselves do poorly.

CORONARY ARTERY DISEASE

Emotional factors have long been associated with the pathophysiology of coronary artery disease, through the "Type A personality," is believed to be at risk for greater incidence of myocardial infarction,[17] and indirectly through smoking and hypertension, recent animal studies[18] implicate psychological factors in the production of atheromatous plaques. In rabbits on a high-cholesterol diet, those that were individually and regularly petted, held, talked to, and played with showed less atherosclerosis than animals given normal laboratory care. Serum cholesterol levels, blood pressure, and heart rate were comparable in both groups.

In addition, clinically significant coronary artery disease can result in overwhelming anxiety and depression. A heart attack is painful and life threatening. It may require changes in work, recreation, and social life. Losses must be mourned and anxieties worked through for optimal recovery. The patient may need to adjust to a new role in his family. For many, this process can be very difficult.

Psychological interventions, including group therapy, have been used as part of a treatment program during all phases of coronary artery disease. Group therapy offers advantages for these patients. Its use may yield some impressive results, including decreased anxiety, decreased mortality, decreased social isolation, and a smoother return to work.[8,19-26] Therapy may induce character changes that might prevent clinically significant coronary artery disease.[17]

The core components of Type A personality are an exaggerated sense of urgency, hostility, and a strong drive to please superiors and peers. These traits may be easily identified in a group setting. Modification of these traits may be facilitated by the patient's wish to please, since the best way to receive approval in a well-run group is to show behavior changes. The group should help the patient understand the urgency as exaggerated. They must learn that it is safe to give up this trait. Economic well-being does not depend on rushing through every action. They may use the supportive atmosphere of the group and the direction of the therapist to reengineer their daily living schedules and explore the basic philosophical assumptions under which they live. The therapist must encourage and guide these patients so they may actively recall past events to balance against their obsessive preoccupation in the present. He must guide the patients to enhance self-observation, self-control, self-instruction, and self-management. He must be active and should not have too many Type A traits himself, or he cannot provide the patient with a usable model.

Rosenman and Friedman[17] report that subjects involved in a pilot study of this type of group therapy were unanimous in their belief that the group facilitated free communication. Many felt they had not communicated so freely for years. For some patients, open communication may uncover convert feelings of anxiety and depression, which may require more traditional psychotherapy, individually or in group. They suggest the training of paraprofessionals to lead this type of group because of the high incidence of Type A personalities among physicians.

Smoking is another risk factor in coronary artery disease which may be modified through group treatment. Halhuber[27] describes an approach that has been successful, especially with patients who have had symptoms of cardiac disease. He attributes the success in these patients to the motivation contributed by pain and Type A's pressure to overachieve.

Smokers should be divided into three groups, based on their self-assessment: the occasional smoker, the habitual smoker, and the addicted smoker. The addict should not be treated outside the hospital. The occasional smoker needs no treatment at all. The habitual smoker, on the other hand, may best be treated in a group led by a nonsmoker. The groups should meet frequently—twice a week—for four to six weeks. Up to about 20 patients may be treated in each closed group.

The first group task is to analyze the motivation for smoking. Smoking may diminish negative feelings, reinforce positive feelings, or facilitate social contact. During the first week of treatment, the patients are asked to observe their smoking habit by writing the time and circumstances for each cigarette smoked. This information must be noted prior to the lighting of the cigarette to eliminate the unconsciously smoked cigarettes and to disconnect smoking from other reinforcers (e.g., coffee).

The data gathered are discussed in the group, as are the resistances to not smoking. Ways to gratify the individual's needs other than smoking are found and the patient is encouraged to stop. Those patients who use smoking to manage anxiety should withdraw gradually until they smoke ten cigarettes a day. At that point, they should stop altogether. Patients who smoke for other reasons should quit "cold turkey" and this avoids the problems caused by an intermittent reinforcement schedule.

The group leader may help the smoker anticipate what will happen when he stops smoking. With knowledge of the stimuli that led to smoking behavior, one may prepare for the impulse to smoke before it arises. Those who quit "cold turkey" should be prepared for the impulse to become stronger for the first three to five days and then to decrease. Patients who cut down should be warned that the impulse to smoke will be stronger for a longer period than if they quit at once. By cutting down, instead of stopping, they put themselves on an intermittent reinforcement schedule. Sometimes the stimulus to smoke has been rewarded with a cigarette, while at other times it has not. This schedule of reinforcement leads to habits that are most difficult to extinguish; hence the recommendation that all but a few quit at once.

For the patient who has suffered a myocardial infarction, group treatment may be helpful not only in modifying his personality and smoking habits, but may also help the patient cope with the stresses ubiquitous to this illness. Groups may be open or closed, brief or long-term, but they should be homogeneous.

When the idea of group is introduced to the patient, the medical functions should be stressed. This leads to greater acceptance since cardiac patients often refuse to consider themselves psychologically needy or ill, and are prone to reject psychological treatment without preparation. Indeed, to mental health professionals who lead their groups, these patients will often seem to be trying to prove how "normal" they are. Nonpsychiatric physicians trained in group dynamics might be the ideal leaders of groups composed of cardiac patients (provided they resist the temptation to become overly involved in the medical aspects of the treatment).

The group may be introduced while the patient is in the hospital or after discharge. CCU patients, three to seven days following admission to the hospital, have been successfully treated in group, with the group allowing for support, ventilation of anxiety and depression, and preparation for the return home.[19] Even in this acutely ill group, there have been no reports of adverse effects, or even chest pain, during group.

Controlled studies have shown group therapy to be beneficial during the rehabilitation phase of treatment. Patients in group showed a lower mortality rate, a high rate of returning to work, and a lower serum cholesterol than controls. Except for the lower cholesterol, these differences persisted years after the completion of therapy.[22]

Integration of therapies focused on the "psychological risk factors" of coronary disease allows patients to concentrate on their areas of success even though they may experience difficulty losing weight or stopping smoking. Satisfaction in one arena may prevent the frustrated patient from leaving treatment prematurely and thus allow more benefit from the overall rehabilitation program.

These patients do poorly with insight-oriented, nondirected therapies. They do best in an educational-inspirational group, with an active, but nonintrusive, therapist.

Patients moving smoothly through rehabilitation may be adequately treated in a short-term group. There should be enough time for each patient to review the events leading up to and following the onset of his heart attack. After this task is accomplished, normally accompanied by some mild depression, the psychological factors leading to the myocardial infarction should be explored. This should include recent life changes, use of denial when the symptoms first appeared, self-imposed job responsibilities, over-competitiveness, intolerance of delay, and a lack of personal satisfaction. Each patient should plan to change these traits. The group provides the supportive atmosphere necessary for discussing the problems and implementing changes.

Work behavior is best discussed before the patient returns to work. This discussion, among other people with the same work habits, is often a valuable experience and provides convincing evidence of the connection between Type A patterns and coronary disease.

For many patients, the return home from the hospital is their first experience since childhood of being home during the day. This experience, combined with the oversolicitousness common among spouses, often arouses anxiety which can be reduced through group therapy.

Confusion about diet, activity level, and sexual relationships may be reduced in group. However, the leader should avoid exclusive focus on the somatic issues, since this is a frequent form of resistance to emotional issues.

Spouses should be involved in the rehabilitation. When they become overanxious, psychotherapeutic intervention may be indicated. Couples groups tend to be more inhibited than separate groups for patients and for their spouses. The spouse needs help in reducing guilt. This may be accomplished by inviting the spouse to one session of the patient's group—the one dealing with the psychological risk factors. This way the spouse may be allowed to ventilate and reduce guilt. If more is needed, individual therapy or admission to a hetero-geneous therapy group might be indicated.

For patients with undue difficulty in the rehabilitation process, we recommend a long-term group. These groups may reduce anxiety, depression, and hypochondriasis so that the patient's self-confidence and positive attitudes toward work can be restored.

Many of these patients seem more inhibited at work after the coronary because of depressive reaction to their myocardial infarction. Others are overwhelmed with anxiety about recurrence. Both these issues must be addressed for successful rehabilitation. The task of the group is to discover the reasons for the inhibition and to work them through.

All patients are anxious about returning to work. Attending group at least once, after going back to work, can be reassuring and valuable. For this reason, it is important to schedule these groups "after hours" or on weekends. Though it might be argued that patients could take an hour off from work for group, it is better not to increase their anxiety at this difficult time.

STROKE

Stroke patients may benefit from group therapy while in the hospital. For the group to be successful, nursing staff cooperation is essential. The patient usually will need to be prepared for group by his nurses and brought to the meeting room. Nursing staff and family might be invited to participate in the group whenever possible. However, it should be noted that where the group norm is for family members to attend, those patients without attending family may become alienated and drop out.

The groups goals should be the working through of depression related to lost function and the facilitation of realistic plans for the future. Patients may benefit from the socialization, even if they are not verbal. Therapists should have some structured supervision or "post-group sessions" to help them deal with the feelings of helplessness and hopelessness engendered by this group of patients.

Family groups may be helpful in allowing the family to better adjust to the limitations imposed by the stroke and plan realistically for discharge. Continued participation following discharge is generally unrealistic because of the considerable problems most of these patients have with mobility.

RHEUMATOID ARTHRITIS

Rheumatoid arthritis has been treated psychotherapeutically for the last thousand years.[28] Psychological conflicts are thought to play a role, though pathogenic mechanisms are not yet clear. It seems a burden of hostility precedes the development of arthritis and that verbalization or acting out of aggression occurs before remission. Many of these patients had a domineering mother, out of which came masochism in the service of others and stoicism. According to Karasu,[29] these patients generally respond best to long-term analytic individual therapy, but group therapy may be helpful.

Udelman and Udelman[30] describe their experiences with a group of hospitalized arthritics. The group met three times weekly. The patients were invited to attend for as long as they were hospitalized. The therapist's goals were educative, supportive-ventilative, and exploratory-dynamic. Udelman and Udelman thought group allowed patients to emerge as people in the hospital, rather than becoming dehumanized patients.

Staff involvement was essential from the inception of the group. They were also involved as members to increase the social integrative function of the group.

Pain was the primary subject discussed. It became clear that chronic pain leads to a modification of personality as old coping mechanisms are discarded. Patients may use their pain to manipulate others or they may adopt a posture of stoic acceptance and masochism toward friends and family. Many psychologically rely on pain and panic when it disappears.

A recurrent finding related to the pathogenesis of arthritis is that aggressive people tended to function effectively for many years with mildly active forms of arthritis. Six months to a year following a significant loss (a job, friend, family member, etc.), exacerbation and general deterioration occur.

For many patients, pain without anatomic changes posed a difficult problems. Once the joints became swollen, they would feel relieved the pain is not "all in the head."

Patients who maintained optimism, were psychologically aware, and showed emotions received the greatest benefit from the group.

REFERENCES

1. Brautigan, W. and Ruppell, A. Group psychotherapy. *In:* Wittkower, E. D. and Warnes, H. (Eds.), *Psychosomatic Medicine: Its Clinical Applications.* New York: Harper & Row (1977), pp. 94-106.
2. Engel, G. L. The need for a new medical model: a challenge for biomedicine. *Science* **196**: 129-136 (1977).
3. Sclare, A. B. Group therapy for specific psychosomatic problems. *In:* Wittkower, E. D. and Warnes, H. (Eds.), *Psychosomatic Medicine: Its Clinical Applications.* New York: Harper & Row (1977), pp. 107-115.
4. Karasu, T. B. Psychotherapy of the medically ill. *Am. J. Psychiatry* **136**: 1-11 (1979).
5. Abramson, H. A. and Peshkin, M. M. Psychosomatic group therapy with parents of children with intractable asthma. III. Sibling rivalry and sibling support. *Psychosomatics* **6**: 161-165 (1965).
6. Reckless, J. B. A behavioral treatment of bronchial asthma in modified group therapy. *Psychosomatics* **12**: 168-178 (1971).
7. Nemiah, J. C. Alexithymia and psychosomatic illness. *J. Cont. Ed. Psychiatry (October):* 25-37 (1978).
8. Hackett, T. P. The use of groups in the rehabilitation of the postcoronary patient. *Adv. Cardiol.* **24**: 127-135 (1978).
9. Friedman, W. H., Jelly, E., and Jelly, P. Group therapy in family medicine: Part I. *J. Fam. Pract.* **6**: 1015-1018 (1978).
10. Kellner, R. Psychotherapy in psychosomatic disorders. *Arch. Gen. Psychiatry* **32**: 1021-1028 (1975).
11. Pattison, E. M., Rhodes, R. J., and Dudley, D. L. Response to group treatment in patients with severe chronic lung disease. *Int. J. Group Psychother.* **21**: 214-225 (1971).
12. Markillie, R. Group psychotherapy in psychosomatic disorders. *In:* O'Neill, D (Ed), *Modern Trends in Psychosomatic Medicine.* Woburn, Mass: Butterworths (1955), pp. 317-332.
13. Rosin, A. J. Group discussions: a therapeutic tool in a chronic disease hospital. *Geriatrics* **30**: 45-48 (1975).
14. Baruch, D. W. and Miller, H. Interview group psychotherapy with allergy patients. *In:* Slavson, S. R. (Ed.), *The Practice of Group Therapy.* New York: International Universities Press (1947), pp. 156-175.
15. Groen, J. J. and Pelser, H. E. Experiences with, and results of, group psychotherapy in patients with bronchial asthma. *J. Psychosom. Res.* **4**: 191-205 (1960).
16. Sclare, A. B. and Cricket, J. A. Group psychotherapy in bronchial asthma. *J. Psychosom. Res.* **2**: 157-171 (1957).
17. Rosenman, R. H. and Friedman, M. Modifying type A behaviour pattern. *J. Psychosom. Res.* **21**: 323-331 (1971).
18. Nerem, R. M., Levesque, M. J., and Cornhill, J. F. Social environment as a factor in diet-induced atherosclerosis. *Science* **208**: 1475-1476 (1980).

19. Frank, K. A., Heller, S. S., and Kornfeld, D. S. Psychological intervention in coronary heart disease: a review. *Gen. Hosp. Psychiatry* 1: 18-23 (1979).
20. Mone, L. C. Short-term group psychotherapy with postcardiac patients. *Int. J. Group Psychother.* **20**: 99-108 (1970).
21. Rahe, R. H., Tuffli, C. F., Suchor, R. J., and Arthur, R. J. Group therapy in the outpatient management of post-myocardial infarction patients. *Int. J. Psychiatry Med.* **4**: 77-88 (1973).
22. Rahe, R. H. Ward, H. W., and Hayes, V. Brief group therapy in myocardial infarction rehabilitation: three to four year follow-up of a controlled trial. *Psychosom. Med.* **41**: 229-242 (1979).
23. Ibrahim, M. A., Feldman, J. G., Sultz, H. A. et al. Management after myocardial infarction: a controlled trial of the effect of group psychotherapy. *Int. J. Psychiatry Med.* **5**: 253-268 (1974).
24. Segev, A., Falik-Elster, E., and Schlesinger, Z. Treatment of stress and anxiety states after myocardial infarction by group rehabilitation. *Harefuah* **88**: 205-208 (1975).
25. Wrzesniewski, K. Some psychotherapeutic problems of patients after myocardial infarction. *In:* Stockmeier, V. (Ed.), *Psychological Approach to the Rehabilitation of Coronary Patients.* New York: Springer-Verlag (1976), pp. 49-51.
26. Soloff, P. H. The liaison psychiatrists in cardiovascular rehabilitation: an overview. *Int. J. Psychiatry Med.* **8**: 393-402 (1977/78).
27. Halhuber, C. Stop smoking training in patients with coronary heart disease. *In:* Hauss, W. H. et al. (Eds.), *International Symposium: State of Prevention and Therapy in Human Arteriosclerosis and in Animal Models.* Opladen: Westdeutscher Verlag (1978).
28. Shafii, M. Psychotherapeutic treatment for rheumatoid arthritis one thousand years ago. *Arch. Gen. Psychiatry* **29**: 85-87 (1973).
29. Karasu, T. B. Psychological and behavior therapies in medicine. *Psychosomatics* **20**: 578-583 (1979).
30. Udelman, H. D. and Udelman, D. L. Group therapy with rheumatoid arthritic patients. *Am. J. Psychother.* **32**: 288-299 (1978).

11
Group Psychotherapy with Psychosomatic Patients

Charles V. Ford, M.D.

The seductive promise of treating patients having psychosomatic ill-nesses with psychotherapy has had, unfortunately, a lesser degree of proven success than the enthusiasm it has engendered. With the evolution of etiologic theories about psychosomatic illness there have been changes in the techniques proposed to treat these very difficult patients. Reports of group psychotherapy methods for psychosomatic patients have been among the few controlled studies reported and for several theoretical and practical reasons this treatment technique deserves serious consideration as a conjunctive if not primary treatment modality. This chapter will briefly review prominent themes in the etiological explanations and proposed therapies for psychosomatic illness, present the rationale for the choice of group therapy techniques, review various types of groups that have been described, and then summarize conclusions drawn from widely varied clinical experience.

PSYCHOSOMATIC ILLNESS AND PSYCHOTHERAPY— A BRIEF REVIEW

The following review emphasizes certain personality and communicative characteristics shared by many psychosomatic patients and their treatment by group therapy techniques. The reader is also referred to other recent reviews of the psychotherapy of psychosomatic illnesses.[1,2,3,4]

What is a "psychosomatic disorder?" Alexander[5] described seven diseases that have become recognized as the "classical" psychosomatic illnesses. These include peptic ulcer, ulcerative colitis, bronchial asthma, atopic exzema, thyrotoxicosis, essential hypertension, and rheumatoid arthritis. Subsequent reports have both extended the number of diseases considered to have a psychologic component and have increasingly stressed the multiplicity of factors involved in the production of disease states. There is also an important reciprocal relationship in that disease states will also influence psychic and social functioning. As a consequence, all illnesses can to some degree be considered psychosomatic or somatopsychic. However, it does appear that some (usually chronic) illnesses are more influenced by emotional factors than others. For the purpose of this chapter, Kellner's[4] definition will be used. He defined the term *psychosomatic disorder* as an "organic disease in which emotions appear to act as precipitating or aggravating factors" and spoke of "psychophysiologic reactions in which the patient is distressed by somatic symptoms in the absence of physical disease."

Early concepts of psychosomatic disease stressed specific etiology. The symptoms of each disease were at one time considered symbolic of an internal psychic conflict and later considered specific for certain constellations of psychological and physiological functioning. From these concepts of etiology it logically followed that the patients should receive psychotherapeutic treatment that would help resolve these specific conflicts. A parallel in medicine would be the treatment of a susceptible pathogenic microorganism with a specific antibiotic. Although anecdotal and individual case reports indicated at least occasional success with this treatment strategem, there has been a lack of well-controlled studies demonstrating consistent therapeutic results. It has been increasingly apparent that despite some overall similarities in a group of patients with a specific disease (e.g., dependency conflicts in patients with peptic ulcer), individuals with a particular disease often differ more from one another than from patients with a completely different disease.

Although the concept of conflict specificity has by no means disappeared from the psychiatric arena,[6] there has been more emphasis on the role of factors nonspecific to a particular disease. These include the importance of life change and stress, such as separation from loved ones, preceding physical illness[7,8] and, more relevant for this chapter, the similarities that psychosomatic patients share in terms of their maturation and communicative capabilities. It is important to emphasize that there are wide variations in the psychological characteristics of patients with any disease, and a description of psychosomatic patients in general is often not at all relevant for an individual patient.

Emphasizing the core personality patterns of immaturity, Ruesch,[9] in 1948, noted that psychosomatic patients showed *arrested* personality development, as opposed to *pathologic* personality development in neurotics. He regarded the somatic symptoms of these patients to constitute an infantile means of self-expression and noted several areas of deficits in personality development. These included insufficient capability to function as an independent unit, unsuccessful social interactions with other people, and defects in self-expression, self-extension, and individuation. He expressed the opinion that insight-oriented psychotherapy is unsuccessful with these patients because they lack the requisite skills for that form of treatment. Rather than insight, he viewed the issue of psychotherapy as one of reeducation, a lengthy process usually requiring years. "The patient has to be permitted to copy, initiate and function in conjunction with the therapist and only as time goes on and very gradually can independent action be initiated." He went on to say, "The whole approach can be summarized by stating that the procedure is really child psychiatry with adult patients." Similarly, Freedman and Sweet[10] used the term *emotional illiteracy* to describe the psychosomatic patient's defective ability to communicate feeling states.

More recently, Nemiah and Sifneos,[11,12] expanding on observations of the French psychosomatists Marty and de M'Uzan,[13,14] have developed the concept of alexithymia. The characteristics of alexithymia (which Sifneos and Nemiah describe as occurring frequently, but exclusively, in psychosomatic illness) include a lack of words for feelings, and a thinking style relatively devoid of fantasies and speech, typified by excessive attention to detail but lacking in emotional depth. These are not "psychologically minded" persons. Why some persons should demonstrate this cluster of symptoms is unclear, but Nemiah[15] has suggested the possiblity that alexithymia, rather than having an underlying psychodynamic explanation, may represent a neurophysiological disorder. Sifneos[12] has hypothesized alexithymia, to be an etiologic factor in psychosomatic illness, theorizing that the patients experience persistent physiological arousal because of their inability to sublimate affects through verbal means or fantasy. Subsequent reports from different centers have confirmed the phenomenon of alexithymia. However, its etiologic relationship to psychosomatic illness has not been completely established and the possibility exists that it is an associative rather than a casual relationship.[16]

Insight-oriented psychotherapy, because it produces anxiety, is regarded by Sifneos[17] as contraindicated for alexithymic patients. Assuming this to be a valid observation, one must be cautious in choosing the form of therapy for a particular patient and this may explain why prior results of psychotherapy with psychosomatic patients, on the average, have not been more impressive despite the fact that some patients seemed to do very well.

Consistent with this line of reasoning, Karush et at.[18,19] in reviewing the results of psychotherapy with ulcerative colitis patients, found individual differences between patients to be very significant in determining the outcome of psychotherapy as well as the somatic course of the disease. Patients who were active and individuated did very well with insight-oriented therapy, but other, more symbiotic patients did better with supportive techniques. The extent of physical improvement in this group of ulcerative colitic patients was related to how well a patient was able to change his environmental situation rather than the acquisition of insight per se. The best psychotherapy results were obtained by therapists who rated high in interest in their patients, empathetic understanding, and optimism.

In view of the above experiences, one must be careful not to make blanket recommendations for the type of psychotherapy indicated for a specific disease but instead carefully examine the ego mechanisms, communicative style, and degree of individuation (maturity) of each individual patient before embarking upon a therapeutic program for that particular patient. However, in doing this, one will most likely find among patients with psychosomatic illness a disproportionate number of persons who can be aptly describe as alexithymic and/or who display little of what is commonly termed "psychological mindedness." This may have some direct etiologic relationship to the illness itself or may represent an associated finding in that there is a higher incidence of both psychosomatic illness[20] and alexithymia[21] in the lower social economic classes. As a consequence, when considering psychotherapy for patients with psychosomatic illness, one must have the ability to provide the type of psychotherapy that will be most effective for that type of person most likely to have these illnesses. There are a number of reasons why group therapy is both a practical and a theoretically sound method of treatment for many of these patients.

RATIONALE FOR GROUP THERAPY
IN PSYCHOSOMATIC PATIENTS

As noted above, a disproportionate number of patients with psychosomatic illnesses are from the lower socioeconomic classes. They have limited financial resources and their medical care is frequently provided by publicly supported health facilities. Group, as opposed to individual, psychotherapy is a less expensive and an efficient method of providing care for large numbers of persons. In addition, with this socioeconimic group, missed appointments are a frequent occurrence and overall group size can be adjusted to compensate for average absenteeism in order that valuable professional time is used most effectively.

Psychosomatic patients, because of their style of relating, such as making dependent demands, being verbally nonproductive or preoccupied with offering mundane details of their lives and illnesses rather than focusing on important emotional issues, are often tedious and emotionally exhausting for therapists to work with. Groups tend to diffuse the dependency and allow for greater interaction between members, and, as a consequence, there is less need for the therapist to be continuously active.

According to Brautigam and Ruppel,[2] another advantage of the process of group therapy is that patients learn to become more responsible for the management of their illnesses. These authors believe that group members, although following the examples of other patients and by the sharing of common experiences, come to realize that they are participants in the recovery process. They also state that group discussions can help break down the resistances to understanding the psychic contributions to their illnesses.

Perhaps most important, in line with the concepts of Reusch,[9] namely that psychosomatic patients have a deficiency in psychic development, the group experience allows a greater opportunity for growth than that of individual psychotherapy. In the group setting, with the therapist acting both as catalyst and benign guardian, group members learn to relate to one another much as in a family, sharing experiences, expressing feelings, and learning new forms of communication. They learn that they are not alone and that others experience similar needs, and they are discouraged from assuming their usual childlike, submissive role to the physician.

Patients may have difficulty relating to a therapist who is of a different socioeducational group (as is usually the case) and who is often more introspective in manner. In this regard, Klein[22] has commented, "It seems to be a fact that less intelligent patients gain insight more easily in a group situation than they do from individual treatment. It may be that the language of the group is more easily comprehended than that of the therapists."

Klein regarded the repression of aggressive and sexual impulses to be an important aspect of psychosomatic dermatological symptoms and noted that group therapy had certain advantages over individual therapy. In the group setting, patients can recognize that certain conflicts are common to all and that certain impulses previously felt as forbidden are experienced by all members of the group. With such recognition comes a lessening of guilt and tension.

TYPES OF GROUP THERAPY FOR PSYCHOSOMATIC PATIENTS

Experiences with group psychotherapy of patients with various psychosomatic illnesses have been reported numerous times in the literature. Usually these reports have involved patients with a similar disease, such as rheumatoid arthritis, peptic ulcer, or asthma. While it would be possible to arrange a discussion focusing on the various results of treatment with specific illnesses, the following outline will instead focus upon the type of therapeutic techniques utilized. The placement of the various reports into different treatment categories is somewhat arbitrary and it is recognized that most therapies actually include multiple modalities. For example, the aspect of socialization is present in all groups, including those with an insight orientation. It must also be noted that published reports of various group psychotherapy experiences vary in their degree of detail concerning the therapeutic style and techniques used and also that successful therapeutic efforts are more likely to be reported than unsatisfactory results.

Educational Groups

This form of "group therapy" for psychosomatic illness is historically the oldest and dates back to the early 1900s, with the educational-inspirational "classes" for tubercular patients initiated by Pratt.[23] Following this tradition, but associated with more scientific evaluation, was the use of group techniques by Chappell et al.[24] to treat peptic ulcer patients. This 1937 investigation deserves attention and an attempt at replication, because the results were impressive and also because it represents one of the few studies where use of a control group was attempted. In this study, patients were divided into two groups, control and experimental (the therapy group). The severity of illness was actually somewhat greater in the therapy group. Treatment consisted of six weeks of daily (seven times a week) sessions centered around lectures. The themes emphasized were control of worry through diversion to pleasant thoughts, control of talking about somatic symptoms, encouragement to think positively, and explanation and insight of both a physiological and a psychological nature. Encouragement of self-assurance and induced suggestion (the patients were told that they were doing well) were also utilized. Results were dramatic. Of 32 patients, 31 were free of all symptoms after three weeks, while all of the controls continued to have symptoms. At the end of three years, results continued to be very good, although some patients had experienced mild recurrences.

Treatment approaches emphasizing a primary educational approach were not reported again until recently. Apfel-Savitz et al.[25] described a group therapy approach with psychosomatic patients who, with one exception (a neurotic patient), had traits of alexithymia. The authors employed a variety of techniques, including guided teaching, concrete visual feedback, such as with videotape, and meditation. A unique feature of this group was the use of the neurotic group member as a "translator" of feelings expressed by the group. The group met bimonthly, and after two years the authors were optimistic that, despite continuation of many long-standing problems, by relating to one another and to the therapists, group members were starting to move out of their alexithymic traits.

Schwartz et al.[26] have described a group setting for patients with rheumatoid arthritis in which dissemination of information about their disease was a major component of therapeutic goals. Rheumatologists acted as co-therapists in the group and served as major sources of information. Other goals included increasing the patients' communication with their families and physicians, and efforts were made to help patients learn to live more realistically with their disease. According to Schwartz et al., many patients were able to modify their life styles, improve meaningful communication with family, friends and physicians, increase compliance with physical therapy and medical regimes and in general learn to live with themselves and their arthritis." Most patients who were regular group attenders appeared to have fewer flare-ups of their arthritis during the eight months of the group, as compared to the preceding year. Of note was the fact that three patients experienced exacerbation of their arthritic symptoms when the group terminated.

In reviewing the experiences of various groups of patients who had suffered myocardial infarction, Hackett[27] has noted that there is resistance to presenting these groups as a "psychiatric" activity. Changing the name to something such as "coronary club" and stressing educational issues increases patient (and perhaps cardiologist) acceptance. Along this line, Buchanan[28] has described a novel, two-phase approach to engaging patients with chronic illnesses into a psychotherapeutic process. These groups, which meet in the medical clinic area, have a time-limited (ten to fifteen sessions) format. The first four sessions are devoted to lectures about the patients' disease (a common shared disease is a requirement for this approach). The discussions following the lecture serve as a nonthreatening method of engaging members into group process. After four sessions, they are invited to continue with the groups for approximately another ten sessions that are devoted to group discussions. About half the patients continue the group meetings, and at the conclusion of these sessions, those patients requesting further psychological therapy are referred to more long-term group or individual treatment.

In summary, although the number of reported studies is small, there has been good acceptance by patients of educational group treatment approaches. Results of this non-traditional treatment technique appear to have been surprisingly good, thereby suggesting that this is an effective and cost-efficient method of therapy.

Insight-oriented Groups

The treatment goal of an insight-oriented group is the acquisition by members of increased knowledge of how prior experiences, especially those from childhood, relate to current relationships and intrapsychic functioning. The analysis and interpretation of transference reactions to other group members, as well as to the therapist, consists of an important aspect of the therapeutic process. Dream interpretation may also be used as a therapy technique.

Insight-oriented, or psychoanalytically-oriented, group psychotherapy is the most reported type of group psychotherapy utilized for psychosomatic patients. Results have been highly variable and this probably reflects the large number of factors involved in therapy, including the personality and style of the therapist, the frequency of sessions, and the degree of deviation from a strictly orthodox analytic treatment approach.

Stein[29] described treating 15 patients who had peptic ulcer disease with insight-oriented group therapy for 18 months of weekly 90-minute sessions. These patients, who were described as having rigid, immature, severely restricted personalities, responded with some lessening of emotional tensions and some loosening of rigid patterns of reaction. The degree of physiological improvement appeared to relate to the degree of psychological improvement. Although the basic personality deformities were not eradicated, the changes that did occur seemed to be enough to favorably influence the course of their peptic ulcer symptomatology. Stein[30] also describes group therapy with a group of women with ileostomies secondary to the surgical treatment of their ulcerative colitis. He noted that "one of the important manifestations of improvement in this group of patients was their ability to become aware of emotions psychologically and to express them by more purely affective means such as anger, shouting and weeping." Stein was impressed that improvement in psychosomatic patients tends to be a little better with group therapy than with individual therapy and pointed to the fact that the intensity of the transference toward the therapist is deflected onto other members of the group. This allows the patients to be less fixed at a regressive passive-symbiotic level and to enter a useful psychotherapeutic relationship.

Treating patients having neurodermatitis with group therapy, Milberg[31] found that almost all had a flare-up of their dermatitis during the first few sessions. However, most patients improved and some remained in the groups even after their skin cleared in an effort to achieve more changes in the personality area. These patients were described somewhat differently than those characteristics usually attributed to psychosomatic patients. Milberg's patients were described as having above average intelligence, perceptiveness, sensitivity, and a drive to get well. Patients were seen in twice-weekly group sessions of 90 minutes after having been seen individually for a number of sessions before joining the group.

Fortin and Abse[32] also noted an initial exacerbation of symptoms in the peptic ulcer patients whom they treated with insight-oriented group psychotherapy. These patients consisted of a fairly homogeneous group of college students, who were described as having infantile personalities with prominent passive-aggressive traits. In response to treatment, the patients first demonstrated improvement in terms of the quality of their academic work and later in the psychosexual sphere as they became more realistic and less solitary. The ulcer symptoms, which had exacerbated during the initial phase of therapy, were reduced in the late therapy and follow-up.

Asthmatic patients treated by Sclare and Cricket[33] were reported to improve in some personality areas but not in their asthmatic symptoms. These authors viewed therapy as helping to increase their patients' tolerance, acceptance, and socialization while reducing their anxiety, tension, and rigidity. Techniques used were those of an insight-orientation, but the therapists placed highest priority on the verbalization of feelings by group members. These authors noted a high turnover in the group initially and also that a productive session was often followed by marked resistance.

Treating patients with multiple somatic complaints with what was described as an analytically-oriented group therapy, Schoenberg and Senescu[34] placed the emphasis upon analyzing somatic complaints as a resistance and deviation from the group contract. Eventually the group members were able to see that the somatic complaints allowed them to avoid dealing with other, more basic problems. These patients, after 18 months of therapy, had a marked decrease in their utilization of medical clinics over the following five years.

Forth and Jackson,[35] using insight-oriented psychotherapy techniques, treated a group of asthmatic patients who were described as having characteristics of alexithymia. They noted a high drop-out rate (over 50%), although some patients who remained with the treatment program seemed to improve. They observed that weekly sessions may not be sufficient to keep the therapeutic process active. Of considerable interest is their clinical vignette of a patient who developed severe respiratory distress in a therapy session. When the patient was taken outside of the therapy room, one of the therapists relaxed her usual professional manner and became very caring in a concrete physical manner. The patient responded with marked improvement, which persisted for many months.

In treating psychosomatic patients with group therapy techniques that emphasized group rather than individual interpretations (the Tavistock orientation), Roberts[36] has made several observations. These included poor patient attendance at group meetings and unrealistic expectations by patients of the therapist. These psychosomatic patients seemed unable to understand the group context and frequently induced the reaction of boredom in the therapist.

In summary, responses of psychosomatic patients to insight-oriented group therapy techniques have been variable. It is not possible to rule out the possibility that factors other than the acquisition of psychological insight were responsible for favorable responses.

Supportive Group Therapy

Although the differences between groups described as insight-oriented as opposed to supportive are often rather arbitrary and/or a matter of degrees, the following reported experiences of group therapy are categorized as supportive because of the apparent emphasis on socialization, group support, and catharsis as opposed to the primary goal of acquisition of psychological insights.

Mally and Ogston[37] found that weekly group therapy for three years significantly reduced medical clinic utilization of women who had complained of multiple somatic complaints. These lower socioeconomic women who possessed few psychosocial assets had been regarded as undesirable psychotherapy patients. Working with a similar type of patient, Ford and Long[16] made a number of observations that are compatible with other reported experiences with psychosomatic patients. These authors were struck with the similarity between not only the various types of psychosomatic illness but also with the similarities between "psychosomatic" and "hypochondriacal patients." These characteristics can be best described as meeting the criteria for alexithymia. In these open-ended groups, which extended over a seven-year period, it was noted that there was a high drop-out rate. This could be ameliorated somewhat by getting patients more personally involved with one of the therapists by scheduling several individual sessions prior to referral to the group. Group members had remarkable sensitivity to expressed affect, and attendance following affect-laden sessions was usually low. The skill of the therapist was required to carefully titrate the level of affect expressed in the group in order that therapy could proceed yet not overwhelm the patients. Therapeutic gains obtained were modest in extent and did not occur for prolonged periods of time. Cautious optimism by the authors was expressed for this type of therapy, but great patience is obviously required.

Treating epileptics in supportive groups, Lessman and Mollick[38] found that while outcome was not universally favorable, there was in general an increase in self-esteem. As a result of the group therapy experience, many patients took their first steps toward assuming new roles. However, one patient, anticipating a loss of emotional support when her group terminated, was hospitalized shortly thereafter with uncontrollable seizures, presumably exacerbated by stress.

An intensive inpatient group therapy program, extending over seven weeks, for chronic pain patients has been described by Pinsky.[39] Although these patients, whose personalities were generally concordant with alexithymia, began the groups with a bias against psychotherapy, they almost unanimously valued the help they received from the group, irrespective of any change in the pain complaint.

Udelman and Udelman[40] report experience with a supportive-cathartic-type group therapy for rheumatoid arthritis patients. This open-ended group, which met three times a week, was available for all hospitalized rheumatoid arthritic patients. Patients were not screened or seen individually prior to attendance at the group. The authors report that some individual patients showed improvement in response to the group but that the average patient attended only 2.6 sessions.

In summary, the results obtained by "supportive" groups appear less impressive than the results of other types of group psychotherapy. This may, however, be an artifact because the descriptions of the patients in these reports indicate that they may have had fewer psychological strengths to begin with than those patients treated by other techniques.

Conjunctive Group Therapy

The groups described in this section have in common, irrespective of the therapists' theoretical bias, the feature that the therapist or co-therapist was also the patients' primary physician or that at least he was present at group meetings. Therefore, the physical and psychological therapies of these patients were conjunctive rather than being parallel. This appears to be an important factor in the almost uniformly excellent results achieved by these groups.

Shoemaker et al.[41] describe weekly supportive psychotherapy for patients with atopic dermatitis. A dermatologist was present and checked the patients' skin condition at the time of the group meeting. These authors reported that those patients who improved were those who were able to increase their aggressiveness and showed decreased evidence of depression. They noted that therapeutic success was to a large extent dependent upon the physician's ability to cope with these patients' heavy demands and unresponsiveness.

The report of Groen and Pelser,[42] in treating bronchial asthma patients, is among the most significant in the psychosomatic psychotherapy literature. This work is unique in that a control group was used for comparison and, in addition, a blind objective method of rating psychological change was employed. The group met twice a week for approximately 75-minute sessions and treatment extended over a period of four years. The therapists were the patients' physicians (supervised by a psychiatrist, Dr. J. Bastiaans). Patients were questioned about their bodily complaints at the time of group meetings and were prescribed treatment as indicated. The authors note that it took about two years before the patients could consciously discuss the possibility and mechanism of a psychogenesis for their asthmatic attacks. Nearly all of the group therapy patients improved, and mortality was significantly decreased as compared to the control group. Those patients who improved most in their "interhuman relationships" were those who also benefited the most in regard to their asthma. The authors stated that their techniques were similar to those used to treat neurotic patients; however, there was some limitation in reenacting conflict situations because of fear of precipitating a severe asthma attack. Blind Rorschach testing of the treated patients compared to controls indicated a significant decrease in the number of "oppression" responses after 19 months of treatment.[43]

Using the family practitioner as a co-therapist, Friedman et al.[44] described the successful treatment of six somatizing women in a relatively short, 20-session, group treatment program. The group met in a family practice center and emphasized a practical daily problem approach rather than a psychodynamic orientation.

In a study mentioned above (see educative groups), the group reported by Schwartz et al.[26] had rheumatologists attending a group program for patients with rheumatoid arthritis. Patients did well symptomatically during the period of time that therapy continued.

In summary, the treatment results for psychosomatic patients using group therapy techniques in direct conjunction with providing medical care are remarkably good. One can speculate that this is because they allow the physician to see the patient as an entire person and conversely they allow the patient to communicate with the physician using means other than somatic symptoms.

ADVERSE REACTIONS TO GROUP THERAPY

If a treatment has the power to influence physical illness in a positive direction, it would seem reasonable to assume that adverse reactions can also occur.[45] Such is the case with psychosomatic patients and group therapy. In the various groups described above, it is important to note that patients have experienced an increase in somatic symptoms with the initiation of therapy[31,32] or with the termination of therapy.[26,38] As a consequence of the potential danger in precipitation of somatic symptoms and/or increasing resistance, some therapists[16,42] have noted the importance of controlling the degree of affective responses in the group setting. In addition to the groups previously mentioned, there are two reports of patients experiencing an increase in the severity of their illnesses in response to group therapy. In one report, the average blood pressure of a group of hypertensive patients increased as compared to the control group in apparent response to group therapy.[46] Specific treatment techniques were not described. In another study, seven out of twelve patients with chronic obstructive lung disease had to quit group therapy because of worsening pulmonary status presumably secondary to the anxiety engendered by challenging psychic defense mechanisms.[47]

CONCLUSIONS

Group therapy, as indicated on the basis of certain theoretical assumptions and on the evidence of empirical data, appears to be an effective method of treating at least some patients with somatizing illnesses. Those patients with "psychosomatic" disease who are well individuated and who would best be described as "neurotic" can, and probably should, be treated as any other potential psychotherapy patient. However, for that large category of somatizing patients who fit the criteria for alexithymia, group therapy with certain modification may very well be the treatment of choice.

Modifications to group therapy programs as usually constituted for neurotic patients should be considered for psychosomatic patients. The following recommendations are based on the author's experience and reports in the literature.

The Therapist

The theoretical orientation of the therapist appears to be of less importance than certain personal qualities. What appears to make a significant difference in successful group therapies for psychosomatic patients is the willingness for the therapist to become involved with his patients. Other very important characteristics of the successful therapists are the capability to accept dependent demands and to be able to tolerate very little change for long periods of time. If at all possible, the patients' primary physician should be present at group meetings, preferably as the therapist or co-therapist.

The Theoretical Orientation of the Group

Successful groups utilizing different stated theoretical orientations have been reported and, as mentioned above, the theoretical orientation of the therapist per se is probably of little direct consequence. Successful therapy appears to be more dependent upon whether or not the patient can learn new ways of expressing feelings and upon how they can influence the quality of their interpersonal relationships with persons significant in their lives. Educative approaches do appear to have considerable value. Information about illnesses and their psychological aspects presented in a didactic manner has a high degree of patient acceptance. Such an approach may be used to get patients involved in a more traditional form of group psychotherapy. Within the group setting, innovative techniques such as teaching patients about emotional expression through the use of played-back videotape may have considerable value. However, one must not forget that learning can also occur by identification with and/or imitation of the therapist and other group members and that new methods of relating to and communicating with others is a major component of most groups. The major issue is that the group process be structured in such a manner so as to facilitate learning in its broadest context. Such a process can vary considerably according to the situation and style of the therapist, much as there are multiple styles of effective parenting.

The Setting and Frequency of Group Meetings

Although most groups have traditionally met once a week, there is suggestive evidence that more frequent meetings may be required for psychosomatic patients. Certainly this appears preferable if practical circumstances permit it. Patients accept group therapy to a greater extent if the group meets in the medical/surgical clinic area rather than in the psychiatric unit. This appears to be related to many patients' concrete need to view therapy as a medical procedure.

The size of a psychosomatic group can be somewhat larger than that of a group of neurotic patients. The reasons for this are: (1) the fact that these patients are somewhat less verbally productive than neurotics and more patients may be needed in order to obtain a "critical mass" for discussions, and (2) one can anticipate a relatively higher rate of absenteeism than with more psychiatrically-oriented groups. Therefore, an overall group size of 12 to 15 may be necessary in order to ensure an average attendance of approximately 8 patients.

Experience indicates that it is also highly preferable for the therapist to have several individual sessions with each patient in order to prepare the patient for the group. For these patients, who on the average have fewer social skills, it is necessary for them to have a good relationship with the therapist so that they can tolerate the anxiety of their initial group experiences. Failure to establish such a relationship prior to their beginning group therapy will result in a high dropout rate.

Precautions

Group therapy, while of potential therapeutic value, may also be associated with adverse effects. One must be cautious not to proceed too rapidly nor attempt to evoke an excessive amount of affect or reenactment of major conflicts, particularly early in therapy. To do so may precipitate an increase in somatic symptoms, sometimes of a life-threatening nature. At the very least, the result of excessive affect is an increase of resistance, possibly resulting in patients leaving therapy. One must also be very sensitive as to how meaningful a group can become for a patient and the necessity to anticipate the effect that the thermination of group meetings may have upon him. Feelings related to termination need to be worked through before the group is discontinued, and some patients will require referral to other psychotherapy treatment programs at that time.

SUMMARY

Although patients with psychosomatic illness constitute a heterogeneous group, a substantial number of these patients can be described as having alexithymic traits and little "psychological mindedness." For these patients, traditional individual psychotherapy techniques may be ineffective or even contraindicated. Thus, group therapy may be the treatment of choice for many psychosomatic patients. Modifications to enhance the effectiveness of group psychotherapy for this type of patient have been presented in this chapter.

REFERENCES

1. Brautigam, W. and Ruppell, A. Group psychotherapy. *In:* Wittkower, E. D. and Warnes, H. (Eds), *Psychosomatic Medicine.* New York: Harper & Row (1977).
2. Cunningham, J., Strassberg, D., and Roback, H. Group psychotherapy for medical patients. *Comp. Psychiatry* **19**: 135-140 (1978).
3. Karasu, T. B. Psychotherapy of the medically ill. *Amer. J. Psychiatry* **136**: 1-11 (1979).
4. Kellner, R. Psychotherapy in psychosomatic disorders. *Arch. Gen. Psychiatry* **32**: 1021-1028 (1975).
5. Alexander, F. *Psychosomatic Medicine.* New York: Norton & Co. (1950).
6. Bastianns, J. The implications of the specificity concept for the treatment of psychosomatic patients. *Psychother. Psychosom.* **28**: 285-293 (1977).
7. Holmes, T. H. and Rahe, R. H. The social readjustment rating scale. *J. Psychosom. Res.* **11**: 213-218 (1967).
8. Schmale, A. Relationship of separation and depression to disease: I. A report on a hospitalized medical population. *Psychosom. Med.* **20**: 259-277 (1958).

9. Reusch, J. The infantile personality: the core problem of psychosomatic medicine. *Psychosom. Med.* **10**: 134-144 (1948).
10. Freedman, M. D. and Sweet, B. S. Some specific features of group psychotherapy and their implications for selection of patients. *Int. J. Group Psychother.* **4**: 355-368 (1954).
11. Nemiah, J. C. and Sifneos, P. E. Affect and fantasy in patients with psychosomatic disorders. *In:* Hill, O. W. (Ed.), *Modern Trends in Psychosomatic Medicine.* London: Buterworth (1970).
12. Sifneos, P. E. The prevalence of "alexithymic" characteristics in psychosomatic patients. *Psychother. Psychosom.* **22**: 252-262 (1973).
13. Marty, P. and de M'Uzan, M. La pensie operatorie. *Rev. Franc. Psychonal.* **27** (suppl.): 1345 (1963).
14. Marty, P., de M'Uzan, M., and David, C. *L'Investigation Psychosomatique.* Paris: Presses Universitaires de France, (1963).
15. Nemiah, J. C. Denial revisted: reflections on psychosomatic theory. *Psychother. Psychosom.* **26**: 140-147 (1975).
16. Ford, C. V. and Long, K. D. Group psychotherapy of somatizing patients. *Psychother. and Psychosom.* **28**: 294-304 (1977).
17. Sifneos, P. E. Problems of psychotherapy of patients with alexithymic characteristics and physical disease. *Psychother. Psychosom.* **26**: 65-70 (1975).
18. Karush, A., Daniels, G. E., O'Connor, J. F., and Stern, L. O. The response to psychotherapy in chronic ulcerative colitis: I. Pre-treatment factors. *Psychosom. Med.* **30**: 255-276 (1968).
19. Karush, A., Daniels, G. E., O'Connor, J. F., and Stern, L. O. The response to psychotherapy in chronic ulcerative colitis: II. Factors arising from the therapeutic situation. *Psychosom. Med.* **31**: 201-226 (1969).
20. Schwab, J. J., Fennell, E. B., and Warheit, G. J. The epidemiology of psychosomatic disorders. *Psychosomatics* **15**: 88-93 (1974).
21. Lesser, I. M., Ford, C. V., and Friedman, C. T. H. Alexithymia in somatizing patients. *General Hosp. Psychiatry* **1**: 256-261 (1979).
22. Klein, H. S. Psychogenic factors in dermatitis and their treatment by group therapy. *Brit. J. Med. Psychol.* **22**: 32-52 (1949).
23. Pratt, J. H. The class method of treating consumptives in the homes of the poor. *JAMA* **69**: 755-759 (1907).
24. Chappell, M. N., Stefano, J. J., and Pike, F. H. The value of group psychological procedures in the treatment of peptic ulcer. *AM. J. Digest Dis.* **3**: 813-817 (1937).
25. Apfel-Savitz, R., Silverman, D., and Bennett, M. I. Group therapy of patients with somatic illnesses and alexithymia. *Psychother. Psychosom.* **28**: 323-329 (1977).
26. Schwartz, L. H., Marcus, R., and Condor, R. Multidisciplinary group therapy for rheumatoid arthritis. *Psychosomatics* **19**: 289-293 (1978).
27. Hackett, T. P. The use of groups in the rehabilitation of the post coronary patient. *Adv. Cardiol.* **24**: 127-135 (1978).
28. Buchanan, D. C. Group therapy for chronic physically ill patients. *Psychosomatics* **19**: 425-431 (1978).

29. Stein, A., Steinhardt, R. W., and Cutler, S. I. Group psychotherapy in patients with peptic ulcer. *Bull. N.Y. Acad. Med.* **31**: 583-591 (1955).
30. Stein, A. Group psychotherapy with psychosomatically ill patients. *In:* Kaplan, H. I. and Sadock, B. J. (Eds.), *Comprehensive Group Psychotherapy.* New York: Williams and Wilkins Co. (1971).
31. Milberg, I. L. Group psychotherapy in the treatment of some neurodermatoses. *Int. J. Group Psychother.* **6**: 53-60 (1956).
32. Fortin J. N. and Abse, D. W. Group psychotherapy with peptic ulcer. *Int. J. Group Psychother.* **6**: 383-391 (1956).
33. Sclare, A. B. and Cricket, J. A. Group psychotherapy in bronchial asthma. *J. Psychosomatic Res.* **2**: 157-171 (1957).
34. Schoenberg, B. and Senescu, R. Group psychotherapy for patients with chronic multiple somatic complaints. *J. Chron. Dis.* **19**: 649-657 (1966).
35. Forth, N. W. and Jackson, M. Group psychotherapy in the management of bronchial asthma. *Br. J. Med. Psychol.* **49**: 257-260 (1976).
36. Roberts, J. P. The problems of group psychotherapy for psychosomatic patients. *Psychother. Psychosom.* **28**: 305-315 (1977).
37. Mally, M. A. and Ogston, W. D. Treatment of the "untreatables." *Int. J. Group Psychother.* **14**: 369-374 (1964).
38. Lessman, S. E. and Mollick, L. R. Epileptic patients in groups. *Health Soc. Work* **3**: 105-121 (1978).
39. Pinsky, J. J. Chronic, intractable, benign pain: a syndrome and its treatment with intensive short-term group psychotherapy. *J. Human Stress* **4**: 17-21 (1978).
40. Udelman, H. D. and Udelman, D. L. Group therapy with rheumatoid arthritic patients. *Am. J. Psychother.* **32**: 288-299 (1979).
41. Shoemaker, R. J., Guy, W. B., and McLaughlin, J. T. The usefulness of group therapy in the management of atopic eczema. *Penn. Med. J.* **58**: 603-609 (1955).
42. Groen, J. J. and Pelser, H. E. Experiences with, and results of, group psychotherapy in patients with bronchial asthma. *J. Psychosomatic Res.* **4**: 191-205 (1960).
43. Barendregt, J. T. A psychological investigation of the effect of group psychotherapy in patients with bronchial asthma. *J. Psychosomatic Res.* **2**: 115-119 (1957).
44. Friedman, W. H. and Jelly, E., and Jelly, P. Group therapy for psychosomatic patients at a family practice center. *Psychosomatics* **20**: 671-675 (1979).
45. Strupp, H., Hadley, S. W., and Gomes-Schwarts, B. *Psychotherapy for Better or Worse: The Problem of Negative Results.* New York: Jason-Aronson (1977).
46. Titchener, J. L., Sheldon, M. D., and Ross, W. D. Changes in blood pressure of hypertensive patients with and without group psychotherapy. *J. Psychosomatic Res.* **4**: 10-12 (1959).
47. Dudley, K. L. and Pattison, E. M. Group psychotherapy in patients with severe diffuse obstructive pulmonary syndrome. *Am. Rev. Resp. Dis.* **100**: 575-576 (1969).

12
Group Communication and Group Therapy with the Aged

Martin Grotjahn, M.D.

America has traditionally been the land of the healthy, the beautiful, and the young. Old people have to compete with young people to be young or to appear so, even if it kills them. "Old" used to mean "from the old country." Native-born Americans of the first generation lived as if they wanted to say: "History begins with us, here in the USA." This led to a denial of old age similar to the denial of death in American culture. However, this attitude seems to be changing. The ever-increasing number of senior citizens and the decrease in immigration has led to a reorientation of the general attitude toward the aged and acceptance of needs rarely voiced before.

The literature contains relatively few guidelines for psychiatry or psychotherapy in the field of gerontology. Butler[1,2] points out that old people can get as hysterical as young people, but that it shows differently. According to him, 80% of all analytic patients are 45 years of age or younger. Old people do not consult psychiatrists.

Butler's claim that psychoanalysis rarely accepts old people for treatment may be true, and one is tempted to say, "But what do old people need a new transference neurosis for?" It may indeed be true that individual treatment is not the answer to the psychiatric problems of the aged. Even where psychoanalysis or individual treatment is feasible for financial reasons, it may not necessarily be the treatment of choice. The implied negative answer to that question, however, suggests the need for a positive approach to problems that continue to persist.

GROUP THERAPY FOR THE AGED

I envision teams of experts, with and without medical background and training, who would go to the homes of old people and conduct group sessions there. Perhaps the term *group therapy* may sound too ambitious or even misleading, for old age itself is not a psychiatric illness. The function of these teams of therapists could be seen in establishing group communication and they could be designated as "communicators."

Optimally, group therapy leads immediately to relief of depression, loneliness, and the feeling of being rejected by the family. The sharing of common worries would help to form group cohesion. Old age, therefore, could be a satisfactory state of the life cycle. The time may come when old people will say: "The last years of my life were the best." Group communication and therapy could help realize this utopian hope.

In such groups, the transference situation, which is the foundation of all treatment, is quite different from that in any individual relationship. In the group, members form a new transference relationship to the therapist (or the team of therapists), to their peers, and to the group as such, which may include the institutions in which the old people live. Such a "divided" transference cannot reach the intensity of a transference neurosis as is essential to standard psychoanalysis.[3]

Lissy Jarvik,[4] in her pioneering studies of old age, shows that continued mental activity is necessary to avoid the main conflicts of aging. Inactivity, both physical and mental, results in deterioration. Group therapy offers continued mental activity. In individual psychotherapy, patients may continue to be lonely, develop further dependency, remain inactive, and feel guilty about it. Group therapy gives almost immediate relief to these symptoms that accompany aging.

If the group therapist has started group communication, he has fulfilled his first assignment. A second assignment would be to induce the group not to deny aging and to accept life as it has been lived. Hand in hand with that goes the final acceptance of death as a natural end of human existence.

There is no reason to glorify old age, nor is there any reason to deny it. One has to accept the past before one can accept the present. This acceptance should be prepared for throughout all of life. People should be aware that they have to live with their pasts. If they could be aware of this they would probably have a better chance of avoiding old age depressions. Americans like to live quite generally in the "existential moment." They do not live for the future as they do not like to live in the past; both avoidances make adjustment to old age difficult.

One great difficulty for the therapist arises here: How shall a therapist accept people who should not and cannot be accepted because they have lived lives of selfishness? It sometimes helps to show them that all human mistakes, short of murder, can be undone.

When a depressed person is rooted in a group, the initial stage of therapy has been mastered and that person is no longer all alone. Then suicide rarely, if ever, occurs. Anyone who has ever worked with groups will agree that group therapy is the treatment of choice for depression, including suicidal depression, at any age.

There are essential differences in the tasks of mastering infancy, childhood, adolescence, maturity, and old age, which is the sublimation of maturity to wisdom. Whereas maturity implies mastery of inner and outer reality, wisdom implies mastery of the existential limitation of human life. Wisdom is the willing acceptance of death as an existential fact.

SOME FACTS OF LIFE

Besides his skill as a group communicator, the group therapist would do well to keep a few psychological facts in mind when treating the aged. As children have to learn the facts of life, so old people must learn the facts of long life. One old woman once told me, with bitterness, but also with some humor: "Nobody ever told me that I, too, would grow old."

Old people have to learn about changes in their sexuality and the group therapist must know about them. One of the first misunderstandings that has to be corrected is that which arises from reading Masters and Johnson.[5] There is not much gained by asking old men about their sexual potency. They almost always lie, the way they used to in puberty. The standard answer is: "If you want to know whether I'm too old to be potent, then you'd better ask somebody older." It is somewhat more promising to ask the partners of old people.

In the first place, a man between 60 and 65 needs an "inviting female." What used to be a joy in former times now becomes a chore. Second, men have to accept retardation in all sexual functions. They have to learn that it is possible and necessary to enjoy sex with orgasm but without ejaculation. Third, sexual pleasure frequently changes in character and turns to a kind of spectator sport. It is astonishing to see that gray- and white-haired people of both sexes enjoy pornographic movies or stripteases; they often constitute the majority of the audience.

The group therapist must know how to correct two misunderstandings: Old people do not live beyond "sin" and they must not expect to function unchanged. Here, the sexual superiority of women becomes obvious once more. A tragic difference in the sexual behavior of men and women must be mentioned here. Old men are frequently attractive to young women and, as a rule, with some skill, have no difficulty in finding sexual or semisexual partners. But although younger women are attracted to older men, who represent fathers to them, older women are rarely attractive to younger men, precisely because the older woman is the symbol of the mother, and as such she is sexually taboo. This incest taboo is a strict and almost absolutely enforced taboo (though obviously it is not *always* absolute). These are not innate psychological conditions. Older women can be attractive and often are, but the taboo forbids younger men to look at older women as sexual objects. It is possible that in the future, when our multiorgiastic young female generation has grown old, a new attitude of sexual equality of the aged can be established.

One last point must be made: Group therapy offers the possibility of discussing problems of death and dying in a much less emotional way than in individual dialogue. Discussions of death between two people soon lead to embarrassment, guilt, and silence. This is not the case in group discussions.

However, talking about death should not be forced. The therapist must allow it to happen and must be prepared. A good place to learn how to deal with such discussion is in groups of terminally ill people. When they have felt initial relief and have gone through the stage of complaining about their environments, about the nurses, who are unfriendly and overworked, about the physicians who always rush away, about the medicine that is never strong enough, about the sedation that is always given too late, and about the family they feel has deserted them (which gives the first meetings the character of unpleasant, boring bull sessions), then a more fruitful and constructive stage of group therapy will be reached and deeper anxieties can be debated. The problem of death will then move into focus. (See Chapter 13)

The first signs of concern with death may become visible in dreams. The therapist should be familiar with the symbols of death. It is tragic that people's most beautiful dreams are usually dreams of death. Beauty and color are the most frequent symbols of death in dreams, but there are many others.

An old man once told his group the following dream, which started with great beauty and ended in a frightful nightmare: The old man dreamed that he took a walk with his grandson, three or four years old. They walked together and came to a high cliff with a balustrade protecting them from falling into a deep and wide canyon below. Both the old man and his little grandson stood still and looked down and saw below them a green valley of indescribable beauty. There was a little pond, which was obviously left over from the drying out of a larger lake. It was surrounded by lush green vegetation. On the water, lotus and water lilies were blooming. A beautiful bird was standing at one end of the pond. He had all kinds of gleaming colors and was built somewhat like a blue heron. There was a second bird standing at the opposite end of the lake. The little boy wanted to see better, so he swung himself on top of the ballustrade, lost hold, flew over it, and fell down, probably to his death. The old man was horrified, hollered for help, and woke up.

The old man was disturbed because he was sophisticated enough to suspect death wishes against the child in himself, which he could not accept. The association showed that the boy symbolized the dreamer's own youth, which had to die. He had to accept the fact that he was old now and getting older. He then realized that the bird was the mythical phoenix, which dies and is reborn from the ashes. That was the reason there was a second bird, the reincarnation of the first one. The pond symbolized the place from which all life comes.

A word of caution may be indicated about any statements concerning "the right to die" in groups of the aged. I have learned not to make any remarks in favor of euthanasia. My attitude will always be on the side of life. I try to analyze the wish to die as a hostility turned against oneself or as an accusation against the family. As long as someone asks for help to die, he is not ready for it.

Immediately after group sessions, medical attention should be available to the group members. Every group session may as well end with medical response to the complaints of its members. This may concern the usual complaints about constipation, sleeplessness, weight loss or gain, lack of appetite, or hypertension. If these questions are treated after the group session, it gives additional stimulus to continued participation. All medical problems should be heard but then referred from the session to the time after the group.

Therapists who work with the elderly must analyze and understand their own attitudes toward old people and toward their own parents in particular. Such therapists should not be unduly loving, have a need to idealize members of the group, or dislike them.

Therapists must be able to stand the great love of their old patients and must be able to accept this love as an expression of their attitude: "My time is mostly over, I will live in you, my therapist, and therefore I love you." Therapists must be able to withstand great hostility, which grows out of the bitter resentment: "I have to go and you will live." Therapists will also find it easier to deal with their responses to these emotions in group rather than in individual sessions.

Group therapy is a great hope for the aged. It also could be a great promise for the final maturation of the therapist who wants to accomplish with the patient the ultimate lesson that the therapist, too, must learn—namely, growing old gracefully.

REFERENCES

1. Butler, R. N. *Why Survive? Being Old in America.* New York: Harper & Row (1975).
2. Butler, R. N. and Lewis, M. I. *Sex After Sixty: A Guide for Men and Women for their Later Years.* New York: Harper & Row (1976).
3. Grotjahn, M. *The Art and Technique of Analytic Group Therapy.* New York: Jason Aronson (1977).
4. Jarvik, L. Thoughts on the psychobiology of aging. *Am. Psychol.* **30**: 576-583 (1975).
5. Masters, W. H. and Johnson, V. *Human Sexual Response.* Boston: Little Brown (1966).

13
Group Psychotherapy with Dying Patients

Carlene Copelan, M.D. and *Frank Kline, M.D.*

The literature contains a host of publications about death and dying, but the topic of group psychotherapy with patients dying of cancer has not been explored in depth. Spiegel and Yalom's[1] work is the best to date. Our work is primarily an existential overview; we hope it will show that this patient population may not only be reached and comforted, but may benefit from an intensive group experience.

The patients were unselected in the sense that all referrals were accepted. The attending physicians asked patients they thought were suitable for the group if they wanted to try it. If so, they were referred. There eventually were patients who came regularly to a once-a-week session of about two hours in duration. Dr. Kline supervised Dr. Copelan's work.

The group resistances were minimal, as the members didn't have time to fool around. Apparently even the unconscious recognizes some realities. The major problems were with the therapist's resistance and countertransference. It is hard to honestly let yourself love and care about the dying. It is not easy to face one's own mortality and it is even more difficult to see that people die feeling unloved and lonely, and with most of their dreams unrealized. Watching relatives withdraw from the dying is painful, especially when you know it will happen to you in your turn. The emotional push and pull of working with the dying is beyond the capacity of the average third-year resident. Fortunately, it was within the capacity of Dr. Copelan.

Obviously, the group described here is *not* for those who still deny their death, although other groups for such patients could be useful, nor should they be put in the same group with patients raging against death. Patients who have arrived at the stage of acceptance—even angry acceptance—and who want to attend a group, should be included. A different group would be suitable for those still raging against death.

CLINICAL OBSERVATIONS

The Beginning

The group of four dying patients began as groups often do, groping for what to talk about, even though the members were isolated and hungry for contact. An added problem was that illness is isolating, and terminal illness profoundly so. This was dramatized in early group work, when the group spent several minutes interacting via the metaphor. They shared vignettes of foreign countries and then said, "It's interesting that people in the same country with different dialects cannot understand each other." The therapist said, "Here you all speak the same language and can understand." The metaphor was dropped, and the group members spoke more openly to one another of their concerns. This direct interaction decreased initial group anxiety and gave permission to the patients to communicate more freely and directly about their concerns.

The first concern of the dying is their ambivalent desire for human contact, yet their family and the physician often respond to only one side of their ambivalence and isolate the patient. All the patients in the group had been isolated and thus started with an anaclitic depression. This was epitomized by Michael, a 57-year-old Mexican-American man, recently divorced and unemployed. He said, "How do I live through this when all I love and all I ever held dear has deserted me?" Michael represented the universal fear of separation and loneliness in the ill and dying. In spite of this, he was also a fighter who never said die. He cheered up other patients and candidly revealed intimacies. For them he was a supportive backbone against death. He did for others what he couldn't do for himself.

Michael began the initial group session with talk about his disintegrating marriage and subsequent divorce. He felt alone. "Yes," he told the group, "I've seen cancer destroy many marriages." Then, with anger: "I can understand why people kill. I told the judge I have cancer. I am a sick man, I said. I can't work and I don't want a divorce." The judge said, "Divorce granted." Did Michael, out of his caring and his guilt, express the other side of his ambivalence and chase his wife away, yet also resent that she accepted his invitation? Dying patients find death as repulsive as anyone might. "Go away, it's better for you," is a common stance among the dying. It is a stance that should be gently resisted.

The group rallied to Michael's support, saying they couldn't understand how a woman could leave a man in need. They reassured him that "all people are not bad." A young woman said, "You don't have to shut off just because someone hurt you, even though it is painful and hard to be abandoned and alone." Michael countered by saying that he carried a gun in his car. "I'm not going to let anyone hurt me without fighting back," he said. One wonders if he personified death as a person who can be fought and destroyed. He told of his dog, devoted and loyal, a perfect companion who had turned vicious and had to be destroyed. Michael was a lonely, depressed man who protected himself but who thought dying might be a punishment for his past and present rage, even punishment for "rage against the dying of the light."[2] In the group, Michael overcame his loneliness and the isolation of illness. The group was his new family, a family that was immortal. Members said, "The group will go on." After each had died, the group would remain. They discovered that being alone and sick and facing death is frightening, and that contact with those we love is essential. The group can, to some extent, replace the missing family. The burden of loneliness and the guilt of survival are reduced. As one patient said, "In a group of dying people I do not feel guilty or ashamed."

Dread of Being Forgotten and Worry about Survivors

Sarah was a 28-year-old Mexican-American woman with a stage 4B Hodgkin's disease that was resistent to chemotherapy. She was married to an alcoholic and had three young children. Her primary concern was, "Will my children remember me? Who will care for them? They are young. The baby is 18 months old. They are girls and will need me." She said, with obvious and real pain, "Will my children know me?"

"Yes," said the group, "they will remember you. Through tapes and through writing you can give your children tangible reminders." The group quoted the Bible: "A house built on sand will wash away in the storm, but a house built on rock will remain."[3] They told her: "Your early years with your children give them a solid framework for their life."

Sarah fulfilled an important role in the group. She expressed the emotions that others struggled to make conscious. She opened the group to rage, anger, despair, and suicidal wishes. By example, she showed the group it could discuss anything and remain strong enough to handle it.

Fear of the unknown was a focal point in this crisis of living with the knowledge of death. Current solutions to life's problems are based on past experience. But in facing death, we have no past experience to rely on.

Anna poignantly represented the fear of the unknown and the effort to master even death. She was a 45-year-old Caucasian woman, married, with three grown children. Her diagnosis was chronic lymphocytic leukemia with a lengthy remission. Initially eager to join the group, she said she had never lost anyone close and did not know how to deal with death. She was saying, "I don't know how to die." She was a woman who firmly and unequivocally stated, however, that she had no fear of death, yet quietly revealed to the group that she secretly read the obituaries daily. She wondered why death for her had been a "bugaboo," something not to be talked about. Anna entered the group to learn how to die. She was verbal and introspective. She often assumed the role of observing ego. For instance, she talked of her son in Israel and said this group came at an opportune time for her. "I have to accept that I may lose my son. Death is very real to me, but it helps to think about history. Thousands of people throughout all time have died—mothers losing children, children losing parents, husbands losing wives." We interpreted this to mean, "One is not alone." Anna validated our interpretation: "If we think of death broadly, it is not as intense." The group here addressed itself to anxiety in the face of the unknown. The patients found solace and comfort in the fact that they were not alone, and while each would die in his own time, they would all eventually die and in a sense all would die together.

Helplessness

Fate makes us all helpless, a theme dramatized by David, a 26-year-old Caucasian who was currently unemployed. His diagnosis was metastatic rhabdomyosarcoma of the prostatic urethra. Recently married and beginning a promising career, his future was consumed by malignancy. After the first recurrence, he made a desperate attempt at suicide. He started the group with a profound depression because of his "lost life." David was the focus of the group. He painfully represented helplessness and intense suffering. We are not masters of our fate. Even the young, who have had no taste of life, can die. He told the group, "This is not the right time for me to die. I don't want to say goodbye to dreams I thought could be. I don't want to lose my wife and child. I'm so alone, yet I can't talk with them it hurts them so." His grief was shared and accepted in the group and he was able to say what he could not say at home.

GROUP PROCESS

Competition was strikingly reduced and giving was relatively uncluttered by ambivalence. For example, the group allowed a session to be dominated by one member whose life situation was intolerable. As the session ended, she asked why the group was silent. A member said, "You needed to get that off your chest. I feel all right and at peace and can wait." Another said "You seemed so pressured and troubled, I can wait." People whose days are numbered seem more patient than those with more time.

Transference

The transference to the group leader was split; she was idealized. Negative transference, rage and anger, was expressed through displacement and was not resolved. Perhaps in the face of death and anaclitic depression each needed to see the therapist as an all-giving, all-loving, all-protective mother. Basic instinctual needs seem stronger in the face of death and this activates the idealized maternal transference as the primary group transference. Members came to the group, where the pain was relieved. For example, group members seen individually often first brought up problems when alone with the therapist and this was then repeated in the group. It was as if a larger source of comfort existed in the group.

Depression and Anger

This group showed more depression and less anger than traditional groups. The isolation and loneliness formed the group framework. Sadness and resignation to separation were far more prominent than rage. Perhaps, as the Spanish say, "Death is the moment of truth." This is not to say that the group did not deal with anger. They raged against doctors and nurses who hid death from them. "We are dying but we are not fragile." They raged against withholding pain medicines because of the concern that they would become addicts. "We won't live long enough to be addicts." They raged at those who encouraged useless painful procedures. "Let them change places for ten minutes and then ask me to sign a consent form."

Confidentiality

Only one group member broke confidence by expressing anxiety about a member to the member's wife. This was discussed and members were able to freely and directly deal with the anger and subsequent guilt and to work it through.

Insight versus Metaphor

Like any insight group, the group of dying patients did not function in a primarily supportive problem-solving manner. It showed it could use insight and interpretations, could work in the here and now, and could employ group interaction as a tool of self-understanding. Thus, interpretations, confrontations, and insight formed the supportive framework. Issues and conflicts were faced directly. Analyzing metaphors was not destructive. For instance, one group member spent a great deal of time talking about her sick dog and his foul-smelling abscess and how he should be destroyed. The therapist interpreted this: "Do you feel that you, with your cancers, are disgustingly repulsive and should be destroyed?" The group then described and discussed other sick patients, who, when bleeding, in pain, and smelling of illness and death, were alone and isolated from human contact.

The therapist said, "Can you accept one another's foul-smelling abscesses?" "Yes," they said, "we will not desert one another."

David's work was a second example of insight work. He was initially depressed and suicidal, and expressed these feelings. This was done in a way that frustrated and annoyed the group. This was interpreted as his need to push others away, to stay isolated and withdrawn. He was able to use this insight and to wonder if perhaps this didn't explain why his family didn't communicate with him.

After some group experience, the group characteristically spoke in the metaphor and then turned to the therapist, saying, "What are we talking about? We can always count on you to make sense out of our nonsense." The group waited for, and expected, interpretations. This was understandable since it was an early group. Eventually they would learn to translate for themselves.

RESOLUTION: WHY?

What was of therapeutic benefit? Was it a decrease in isolation, loneliness, and depression, because the patients were no longer deprived of human contact? Were members able to face the unbelievable and unacceptable? Did they begin to work through, together, the overwhelming separation anxiety of death? Were old nurturing introjects activated, through transference, and did this in turn reduce depression?

We feel all of these occurred, and, as the group became a family, fear of the unknown decreased. "We will not die alone." Self-esteem increased. "We are not useless and worthless." They shared conflicts and helped others to endure what they had already experienced. They had value. Even though weak, deformed, and physically changed, they knew they had worth. "We are needed by other members of the group." Knowing they would be missed enhanced their self-esteem and decreased depression. "If we are going to be missed, we must be loved." Finally, they saw one another's courage and gained strength. The depression was reduced. The group as a whole became the all-loving, all-protective preoedipal mother who accepted the bleeding, wounded patients, taught them to accept, and showed them they had a worth beyond immediate physical existence.

Group cohesiveness, universality, catharsis, the group as surrogate family, and insight were, for this group of dying patients, as for any insight groups, the therapeutic, curative factors.[4]

The authors of this chapter were reluctant to use the past tense to describe the group, but we had to agree that it was correct and so it was done. Was our reluctance only our attempt to deny the group's collective and individual death, or something more? Did the group become a part of our psyche in a more significant way than most people do? We think it did. Even though the group's process and useful techniques were very similar to those in the usual insight group, the countertransference problems were more severe. The therapist had to analyze and contain the desire to avoid the patients and their death. She also had to avoid becoming excessively gentle and protective.

REFERENCES

1. Spiegel, D. and Yalom, I. D. A support group for dying patients. *Int. J. Group Psychother.* **28**: 233-245 (1978).
2. Thomas, D. *Collected Poems.* New York: New Dimensions (1952).
3. Matthew 7:24. *The New English Bible.* Oxford Univ. Press. Cambridge Univ. Press (1961).
4. Yalom, I. D. *The Theory and Practice of Group Psychotherapy.* New York: Basic Books (1970).

14
Group Therapy for Substance Abusers

Edward Kaufman, M.D.

This chapter presents the specific group therapy techniques and approaches utilized in the treatment of substance abusers. Substance abuse is defined as the use of a psychoactive drug, alcohol, or a combination of the two to the extent that it seriously interferes with an individual's physical health, social relationships, or vocational functioning.* Group therapy techniques are particularly relevant to substance abusers and are generally considered the preferred method of psychotherapy by both clinicians[1] and clients.[2] However, no type of psychotherapy with these clients is effective unless it is a part of a comprehensive treatment system.

The specific techniques presented here are most necessary in the early and middle phases of psychotherapy groups with substance abusers. In the later phases, these patients require group techniques that are similar to those used with most neurotics. Although different techniques are used in the early phases of groups of alcoholics than with groups of drug abusers, as treatment progresses, these techniques become more similar. In addition, both alcoholism and drug abuse are multidetermined final common pathways that may develop from

---

*DSM III classifies the syndrome as *substance use disorders* and divides the problem into *substance abuse* and *dependence*. DSM III criteria for abuse are: a pattern of pathological use, impairment in social or occupational functioning due to substance use, and a minimal duration of disturbance of at least one month. Substance dependence involves tolerance or withdrawal and, for alcohol dependence, a pattern of pathological use and social or occupational impairment. Thus we use the term *substance abuse* instead of the as yet unfamiliar *substance use disorders*. Its use here includes substance abuse and dependence.

personality, neurotic, psychotic, antisocial, or cultural factors. These individualized antecedent factors must be dealt with by other modalities, as well as by variations in group techniques. In fact, an individual patient's age, social class, ego strength, and underlying psychopathology will say more about needs for specific group and other therapeutic techniques than the choice of substance abused.

It has been my experience[3] and the experience of others, particularly Yalom,[4,5] Fox,[6] Casriel,[7] and Rosenthal,[8] that there are specific group techniques that work best with specific groups of drug abusers and alcoholics. There are also many different types of group approaches to these patients, including Alcoholics Anonymous (AA), Narcotics Anonymous (NA), instructional, multifamily, spouse, and couples groups, as well as many systems of open and closed psychotherapy groups.

GENERAL PRINCIPLES OF GROUP TREATMENT FOR SUBSTANCE ABUSERS

No group approach for substance abusers will be successful unless the abuse of substances is a critical issue in treatment. Individuals who abuse drugs or alcohol to a point where intellectual functioning is frequently impaired during therapy sessions, or when their lives are totally preoccupied with obtaining drugs,* are virtually untreatable as outpatients. Frequently an individual can be detoxified from drug dependence or alcoholism in a hospital and can then engage in meaningful treatment. At times this detoxification must be repeated several times before successful treatment can occur. Drug abusers or alcoholics who are not physiologically dependent may be treated as outpatients, particularly if they are capable of building a therapeutic alliance and transferring their attachments from drugs to a therapist or therapeutic team. Patients who repeatedly continue to abuse substances or revert to dependence after detoxification can only be treated in a controlled and drug-free setting such as a residential program or a hospital.[3] Thus, the first step and the common denominator in the successful treatment of substance-dependent patients is to get them to give up, at least temporarily, their pattern of drug abuse. Once this is accomplished, whether through a residence, hospitalization, detoxification, drug

---

*Since alcohol is a drug, the term *drug* here will include both drugs and alcohol.

maintenance, AA, Antabuse, transference, or self-determination, there must be an individualized treatment plan that offers a full range of therapeutic and vocational services.

Psychoanalytically-oriented therapies, particularly those in which the therapist maintains a passive role, are not generally successful with alcoholics or drug abusers.[3] "This is because individuals who are used to . . . the immediate effects of drugs frequently find the slow, tedious process" of such therapies ". . . to be excruciating."[9] Thus, dynamic therapies, such as Gestalt, encounter, transactional analysis, and structured psychodynamic approaches, tend to be more successful, in part because they are more immediately rewarding. However, if these therapies are not based on individual need and psychodynamic principles, they tend to be of only short-term benefit. What makes any psychotherapy successful with these patient is the therapist's active use of his own experiences and emotions. He must use a variety of directive techniques and methods of confrontation to break through emotional barriers. The therapists should also offer themselves as a model of existential choice and action.[3]

Another aspect of successful therapy with substance abusers is limit-setting, particularly about drug and alcohol abuse and other antisocial behavior. Such limits are necessary but with voluntary outpatients should be delayed until after a therapeutic alliance is established or the patient will be driven out of treatment. On the other hand, if these limits are not established early in treatment, drug use can make patients unreachable. In nonvoluntary patients and in residential settings, these limits are more easily established, but must be done with love and concern. This type of balance is the essence of the art of psychotherapy. Groups where patients continue to use drugs have been consistently unsuccessful. However, there has been some success in treating patients with intermittent alcohol abuse. This may be because alcohol is legal and therefore less conducive to continued antisocial activities or perhaps because special techniques have been developed to deal with drinking in groups. Brown and Yalom[5] emphasize the use of videotapes and typed group summaries that confront the alcoholic with their behavior and permit the sober integration of material obtained during inebriation.

It is my experience that if a patient is dependent on drugs or alcohol at the time he enters treatment, then an initial period of at least 28 days in a specialized residential (or hospital) substance abuse program greatly enhances the success of subsequent outpatient group psychotherapy. Such a program not only provides the patient with detoxification but immerses the patient in an environment that supports a substance-free state through AA, NA, Antabuse, family treatment, vocational planning, relaxation, and recreational techniques and by providing medication where necessary for other underlying disorders. Patients who refuse hospitalization, including psychotherapy, may accept it later. They should be offered alternatives to a substance-free state on an outpatient basis. If substance abuse returns to a level where it leads to dependency, is life threatening, or is otherwise disruptive, then hospitalization is insisted upon as a condition for continuing treatment.

Substance abusers do well in treatment that is motivated by significant others or legal pressures. In fact, many substance abusers will not participate actively in treatment unless it is mandated by the legal system or by their families' and/or their employers' sincere threats to abandon them if they don't accept treatment and the promise to accept them after completion.

MATCHING THE GROUP THERAPY TECHNIQUE TO THE INDIVIDUAL

Treatment techniques must be geared to specific causes in specific individuals as well as to types of substance abuse. When social factors are prominent, as in urban ghettos, a treatment approach should emphasize educational, vocational, recreational, and housing factors. However, group and individual therapy are frequently necessary when personality difficulties prevent the client from achieving these social goals. Among ghetto addicts, 5% to 10% demonstrate serious psychopathology and thus require the special techniques used with such patients (described later). The incidence of severe psychopathology is even higher among middle and upper class addicts and these patients require appropriate psychiatric intervention.[10] Likewise, alcoholics may be schizophrenic, sociopathic, neurotic,[11] or, most commonly, without other significant psychopathology and require distinctly different techniques.

PSYCHOLOGICAL CHARACTERISTICS OF SUBSTANCE ABUSERS

As mentioned, substance abuse is a final common pathway for many different types of individual with varied diagnoses. However, there are personality characteristics that are specific to alcoholics, others to drug abusers, and some that are seen in both. When one considers that over half of alcoholics abuse drugs and half of drug abusers misuse alcohol,[10] it becomes even more difficult to tease out personality factors that are unique to one group or the other. There has yet to be a study that demonstrates that these personality patterns antedate substance abuse and dependence, but many studies have quantitated these characteristics after dependence has been established. Knowledge of these personality factors is crucial to group therapists because they must be understood and shifted if the substance abuser is to change. When these are dealt with, then the focus of treatment can shift to underlying neurotic features.

Exclusive Personality Aspects of Alcoholics

These aspects include the use of rigid denial, which does not respond well to confrontation, and an underlying sense of ego fragility; a strong archaic, punitive superego with harsh self-condemnation and a sense of unworthiness and guilt leading to masochistic, self-punitive behavior;[6] sexual immaturity, impotence, fragility, and homosexual conflicts;[6] and a tendency to become overly dependent on a therapist, which is more appropriately diffused in groups than dealt with in individual therapy.

Exclusive Personality Aspects of Drug Abusers

Although a minority of drug abusers and addicts have strong superegos (and these individuals have a good prognosis), the majority have absent or severely lacunaed superegos. They tend to respond well to early confrontation, particularly if the techniques described later in this chapter are employed. They tend to be more overtly aggressive when not intoxicated than alcoholics. Although many drug abusers use drugs to overcome or mask sexual conflicts, they tend to have fewer underlying conflicts about sexuality than alcoholics. The illegality of most drug use forces them into greater antisocial acts and resultant extended incarceration leads to reinforcement of antisocial behavior. Although they form dependent relationships, they shift their dependency readily from one person to another.

Common Personality Aspects of Drug Abusers and Alcoholics

In more disturbed individuals, these drugs substitute for a lack of internal homeostasis. Drugs and alcohol are used to diminish anxieties about self-assertion in work and social life. Sedative drugs and alcohol are used to obliterate anger and hostility, which are then released during intoxication. There is a low frustration to tolerance and an inability to endure anxiety or tension. There is schizoid adjustment with social fear and low self-esteem[6] (covered over during intoxication). Both groups share repressed or conscious feelings of omnipotence, grandiosity, and extreme narcissism,[6] yet they have little ability to persevere. Marked unaccountable mood swings are present (and not indicative of mood cycle disease). There is a constant inner battle between passivity and aggressiveness with conscious or unconscious rebellion, a strong tendency to act out aggressive and sexual impulses, and strong dependent needs, which are inevitably frustrated, leading to depression and despair or hostility, rage, and fantasies of revenge.[6] Both groups use the defenses of regression, denial, introjection, projection, and rationalization. When they give up their substances, there is a prolonged period of physiological withdrawal (6 months) and of mourning for the lost substance. They expect all kinds of rewards for doing this, and become furious when rewards are not received.

SPECIFIC TECHNIQUES FOR DRUG ABUSERS

Many of these techniques have been developed by ex-addict therapists, as well as by professionals. The group techniques developed and utilized by ex-addicts include identification, love and concern, confrontation, responsibility, acting "as if," reward and punishment, stratified groups, and emphasis on the present.[3] These techniques have their roots in residential programs such as Synanon and Phoenix House.

Identification[3]

As a substance abuser matures through a program of graduated levels, he identifies with varying kinds of therapists.

In most programs, the first therapist the client meets is a rehabilitated former substance abuser. The therapist is very much like the client in attitude and language, yet he has "made it." That is, he has stopped using drugs and alcohol even though he came from an environment identical to that of the patient's. He may offer a highly emotional catharsis of his own struggle to give up drugs with which patients can identify. He may share difficult experiences from his own life prior to his giving up drugs. He demonstrates that he is not where he is through magic. Frequently, the addict is quite "hungry" for an identification with a strong accepting male figure because his prior contacts with such individuals have been limited. Because of the similarities between therapist and client and the relationship hunger of the latter, these identifications are made quite rapidly. This identification may be risky, especially if the therapist is inexperienced, as it can rapidly develop into over-identification.

In the final phases of the program, the patient identifies with the professional therapist, who may come from a totally different sociocultural environment.

Love and Concern

"Love and concern" is given only as a reward for adult and giving behavior on the part of the members. In nonresidential centers, it may be necessary to give more of this kind of direct gratification in the initial phases of treatment to entice the patient into therapy, as well as to provide immediate gratification as replacement for drugs. This kind of gratification is gradually withdrawn when the individual is motivated to maintain adaptive changes in his personality. Synanon initially provided a prolonged period of "unconditional love," which was soon shortened to only the time when the individual kicked "cold turkey."[7] The giving of unconditional love is controversial in all forms of therapy. When this love was limited at Synanon, the original maternal figure and several of her followers left the program.[7] Addicts have a need "to be close to a mother-like figure able to satisfy their every need even without their asking for it."[12] The difficulties of directly gratifying the addict's primitive need for love are always kept in mind. An attempt is made to deal with these difficulties by giving the love only in return for the addict's meaningful attempts to understand or change himself.

At times the love and concern are expressed by reassuring physical gestures such as hand-holding or embracing. The therapist sets the tone for this kind of interaction but most of it goes on between group members. This touching should only take place following significant insight or meaningful emotional interaction. It should not have the rehearsed quality frequently attributed to encounter techniques. Touching is used as a natural part of any warm ongoing relationship, to convey a sense of being accepted, to convey reality, or as a necessary modality when verbal communication is unavailable or inadequate.[3]

The therapist should communicate to the members the feeling that although he is accepting them, he is simultaneously demanding more and more. The therapist may also express love and concern by listening carefully and paying attention to the members and not ridiculing the members' difficulties or productions.[3]

Confrontation[3]

Because of its alleged brutality, this technique is one of the most controversial of ex-addict techniques. When precisely done, confrontation is most effective and perhaps essential to changing the addict. A correct confrontation is accurate and substantiated, delivered with genuine love and concern, relevant, timely, and considers the ego strength of the client. Group members confront one another with their behavior and its impact on others until, layer by layer, these defenses are removed.

A very valuable form of confrontation is one that includes sympathetic clarification of the rationalizations for drug use. This technique is used by the therapist to gradually strip away defenses while identifying with the feelings underlying these defenses. Examples of defenses that must be stripped early in treatment are, "I am an addict whose only problem is drugs," or "I use drugs because I am the helpless victim of an insane society." Ex-addict therapists are particularly adept at overcoming these rationalizations and reaching the underlying anxiety.

Responsibility[3]

The existential approach of assuming responsibility for oneself and for changing is another crucial attitude the group must learn. Responsibility for self-improvement and for the success of the group are utilized as cornerstones of permanent change. This responsibility removes a "we-they" dichotomy from treatment. The existential approach asks the individual what he has done to produce a situation and what he can do to change it, and prevents using uncontrollable externals, past and present, as an excuse for the problem, and a justification for not trying to improve.

Acting "As If"[3]

This is a concept utilized by most programs and attributed to Casriel.[7] He states that after three to six months of acting "as if" they were the men they want to be, the addicts will start to actually become those men. Even before patients have any insight, there are some areas where they are asked to perform "as if" they did. They are asked to abstain from alcohol, drug use, lateness, and grossly inappropriate and antisocial behavior. The individual is taught that to change his behavior he must first form an image of the kind of man he wants to be, and that with effort he can carry out his plan. The group member begins to abandon his self-destructive behavior and to look for positive ways to live. He acts "as if" he is the person he wants to be and eventually his feelings begin to mirror the desired attitudes. Each step he makes in a positive direction is rewarded and acknowledged. As the time since the last negative act passes, positive behavior is actively reinforced, particularly by others in his group who are also struggling.

Reward and Punishment[3]

Although the principle of reward and punishment is utilized in all therapies, it is a basic method in all ex-addict approaches. Status and approval are given as basic rewards. Any member can rise as high as his abilities will take him. Punishment is frequently administered through verbal confrontation. Another crucial punishment deprives an individual of his status. Attempts are made to have the individual see demotions in level as learning experiences and evidence that he is not really ready to function at a given level. However, the punishment aspect of such demotion can never be denied, particularly when promotions are utilized as rewards. In addition, "love and concern" are given as a reward whenever an individual actively works to change himself. All successful programs use stratified therapies with promotions and demotions as important parts of the reward and punishment system. Interestingly, most programs have four levels of group (described below) and require 18 months for completion of the program.

Stratified Groups

This principle has been discussed as part of each of these techniques. It involves groups that initially deal with drug abuse and later deal with underlying factors. As I have described, at Reality House,[13] the groups begin with orientation. They then progress from pretherapy to therapy to a psychodynamically-oriented final level. The shift from ex-addict therapist to professional at later phases also emphasizes a shift from identification and confrontation to psychodynamically-oriented treatment. These phases are similar to those in groups for alcoholic patients.

Emphasis on the Present[3]

Most programs emphasize the here and now. The past is buried and the patient is not permitted to use it as a reason for not changing. The past may be explored when it is clearly relevant, but a "now what" posture is stressed. The resources, available to the patient that permit him to cope effectively, are emphasized. The patient is challenged to begin to change today.

Use of Ex-addicts as Co-therapists[13]

Ex-addicts are valuable as co-therapists particularly in the early stages of groups or even as primary or sole therapists at this stage. Commonality of experience with the client, by itself, does not qualify an individual to be a therapist. The techniques that help ex-addicts become experienced therapists are best learned gradually and under close supervision, preferably by both experienced paraprofessionals and professionals.

As the patient progresses through therapy, reconstructive group techniques as practiced by professionals are extremely helpful and essential if significant shifts in ego strength are to be accomplished. Another helpful pairing in co-therapy is male-female pairing, which provides a balance of male and female role models and transference.

RECENT DEVELOPMENTS IN THE GROUP THERAPY OF DRUG ABUSERS

Some therapists now utilize adaptations of primal therapy with addicts.[14] Here peer pressure and the urging of the therapist are used to reach the deepest physical levels of emotional expression possible at each point in therapy. The patient is, therefore, urged to experience emotion by screaming progressively louder and by tapping feelings that symbolically are locked deeply in the abdomen and chest. These techniques should not be used mechanically but only when the patient is beginning to express genuine emotional pain. They should be avoided or modified in individuals with a history of overt or borderline psychotic symptoms. Most therapists who use these modifications of primal techniques do not reach early levels of primal pain and should not attempt to do so unless the therapist is thoroughly trained in this technique.

Gestalt techniques are particularly useful in helping patients to experience feelings rather than talk about them. To this end, such techniques as expressing one's feelings to an empty chair as if it were the object of the emotions can lead to a fuller emotional experience. Gestalt dream work, in which the client tells the dream as if he were each individual and object in the dream, leads to a more complete experience of the dream and all of its components.

Psychodrama is helpful and easily grasped and utilized by addicts. Family sculpture, where group members recreate their family by having other group members play the roles of their family, emphasizes nonverbal aspects and can tap deeply buried feelings. Videotape can also be extremely helpful in confronting patients with denied nonverbal communications and emotions.

Tuning in to body language, particularly the somatic equivalents of depression and anxiety, is also important. At times feelings may be released by tapping bodily components before intellectual insight has occurred. Thus, techniques such as breathing exercises and massage are helpful in releasing blocked feelings. These techniques are often preferred by drug abusers because they provide immediate gratification.

All of these therapeutic techniques can be beneficially applied in marathon groups of 24 to 48 hours. This type of intense experience helps overcome denial and resistance and facilitates group catharses.

Family evaluation and therapy is rapidly becoming an essential aspect of therapy with these patients. Multiple family therapy and couples groups are particularly effective as family members are able to identify and change certain basic trends that create and perpetuate drug abuse. These family group techniques are similar to those used with alcoholics and will be discussed later.

SPECIFIC PROBLEMS IN GROUP TREATMENT OF DRUG ABUSERS

Group Therapy in Methadone Programs[15]

It is generally difficult to motivate methadone patients for group therapy, but it is particularly difficult when group is not mandatory. In addition, many methadone patients failed in previous therapeutic community experiences because they were unable to tolerate confrontation and encounter. They are afraid of any group in which they think these techniques will be used. Therefore, groups must be set up so that patients are not frightened by early confrontation in a nonsupportive atmosphere. There are several principles that can be used to establish working groups in methadone programs.

1. Select as group leader a person with high status in the program, such as a program director or respected psychiatrist or psychologist.
2. Time groups to coincide with methadone dispensing. (Most patients are not motivated to return a second time in a day or on a day they do not receive methadone.)
3. Use the patient's negative feelings as an impetus to start groups. Thus, groups can be started with patients who complain about conditions or who "hang out" around the program.
4. Have counselors draw their group from patients in their own caseload so there is an established therapeutic alliance.
5. Begin some task-oriented groups; i.e., women's groups, patient government, socialization, health and sex education, detoxification, "rap" or discussion.
6. Group leaders should be consistent and hold groups if even only one member appears. A co-therapist should direct the group if the primary leader is absent for any reason. (This is particularly important in the early phases of such groups.)
7. The milieu of the clinic must shift from getting methadone, with as little effort as possible, to participating in as many helping activities as possible.
8. Avoid placing patients in the same group who have severe conflicts with each other outside of the program.
9. Use pretreatment group experiences to prepare patients for the working group (e.g., verbal skills, trust in leader and other pa-

tients, support and reassurance, exploring fears). Once these groups are established, the therapeutic techniques described in this chapter can be gradually introduced.

Therapeutic Community (TC)[15]

Substance abusing residents in a TC are a captive audience, and it can be assumed there is sufficient motivation or external coercion to facilitate their participation in the therapeutic experiences described in this chapter. Encounter and confrontation techniques are also used in outpatient mental health clinics, but rarely in groups with methadone maintenance patients. However, the general treatment principle that the sicker or less motivated the client, the less harsh the confrontation, is applicable.

Outpatient Clinic[15]

In "drug-free" mental health clinics, patients are usually more motivated than typical methadone patients, but less motivated than TC patients. A mental health clinic may also attract highly motivated patients with sufficient ego strength who do not require a therapeutic community for intensive psychotherapy. Most of these patients can be treated successfully by one to five groups weekly over one to two years and are able to continue their gains with one follow-up group session weekly for support and crisis solution.

The Psychotic Addict[15]

The psychotic addict presents special problems in group treatment. Some solutions developed for overtly psychotic patients are applicable to borderline psychotics, adolescents, and/or multiple drug abusers. The setting for these groups should be a structured environment such as a specialized residence or day program. The therapist must be experienced as a reliable, predictable part of the patient's schedule. The therapist must be quite supportive and urge each group member to support others and to expect support in return. The therapist must acknowledge and encourage the most minute expression of mutuality in thought and experience and foster interest in one another's welfare. The therapist must, through speech and action, demonstrate care about each group member and the success of the group. Ultimately, the caring quality of the therapist is incorporated by the clients who in turn nurture others.

Summary

This section has delineated an individualized approach to the group treatment of drug-dependent clients. Treatment must vary according to the psychopathology and other specific reasons for drug dependence. This treatment should, in all cases, be directive, active, and limit setting. Treatment generally does not begin until the pattern of illicit drug dependence is interrupted. Once the individual is engaged in treatment, a variety of therapeutic techniques can be utilized. Therapeutic communities have developed a number of valuable techniques for use with these clients. More recently, such approaches as Gestalt, psychodrama, and family therapy have been used to help achieve the personality changes that lead to abstinence from drugs as well as to social and vocational success.

GROUP THERAPY OF ALCOHOLICS

There are many different group approaches to alcoholics, many or all of which may be useful and necessary with each patient. These include multifamily, couples, spouse, and "significant others" groups in addition to groups exclusively for the alcoholic. These groups may be educational, inspirational, psychoanalytic, Gestalt, psychodramatic, etc. In part, the emphasis on the group treatment of alcoholics may have evolved from the "spectacular success of the group approach of Alcoholics Anonymous."[6] After many years of treating alcoholics in mixed groups with other drug abusers, I shifted to treating them *only* in conjunction with a system of three other groups that meet weekly— multifamily, couples, and spouses. The alcoholic and his spouse and children are encouraged to simultaneously participate in AA, Al-Anon, and Al-Teen.

GROUP THERAPY TECHNIQUES WITH ALCOHOLICS

Beginning Phase

I prefer to establish a contract with the alcoholic that limits continued drinking. As their part of this contract, the alcoholic must agree to attend AA regularly and/or take Antabuse and return to a detoxification program if drinking continues or reoccurs. Most alcoholics are not internally motivated for therapy. They participate when seriously threatened with an important loss such as family, prestige, job, physical health, or driver's license. They generally do not want to stop drinking. They minimize or deny the extent of their drinking and its consequences. They project the blame for their problems on those closest to them and onto society in general. They build elaborate systems of rationalizations and react with hostility to those who insist that they stop drinking.[6] One advantage of the specialized type of 28-day residential program described earlier is that the group therapy can be started immediately after drinking stops. In the first few sober days, the alcoholic is so needy that his resistance to groups is low. After a few days of sobriety, defenses resolidify and therapy is resisted. Without alcohol to relieve life's problems, the alcoholic is depressed and frightened. He feels he has nothing to contribute to society or to a group, yet he desperately needs support. At this stage, the therapists and the group should show the alcoholic how to borrow the confidence that life without alcohol is possible and better than life with it. This is best done by a therapist or co-therapist who is a recovered alcoholic. There may be a honeymoon stage after drinking stops, during which all problems are denied and there is a sense of well-being. This lasts until the alcoholic realizes that the rewards anticipated for staying sober are not possible.

During the early sessions of group therapy with alcoholics, the focus is on the shared problem of drinking and its meaning to each individual. The therapist should be more active in this phase, which should be instructional and informative as well as therapeutic.[6] Alcoholics need to know a great deal about their condition, including its definition, causes, symptoms, effects on bodily functions, and treatment. This may be done in a separate didactic experience or in the group. These didactic groups are a good introduction to group therapy. A checklist of 20 symptoms and signs, which requires only three positive responses for a diagnosis of alcoholism, may help aid in the recognition of the serious problems.

Alcoholics tend toward confessionals and monologues about prior drinking. These can be politely interrupted or minimized by a ground rule of "no drunkalogues."

The desire to drink and the fear of slipping is a pervasive, early concern in these groups.[5] The patient's attitude is one of resistance and caution combined with fear of open exploration. Members are encouraged to participate in AA, yet the "high support, low conflict, inspirational style"[5] of AA may inhibit attempts at uncovering interactional therapy. Therapists should not be overly protective and prematurely relieve the group's anxiety since this fosters denial. On the other hand, the members' recognition of emotions and responsibility must proceed slowly since both are particularly threatening to alcoholics. There evolves a beginning awareness of the role of personality and social interactions in the use of alcohol. Patients are superficially friendly, but do not show real warmth or tenderness. They are afraid to express anger or to assert themselves. However, sudden irritation, antipathy, and anger to the leaders and other members inevitably begin to show. Gradually tentative overtures of friendship and understanding become manifest.[6] There may be a conspiracy of silence about material that could cause discomfort or lead to drinking. The therapists can point out to the members that they choose to remain static and within comfortable defenses rather than expose themselves to the discomfort associated with change.[5] Patients usually drop out early if they are still committed to drinking. Other patients who drop out at this stage do so because they grow increasingly alarmed as they become aware of the degree of discomfort that any significant change requires. Fear of intimacy or of giving up a long-term, vital, but conflictual relationship also leads to early dropping out.

Middle Phase

This phase may last from six months to several years. The alcoholic who successfully completes this phase will express and work through feelings, responsibility for behavior, interpersonal interactions, and the functions and secondary gain of alcoholism. He will become able to analyze defenses, resistance, and transference.[6] The multiple transferences that develop in the group are recognized as "old tapes" that are not relevant to the present. Problems of sibling rivalry, competition with authority, and separation anxiety become manifest in the group and are recognized as transference. Conflicts are analyzed on both the intrapsychic and interpersonal levels. Ventilation and catharsis take place and may be enhanced by the same role playing and nonverbal methods used with drug abusers. There will be group identification and acceptance as well as reality testing of old and new concepts. Excessive fantasy is abandoned.[6]

Alcoholics can be expected to show cycles of improvement and alternate retreats into former behavior, including drinking. The therapists should not be punitive nor should they condone drinking. An initial contract about AA or Antabuse can be reinforced at this time. These cycles have a crisis flavor and the therapist should not participate in or contribute to them by showing discouragement or undue optimism.

Alcoholic dependency may be expressed overtly or counterphobically. Those who express dependency directly more easily understand their dependency conflicts. Their needs and frustrations are greater than those in neurotic patients so they repeatedly feel frustrated and disappointed. They demand praise, advice, and solutions, which should be given initially, then slowly withdrawn as the patient becomes capable of insight.[5] The sick role may become an important source of identity and may be reinforced by AA's concept of alcoholism as a disease. This must be gradually relinquished since it lowers self-esteem. Counter-dependent behavior, such as the need to control or deny feelings, is also gradually confronted and given up.

Alcoholics are ambivalent about positive feedback. The beg for it, yet reject it when it is given. They repeatedly ask for physical reassurance such as a hug, but panic when they receive it because of fear of intimacy and a reexperiencing of their unmet past needs. There is a fear of success and a dread of competition—in life, and in the group. Success means destroying the other group members (siblings) and loss of therapist (parent). Rigidity and denial are greater in groups of alcoholics than in any other groups except those of chronic schizophrenics. They are afraid to talk about unpleasant experiences because they are afraid they will be overwhelmed by their previous pain. They are reluctant to explore fantasies since the thought makes them feel as guilty as the act. They view emotions as black or white. This makes them withhold critical comments because they fear their criticism will provoke chaos and alcoholism in other members. This withholding may be on a conscious or unconscious level. They are frequently overly conscientious. They have often felt that they had to be the responsible member of their family even when they were children. Thus they assume blame and guilt for the emotional pain of other group members. Rage is expressed either explosively or not at all. Its eventual expression in group should be gradual. Expression of anger can be facilitated by waiting until these patients have a good reason to be angry, and then challenging them. The challenge will add to the inner anger until its nonverbal expression makes the anger clear to the group and to the patient.

There is resistance to any open discussion of sexual issues in groups of alcoholics, and this topic should be gradually introduced by the therapist. Involvement of the spouse in therapy facilitates discussion and resolution of sexual issues.

The other crucial affect that must be dealt with is depression. There is an initial severe depression, which occurs immediately after detoxification. This appears vegetative in its severity, but usually remits rapidly, leaving the alcoholic with a chronic, low-grade depression, frequently expressed by silence. These patients should be drawn out slowly and patiently. Ultimately, they must be encouraged to cry or mourn.[16] The empty chair technique may be used to facilitate mourning, by expressing the grief and the anger toward lost love objects. A distinction must be made between helping these patients deal with despair and rushing to take it away from them. Patients must experience and live through their depression.[5]

Role playing or doubling may facilitate expression of anger. In doubling, the therapist or another group member will sit behind the patient and express feelings that seem obvious yet are dammed up. When the patient finally expresses anger, he should be cheered and rewarded by the group.[16] Assertiveness training may increase the ability to express anger and to accept it.[17]

The success of the middle phase of group therapy with alcoholics depends on the therapist's and the group's ability to relieve anxiety through group support, insight, and the use of more adaptive, concrete ways of dealing with anxiety. Alcohol must become an unacceptable solution to anxiety. In this vein, it is important not to end a session with members in a state of grossly unresolved conflict.[16] This can be avoided by closure when excessively troubling issues are raised. Closure can be achieved by the group's concrete suggestions for problem resolution. When this is not possible, group support, including extra group contact by members, can be offered.

Closing Phase

By the time alcoholics have reached this phase, they have achieved the same changes as neurotic patients. Thus, alcoholics in this phase function like patients in neurotic groups and work on their underlying neurotic core. Those alcoholics who survive a high initial drop-out rate stay in groups longer than neurotic patients,[4] so many alcoholics will reach this phase. By the closing phase, the alcoholic has accepted sobriety without resentment and works to free himself from unnecessary neurotic and character problems.[6] He has developed a healthy self-concept, combined with empathy for others and has scaled down his inordinate demands of others for superego reassurance. He has become effectively assertive rather than destructively aggressive and has developed a reasonable sense of values. More fulfilling relationships with spouse, children, and friends can be achieved.[6]

When members leave the group, the decision to leave should be discussed for several weeks before a final date is set. This permits the group to mourn the lost member and for the member to mourn the group. This is true regardless of the stage of the group, but the most intense work is done when termination is in the later phases. In open-ended groups, the leadership qualities of the graduating member are then taken over by others, who may transfer these qualities to life outside the group.

Although these phases are described for alcoholics, they are also characteristic of groups of drug abusers, even though they are achieved through different techniques in early phases.

MULTIPLE FAMILY GROUP TREATMENT (MFT)[18]

This is a technique that can be used in any treatment setting for substance abusers, but is most successful in residential settings, where family and patient are usually more available. In a residential setting, the group may be composed of all of the families or separated into several groups of three or four closely matched families. My experience is with the former type of group, and I regard the group of families as one community.

There may be as many as 10 to 15 families and 40 to 50 individuals in the weekly family group. Families should be oriented and interviewed prior to entry in the group. The group includes identified patients and their immediate families as well as any relatives with significant impact on the family. Friends and lovers are included if they are an important part of the addict's network and are drug-free. If they abuse drugs or alcohol, they are excluded from the group until they control this symptom, otherwise they are disruptive or destructive in group. However, there are no rigid guidelines about excluding family members or friends since meaningful material and a true picture of the family may come from anyone who knows the patient.

An experienced family therapist works with program counselors as co-therapists. The total group frequently functions as adjunctive family therapists. Usually family members take their cues from primary therapists and will be appropriately confronting, reassuring, and supportive. At times the family's own needs prevent this and their anger at their child will spill over onto other identified patients in the group. At other times, the family's protective and possessive qualities may be inappropriately directed toward group members. Families also share experiences and offer help by acting as extended families to one another and to the residents outside the actual therapy hours. Residents who accompany each other on home visits serve as supports in the home and behavioral reporters in MFT groups, and may help the identified patients with their family "homework" at home and in the MFT.

In meetings, the group is seated in a large circle with co-therapists distributed at noon and six o'clock to provide observation of the total group. Families sit together and their seating arrangements are carefully observed, since they usually follow structural patterns. They may be asked to separate if their is a great deal of whispering or disruption. The group begins with everyone introducing themselves and identifying their role in the group. A group member will describe the purpose of the group, generally stressing why families need to communicate honestly and express their feelings openly. At times, the description emphasizes the importance of understanding and changing the familial forces that contribute to substance abuse. After introductions and orientation, we usually work intensively with one family at a time. The first family selected is the central focus for about an hour. The problems they describe set the emotional tone and influence the topics discussed by the entire group. Many other families will identify with these problems, express feelings, offer support, and work on their own similar conflicts. Generally, three or four families work intensively in one night and almost all the families participate verbally. Usually all the families are emotionally involved.

The informal contacts that take place before and after group are crucial. Therapists should mingle and interact during these pre- and post-group gatherings. Many pre-session contacts are excellent grist for therapeutic mills. Post-group interaction may confirm insights and validate feelings or, if not monitored, undermine therapeutic work. Families of clients who leave may continue to attend group to maintain their structural shifts and encourage the identified patient to return to treatment.

The therapeutic team must include a primary therapist who is experienced in group and family therapy and confortable in large groups. There should also be several co-therapists who are an integral part of the treatment program and can provide feedback from group to program and from program to group. The group should be used to train therapists in the dynamics of families and in the techniques of group and family therapy.

MFT is a stimulating and rejuvenating experience for therapist, treatment program, and family. The therapists become the paternal/maternal figures for a host of families who become a single family network and in ways a single family. The therapists assume temporary parental control of all of these families and at the same time are the children of each family. Thus the therapists project, introject, transfer, and are transference objects of a multitude of parental and childlike roles. At the same time, the therapist must step away from emotional entanglement and be objective. The primary therapist must always keep in mind that a critical function is to be a supportive ally to every member of the group. The therapist must also feel the capability and right to interrupt destructive or disruptive communication.[18]

In the early phases of treatment, the families support one another by describing the pain they experienced having a substance abuser in the family. The family's sense of loneliness and isolation, in dealing with this major crisis, is attenuated by sharing the burden with other families. The ways in which the users manipulated them are quite similar and help form a common bond. Group members commiserate over each family's suffering. Each family must be encouraged to break the pattern of perpetuating substance abuse through overprotection. The family learns to see the hostile aspects of this, rather than its benevolence. Many patients who have difficulty with the demands of residential treatment will try to convince their families to take them home and "protect" them. Intervening, in this system, helps prevent early "split-ups." Many families are able to do this merely through group support. Others must learn to recognize and reduce the pattern of mutual guilt induction and enmeshment before they can stop the cycle of symbiotic reinvolvement. An initial period of ventilation of anger and resentment may be necessary before strategies for change can be introduced. The group creates an atmosphere in which all families are encouraged to be open and tactfully express everything about everyone. This does not give a family permission for sadism under the guise of honesty.

Giving food may be the center of an important family transaction. Food may also be limited to gifts to the entire group. This helps create a feeling that the group is one family. This may alleviate guilt and permit giving without infantilizing.[18]

As therapy progresses, the role of the family in producing and perpetuating substance abuse is identified. Patterns of mutual manipulation, extraction, and coercion are identified and corrected. The family's need to perpetuate the patient's dependent behavior through scapegoating, distancing, protection, or infantilization is discouraged and new methods of relating are tried and encouraged. Families tend to feel guilty when the patient confronts them with their role in the addiction cycle. This confrontation has occurred in the home and reoccurs in the early phases of multiple family therapy. If the therapist does not intervene, the family will retaliate by inducing guilt or undermining growth and ultimately pull the addict out of treatment. Substance abuse is viewed as a total family problem; there must not be scapegoats. Parents must be given a great deal of support in family sessions because of their own guilt and the tendency of patients and untrained therapists to attack them. For some parents, even the public admission that there are family problems leads to shame and reactive hostility. Such parents may require individual family therapy sessions and individual support. When they can overcome their embarrassment about expressing feelings in "the public" group, they have made a valuable step toward more open and honest expression of feelings in general.[18]

Multiple family therapy groups help patients achieve and put into practice insight about their family. Many families learn to express love and anger directly, for the first time, in these groups. Deep emotional pain is expressed when appropriate and other family members are encouraged to support such expressions rather than nullify or deny them. Sometimes group support is expressed by the tears of the entire group or by appreciative applause. While kissing, hugging, and rocking are ways families may use to obliterate pain, under the guise of giving comfort, emotionally isolated families may need encouragement for emotional exchange and physical affection.[18]

Therapeutic homework is frequently assigned to reinforce family structural changes. Family tasks and family roles are assigned to restructure the family. Weak ties between family members can be strengthened by suggesting joint activities to build closeness and identifying the fears and patterns that led to weak ties. Strengthening realistic ties will help deintensify enmeshed relationships. Overwhelming family members may be asked to withdraw from group for several weeks in order to strengthen other ties. The family pain caused by having an addicted member can be used to motivate over-involved family members to work toward more adult interactions.[18]

The group is encouraged to consistently focus on inaccurate communication, and delineate individual boundaries by not permitting family members to speak for one another. We point out nonverbal coercive communications that may overwhelm family members, inhibit expressiveness, or produce double binds. We ask that messages be stated clearly and the underlying meanings made explicit. We also assign individuation tasks to family members. It is important for single parent mothers to enjoy their own lives and for couples to learn or relearn to enjoy each other. Grandparents may need to be included, and intergenerational patterns demonstrated, before parents can change. Interpretations that simultaneously focus on the responsibility of both parties are effective and diminish guilt and scapegoating. They also help maintain the therapist's position as the family's ally instead of an individual's advocate.

In the later phases of MFT, families may express intense repressed mourning, a response essential to a healthy family adaptation. The mourning focuses on externals, but its source is in changing or abandoned objects. Mourning is most easily expressed about a sibling who died from an overdose. In still later phases, lost parents may be mourned. Family secrets and myths are also revealed in the later phases of MFT. Families and individuals rarely understand that the real source of mourning is from lost opportunities, lost objects, and unexpressed affect. When the anxiety stirred up by early shifts has been resolved, more advanced tasks can be assigned. In the final phases, the family and identified patient are separated from the group.[18]

Families in the MFT act as supports for one another outside the session. The multitude of cultures and languages in our families is frequently bridged by the universal aspects of the problems, but it also presents difficulties that are minimized when there are therapists from several different ethnic groups.

In some cases, working distance between family members is a necessary goal. In many families, the goal is a restoration of the family homeostasis. Multiple family therapy is unique in contemporary society in that families expose themselves to one another and try to have a significant effect on one another's way of life. MFT enriches and stimulates any therapeutic program that utilizes this technique.

In my experience, MFT reduces the incidence of premature dropouts, acts as a preventive mental health measure for other family members, builds an extended "good family" subculture, and creates and supports structural family changes, which help prevent substance abuse.

Couples groups are generally either composed of the parents of younger substance abusers or older patients and their spouses. After couples have been part of an MFT for several months, they usually request couple sessions. The frequently stated rationale is that there are problems that relate only to the couple which cannot be resolved with the children present. Couples often have difficulty assuming responsibility for family dysfunction with the children present.[19]

When the presenting problem of substance abuse is resolved, content shifts to marital problems. It is often at this point that parents want to leave the multiple family therapy group and attend couples group. In couples group, procedures are reversed. Couples should not speak about their children; they must focus on the relationship between themselves. If material is brought up about the children, it is allowed only if it is relevant to problems that the couple have. Invariably, four issues are emphasized: control, money, sex, and intimacy.[19]

In a number of cases, the husband or the lover has beaten his mate while frustrated and angry. This is noted but not specifically examined. Instead the group helps the couple "exhume" tender feelings that may have existed and been buried in the family strife. Couples are taught to fight creatively and to resolve problems. Members who have been in the group for a while encourage others to talk about their sexual life. For many couples, sex has become an abortive experience and a source of pain rather than pleasure.[19]

A number of divorced parents have attended the couples groups with their new husband, wife, or lover. When this occurs, the divorce becomes a reality during the group experience and both parents are free to make a more lasting commitment to their new partners. As the couples begin to get pleasure from their own relationship, the use of children as a battlefield diminishes. The couples are able to solve the problems between themselves. The generational distance between parents and children becomes appropriate and realistic. They also begin to separate themselves from their family of orgin.

In the couples group, the pronoun "we" is gradually used more and more, especially when couples talk about their problems with their children. They are often amazed to see how easy it is to manage the children if the parents are in agreement. From this they develop constructive ways to talk to one another about the children and, consequently, their general communication improves.

Couples speak about generational boundaries—not in those words, but they express different ideas about distance and closeness. Occasionally, a mother may want to see herself as her daughter's friend or a father as his son's pal. Other members of the couples group may talk about parenting and the desirable and necessary distance between the generations. As the couple develops a greater investment in each other, and less in the identified patient, there are fewer crises. Members of couples groups are alert to convert alliances with children and readily point these out to one another. The members of the couples group become increasingly aware that they, the parents, are the center around which the family revolves. As long as these two feel good about themselves and each other, problems with and between the children will be minimal. In the group sessions, the couples monitor each other and share experiences. They also alert each other to "slippage." Sexual problems that were difficult to discuss in multiple family therapy group are the subject of many couples sessions.[19]

Another type of couples group should be utilized when one spouse is the identified patient. This group is composed of clients and their spouses and includes in-house couples. The MFT group is used as a screening device to evaluate the viability and therapeutic potential of the relationship between the identified patient and the spouse. If no member of the family of origin is available and the client-spouse dyad is thought conducive to a drug-free, health state, then the pair can be added to the couples group. This should be done only after four to ten sessions in MFT. When the family of origin is available, a great deal of work must be done with the client in MFT before or concurrent with the couples group.

Another issue that can be dealt with in the MFT prior to couples group is the parenting function of the client. MFT offers an excellent opportunity for helping the patient become a parent again. It also helps the patient develop a united parental subsystem with his spouse. If the spouse's behavior contributes to, or provokes, drug abuse, this behavior is identified and shifted. The couple is not encouraged to detach emotionally or physically, but to establish a mutual, loving relationship.[19] In most cases, the couples who reached the stage of couples therapy have a potentially constructive relationship.

Many traditional family therapy techniques are used with couples. Some techniques, such as examining and shifting triangulation, are particularly suited to a couples group. The therapist must be aware that couples will tend to suck him into a triangle, using their relationship with the therapist to replace issues of children, money, power, drugs, alcohol, and affairs. It is important to examine hidden agenda and rule-governed behavior. One should remember that partners tend to balance each other. Balancing may be more important than the role either spouse occupies at the moment. The stereotype of female spendthrift and male tightwad is frequently reversed in couples where there is a male substance abuser. However, if he gives up spending money on drugs, he rapidly becomes the tightwad, which may push the spouse into becoming a spendthrift. Another rule is that spouses tend to provoke each other into escalating quarrels, which can only be abated by pulling in a third party (in-law, child, therapist). In the substance abuser-spouse pair, there is frequently competition over who is the sickest and most needy. This may be a source of many quarrels and may continue when the identified patient is drug-free.[19]

Spouses tend to communicate through third parties. This is called triangulation. It can be dealt with even if that person is not a member of the group, since couples who are used to this pattern will find someone in the group to complete the triangle. Frequently the problem a couple presents is not the real problem. The presenting problem may be a device to keep the marriage going, such as an affair to provide needed distance, tapping anger to alleviate depression, or provoking substance abuse. Substance abuse may be provoked or supported in the potential addict because of the spouse's need for self-punishment, to control someone who is weak, to have someone to punish, or out of a need for love that is so desperate that the love object must be rendered helpless and incapable of leaving.[19]

The therapist must try to avoid becoming the subject of the couple's triangulation and work to resolve the triangle when it develops. He must not join either spouse against the other—or he will become a part of the problem rather than its solution. The therapist must also realize that despite similarities, all partnerships are different and, in particular, different from his own domestic relationships.[2]

When one partner gives up substance misuse, this is a critical period, for the nonusing partner must adjust the way he relates to the using partner. There are totally new expectations and demands. For the first time there is communication, an art that neither spouse may have learned. Couples must support each other while learning the basic tools of communication. Sex may have been used for exploitation and pacification so often that both partners have given up hope and have stopped serious efforts toward mutual satisfaction. In addition, drugs and alcohol physiologically diminish the sex drive. Sexual communication must be slowly redeveloped. Difficulties may arise because the recovering abuser has given up the most precious thing in his life (drugs or alcohol) and expects immediate rewards. The spouse has been "burned" too many times and is unwilling to continue to provide one more reward. We encourage spouses to once more trust and provide rewards while at the same time we ask the ex-abusers to reevaluate their expectations.

Couples groups in either an adult or adolescent program provide a natural means for strengthening intimacy. It is critical that shifting a couple to a couples group not be done simply because such groups exist, but with the full knowledge that the group will support some systems and weaken others. If this is kept in mind, the specialized couples groups can be extremely helpful and, in some cases, essential.

Couples groups with alcoholics have been used even more widely than with drug abusers, and the techniques are similar to those described above. In addition, the spouse is encouraged to attend Al-Anon, which facilitated an attitude of loving, detached acceptance. Ablon[20] states that the chief dynamic of the group process of Al-Anon "is a learning experience resulting from a candid exchange and sharing of reactions and strategies for behavior related to living in a household with a problem drinker." The experience of others provides a basis for a comparison and a stimulation of self-examination leading to new insight in all areas of life experiences. However, Al-Anon is frequently not enough for the spouse, perhaps because the approach is not individualized. Hence, spouse groups may be an essential, additional resource.

Another group that may be used is a significant others group. This group may include parents, lover, employers, close friends, and other important members of the substance abuser's network. In addition, separate groups for adolescent and younger children of substance abusers offer support and an opportunity to discuss their speical problems.

Many studies have demonstrated that spousal involvement facilitates the alcoholic's participation in treatment and aftercare.[22] In addition, it increases the incidence of sobriety and enhanced function after treatment.[22] Further, the greater the involvement of the spouse in different group modalities (Al-Anon, spouse groups, etc.), the better the prognosis for treatment of the alcoholic.[23] The author's work with Pauline Kaufmann demonstrated that involvement of the family of adolescent drug abusers in MFT and couples groups cut recidivism from over 50% in families without family group treatment to 20%.[18]

CONCLUSION

In 1975, after 15 years of experience with groups consisting of substance abusers without their families, I shifted to an approach that emphasizes group treatment methods for the entire family. During the time when I provided nonfamily group treatment, I frequently shared with other therapists the frustrations associated with providing group therapy for substance abusers. The effectiveness of group treatment improved as a result of the specialized techniques described in this chapter. Enlisting the family as therapeutic allies and learning to regard the family as a patient that desperately needs and wants help will substantially alleviate the frustration of working with these patients. When one uses these techniques and involves the family, the group treatment of substance abusers becomes meaningful, exciting, and more successful.

REFERENCES

1. Cahn, S. *The Treatment of Alcoholics: An Evaluative Study.* New York: Oxford University Press (1970).
2. Hoffmann, H., Noem, A. A., and Petersen, D. Treatment effectiveness as judged by successfully and unsuccessfully treated alcoholics. *Drug Alcohol Depend.* 1:241-246 (1976).
3. Kaufman, E. Group therapy techniques used by the ex-addict therapist. *Group Process* 5:3-19 (1972).

4. Yalom, I. D., Bloch, S., Bond, G., Zimmerman, E., and Qualls, B. Alcoholics in interactional group therapy. *Arch. Gen. Psychiatry* **35**:419-425 (1978).
5. Brown, S. and Yalom, I. D. Interactional group therapy with alcoholics. *J. Stud. Alcohol.* **38**:426-456 (1977).
6. Fox, R. Group psychotherapy with alcoholics. *Int. J. Group Psychother.* **12**:56-63 (1962).
7. Casriel, D. *So Fair a House: The Story of Synanon.* Englewood Cliffs, N.J.: Prentice-Hall (1963).
8. Rosenthal, M. S. and Biase, D. V. Phoenix Houses: therapeutic communities for drug addicts. *Hosp. Community Psychiatry* **20**:26-30 (1969).
9. Smith, D. E. and Wesson, D. R. Editor's note: the Federal approach to poly-drug abuse. *J. Psychedelic Drugs* **7**:111-114 (1975).
10. Kaufman, E. The abuse of multiple drugs. 1. Definitions, classification, and extent of problem. *Am. J. Drug Alcohol Abuse* **3**:279-292 (1976).
11. Scott, E. Group therapies utilized for alcoholics. *In:* Scott, E. (Ed.), *Struggles in an Alcoholic Family.* Springfield, Ill.: Charles C. Thomas (1970), pp. 64-125.
12. Chessick, R. D. The "pharmacogenic orgasm" in the drug addict. *Arch. Gen. Psychiatry* **3**:545-556 (1960).
13. Kaufman, E. A psychiatrist views an addict self-help program. *Am. J. Psychiatry* **128**:846-852 (1972).
14. Janov, A. *The Primal Scream.* New York: Dell (1971).
15. Kaufman, E. Individualized group treatment for drug-dependent clients. *Group* **2**:22-30 (1978).
16. Blume, S. B. Group psychotherapy in the treatment of alcoholism. *In:* Zimberg, S., Wallace, J., and Blume, S. B. (Eds.), *Practical Approaches to Alcoholism Psychotherapy.* New York: Plenum (1978), pp. 63-76.
17. Adinolfi, A. A., McCourt, W. F., and Geoghegan, S. Group assertiveness training for alcoholics. *J. Stud. Alcohol.* **37**:311-320 (1976).
18. Kaufman, E. and Kaufmann, P. Multiple family therapy: a new direction in the treatment of drug abusers. *Am. J. Drug Alcohol Abuse* **4**:467-478 (1977).
19. Kaufmann, P. and Kaufman, E. From multiple family therapy to couples therapy. *In:* Kaufman, E. and Kaufmann, P. (Eds.), *Family Therapy of Drug and Alcohol Abusers.* New York: Halsted Press (1979), pp. 95-103.
20. Ablon, J. Al-Anon family groups. *Am. J. Psychother.* **28**:30-45 (1974).
21. Corder, B. F., Corder, R. F., and Laidlaw, N. D. An intensive treatment program for alcoholics and their wives. *Q. J. Stud. Alcohol.* **33**:1144-1146 (1972).
22. Cadogna, D. A. Marital group therapy in the treatment of alcoholism. *Q. J. Stud. Alcohol.* **34**:1187-1197 (1973).
23. Wright, K. D. and Scott, T. B. The relationship of wives' treatment to the drinking status of alcoholics. *J. Stud. Alcohol.* **39**:1577-1581 (1978).

Part V:
Training in Group Therapy

15
Teaching Group Psychotherapy

Tracey McCarley, M.D., Joe Yamamoto, M.D.,
Alan Steinberg, Ph.D. and *Marion V. Anker, Ph.D.*

Since group psychotherapy attempts to bring about relief of symptoms and personality change through mobilization and utilization of group forces, the mental health trainee cannot merely transfer his learned skills in individual therapy to the group situation. He must develop an understanding of group phenomena, learn to promote group cohesion, and learn to be comfortable and effective in a leadership role. In this role he will experience powerful affects as he is, at various times, adored or hated by the group. The group will at times endow him with omnipotence and at other times ridicule and derogate him. For these reasons, the personality and the countertransference reactions of the neophyte group therapist must be an important focus of the training.

Dies[1] has surveyed practicing group psychotherapists in order to get their opinions about various training methods. The clinicians were asked to evaluate twelve specific techniques based on four training components. The results, presented in order of "most" to "least" helpful as training experience, were as follows.

1. Co-therapy experience with a qualified therapist.
2. Discussion of your own therapy tapes with a supervisor.
3. Supervised experience in individual therapy.
4. Co-therapy experience with a peer, followed by sessions with a supervisor.
5. Attendance at a group psychotherapy workshop.
6. Attendance at a T-group training workshop.
7. Participation as a patient in a therapy group.
8. Discussion of films or videotapes produced by experts.

9. Careful analysis and discussion of audiotapes produced by experts.
10. Serving as a recorder-observer in a group.
11. Didactic seminars (therapy, research, case study).
12. Learning by doing, self-taught (practice, reading).

Dies notes that the first four items relate to supervision, the next three to experiential learning, the succeeding three to observations, and the remaining items to didactic instruction. Thus, the preferred training comes from active participation as opposed to procedures that remove the trainee from actual group involvement.

Dies believes that to design a proper group psychotherapy program geared effectively to prepare the trainee, the study of important research on the pervasive problems encountered by trainees is necessary and valuable. Trainees ought to be confronted with their misunderstanding about the differences between group and individual treatment. Didactic seminars and observations of ongoing groups might incorporate readings and instrumentation that emphasize group process phenomena. This will help combat their tendency to conduct one-on-one therapy in the group setting.

Focus should be placed on participation in experiential groups and supervisory models employing a group process. The experiential groups and supervisory models might also focus more systematically on trainees' interpersonal and leadership styles to foster greater self-understanding, and to lessen many of their uncertainties about their public image. This will help in reducing their need for contrived therapeutic roles. Dies further suggests that more communication among clinicians is necessary in order to assess new possibilities that may be effective.

There is a limited interchange and collaboration among researchers and practitioners. An overwhelming majority of clinicians failed to include research-oriented references in their recommended readings for beginning group psychotherapy supervisory programs (e.g., inventories, rating schemes, leadership, and group assessment techniques). The trainees should learn to appreciate the potential value of research techniques and findings for the practice of group psychotherapy for their own development as group leaders.

Stein[2] emphasizes that in addition to basic knowledge in his field, the trainee should have a well-rounded experience with a wide variety of psychiatric cases, and be well versed in psychiatric diagnosis. This should take two to three years to acquire, and should be a prerequisite for beginning group psychotherapy training; the trainee should have had well-supervised and adequate experience in individual psychotherapy; personal analysis or personal psychotherapy is essential to avoid areas of conflict leading to blind spots in the therapist and to help him become aware of the nature of his emotional reactions.[3]

Proper teaching of group therapy demands a program that will equip the therapist with relevant theoretical knowledge combined with the technical and practical skills necessary to enable him to guide the group members in achieving the intended goals. The therapist who attempts group therapy must become knowledgeable regarding issues specific to the therapeutic group. These issues are: (1) appreciation of the group *per se* as a potential curative force; (2) attention to the unique character of the group as a medium for therapy (group culture, pressure, role assignment, resistance, regression); (3) the need to learn how to operate as a nonauthoritarian group "conductor"; (4) the greater complexity of transferences and countertransferences in the group; (5) the trainee's fear of group emotion, anger, and dependency; (6) the therapist's need to be liked by the group; and (7) the vulnerability and greater exposure of the therapist in the group.[3]

The most comprehensive model for training group psychotherapists is the *Guidelines for the Training of Group Psychotherapists,* by the American Group Psychotherapy Association.[4] These guidelines specify a certain minimum numbers of hours to be devoted to didactic seminars, supervision, practical experience, and personal group therapy.

Yalom,[5] in his book, *The Theory and Practice of Group Psychotherapy,* describes four major components for an effective group psychotherapy program. They include (1) observation of an experienced group therapist at work; (2) close clinical supervision of trainees' groups; (3) a personal group experience; and (4) personal psychotherapy (self-exploratory work). Roman and Porter[3] describe an approach that is used at the Albert Einstein College of Medicine, which combines, in a fairly structured way, experiential and didactic aspects of group therapy training.

As a prerequisite to group therapy training, the trainee needs to have a basic understanding of the nature of man through studying 1) human growth and development, 2) abnormal behavior/psychopathology, 3) neuroscience, 4) aspects of anthropology, sociology, and psychology, and research techniques to assist in understanding and evaluating human behavior. The trainee also has to develop an understanding and competence in modifying individual or group adaptational systems. The neophyte group therapist should follow a curriculum of studies that incorporates didactic and theoretical knowledge with experiential and practical skills of psychotherapy. To accomplish these goals, the program should consist of the following components.

Didactic Seminars. The neophyte group therapist, who tends to be greatly concerned with learning exactly how to proceed, should first of all be given a broad overview of the various approaches to group therapy as a means of orientation. These approaches can be presented, as Parloff[6] has done, under these three headings: intrapersonal, interpersonal, and integralist (group as a whole).

Emphasis is placed on learning group dynamics and group process, including issues of leadership, norms, social roles, and ingroup-outgroup membership and concerns. This part of the program should be geared to serve as a model of how groups act in general and should focus on the characteristics and dynamics of different groups.[3] The trainee should be introduced to the literature of group therapy and be acquainted with some basic principles on which to base his actions as a group leader.

There should be thorough discussion of the rationale and technique of the leader's interventions. The interventions to be covered should include:

1. *Supportive comments.* These are used when the level of anxiety or other painful affect is so high as to interfere with the progressive unfolding self-revelatory work of the group. For example, after a member has made a particularly painful or embarrassing revelation, the group may fall silent and seem "stuck." At this point the leader may choose to express his empathy—for instance, by stating that some revelations are very difficult to make and may touch some deep chords in the whole group.
2. *Confrontation.* This intervention consists of commenting on observed behavior in group. For instance, the leader may point out that a member is always apologizing, or that two members frequently look at each other and giggle, etc. A confrontation is the

beginning of a process in which the leader and the group thougt-
fully examine their behavior in the here and now.

3. *Interpretation.*   This is a comment made either to individuals
   or the group in which the leader not only points out behavior but
   gives his ideas about its meaning, purpose, and, perhaps, origin.
4. *Directive.*   These are interventions, necessary at times, to halt
   potentially traumatic destructive attacks.
5. *Group cohesion enhancing.*   These include techniques aimed at
   enhancing group cohesion by, for example, pointing out similarities among the members, or helping members to accept differences.
6. *Questions.*   These can be used to encourage the group members
   to become full participants as co-therapists for one another, including such questions as, "What do you (the group) think about
   what Mary has been telling us?" or, "How is it that no one has
   commented on Joe's silence?"

This emphasis on studying leader intervention meets the neophyte's
needs well, since he is often very anxious about what he is to do
when he starts the group.

Finally, this segment of the training program should present some
practical suggestions on how to proceed in selecting patients, and on
forming and conducting a group.

For a thorough knowledge of psychotherapeutic techniques and
dynamics, a series of six to eight weekly 90-minute small discussion
groups is satisfactory. The training group should be small enough to
allow members to participate actively. Readings should be assigned
prior to the beginning of the course. Some may see this as a very brief
time to cover such a complex subject; however, one should keep in
mind that the purpose of this seminar it to introduce the learner to
the intellectual underpinnings of group therapy practice.

The use of pertinent examples from clinical practice of either the
teacher or the learner is desirable. The emphasis should be on illustra-
ting a general principle as well as on helping the learner to deal with
a current problem per se. There will be constant pressure from the
participants for practical advice. At such times it is appropriate for
the instructor to describe how he handles specific situations. However, he should not just serve as a model for the neophyte to imitate.

He should show clearly the abstract concepts that dictate strategies. Sometimes the handling of a situation may be based on a "feel" for what's happening rather than intellectual understanding of it. Intuitive leader-behavior should be explained in light of the general underlying principles of group work. Lectures should not only summarize the reading, but attempts should be made to clarify them with examples.

The trainee should be encouraged to explain areas of disagreement he may have with the authors. Further, the instructor should bring his own clinical examples to be used in this part of the discussion. The latter part of each seminar should be devoted to a discussion in which participants are invited to examine how the ideas apply to their clinical experience.

The use of brief videotape segments of group work is very helpful in these didactic seminars. The leader's interventions can be pointed out and the response of the group observed. Thus the trainees can see which interventions facilitate the therapeutic process and which ones slow it down. According to Berger,[7] the use of videotape in group therapy training will allow the therapist to assess important nonverbal aspects of behavior. It will also illustrate various techniques used in psychotherapy as well as enable the therapist to study crisis situations. At the same time, it allows certain aspects of the sessions to be viewed several times. (For a discussion of the advantages and limitations of this method, see Appley and Winter.[8]) These segments should be brief, and should be carefully selected to focus on particular points.

The integration of the presentation of didactic material with a simulated group experience, as described by Roman and Porter, has appeal to trainees. Use of role-play procedures can help the trainee to integrate conceptual knowledge.[9]

In summary, the didactic seminars should be organized and well planned, involve assigned readings, include an introductory overview of group therapy theory, and present the basic principles that a group leader uses in his attempt to mobilize group forces for bringing about individual therapeutic change. Stephen R. Perls,[10] in his 1979 survey of group therapy training in psychiatric residencies, said programs should present theories including psychoanalytic, psychodynamic, and Gestalt approaches. He feels that a reasonable understanding of the theoretical constructs and techniques of these particular therapeutic modalities should be a minimum requirement. We would add that within the psychoanalytic or psychodynamic category, understanding of intra-personal, interpersonal, and group dynamics should be developed.[6]

Observation. Group psychotherapy observation constitutes another important element of the training program. It is used more universally as a teaching method than is observation of individual therapy, probably because patients in a therapy group have already given up their privacy by joining the group and are less intimidated by an outside observer. Observation can be done by having the trainee observe a session from behind a one-way screen or seated in the room with the group.

The observer in the room is often used by the group to split the transference, and he can become the focus of negative feelings because he is often seen as a judging, disapproving projection of the members' superegos. This group phenomenon can be used by the group leader to enhance the insight of the group members, but the role of passive observer may be uncomfortable for the learner because he is the recipient of these projected feelings. The prohibition against participating verbally in an emotional situation of which he is nevertheless a part may prove stressful. Since it is usually not possible to accommodate several observers in the room, the one-way screen has advantages.

Observation of a group session from behind a one-way mirror allows the trainee to see how an experienced therapist conducts a group. The strengths and limitations of the leader will become apparent. The advantage of this method of observation is that it gives several trainees the opportunity to observe the same group at the same time, thus providing the opportunity for discussion of different points of view of common observation. When the instructor is present with the observers, the trainees have the added advantage of being able to discuss questions and comments that arise during the session. In addition, through the observation and discussion of a variety of group sessions conducted by different group leaders, the trainee will be helped to find a style most appropriate for himself. The student also should be exposed to the experience of hearing and seeing two different instructors discuss their different approaches and their different points of view. When several trainees are present for an observation of a group session, they can share and discuss their different reactions to the same observed patient behaviors. In this way, the trainee can examine his particular, individual reactions.

The disadvantage of this method of observation is that many train-ees find it quite uncomfortable to be involved emotionally, and yet be unable to have any impact on the developing situation in the group. This frustration is often expressed through criticism of both the leader and the patients. The leader is enmeshed in the dynamics and cross-currents in the group, and his experience, therefore, is different from the trainee, who is separated by a glass partition.

Observation of a group demonstrates the excitement, challenge, and opportunity to exert therapeutic leverage in a way that reading, listen-ing to lectures, and discussions can never do.

Experiential Learning.   During this phase of the training, the trainee participates in the group as a member, an experience that is uniquely valuable because it allows identification with patients. The trainee learns to feel anxiety over self-revelation. He may also experience the feeling of hostility that the group members display toward the leader and among themselves. Most important is the fact that he learns and understands the dynamics of group support. He may experience distor-tions of perceptions in his transference to the leader, and the strength of cogent observation made about him by the group members.

The experiential component in training has two major aspects: The first is therapeutic in nature, the second educational.   Provision of ther-apeutic experience is recommended in the guidelines of the American Group Psychotherapy Association because it allows the trainee to ex-plore his personal problems in depth with persons who are strangers. The leader should be someone with whom he has no social or profes-sional relationship.   Here he gains experience that will deepen his un-derstanding of what it feels like to be a patient. The group leader in sessions with trainees must exert careful control over the degree of regression that occurs.

Hadden[11] notes that students in an actual psychotherapeutic group, through an examination of their own behavior and reactions in a group, learn not only group psychotherapy, but other aspects of psychiatry, psychotherapy, and related matters as well. The efficacy of this me-thod in training was confirmed in reports by Ganzarian and his co-workers.[12]

The use of experiential group psychotherapeutic technique in teach-ing allows treatment to a greater or lesser degree to be carried out at the same time.   The therapeutic effects obtained in this manner have a great impact in helping students to understand the total spectrum of feelings. Not only are resistances and defensive inhibitions (blocks to learning) lessened, but increased awareness of their own reactions enable the students to see and understand what is occurring in patients.[11,13,14,15]

Berger,[16] a strong advocate of the experiential approach to training, states that "group psychotherapy and group training experience are essential for, and most useful in, group psychotherapy training." Sadock and his co-workers[17,18] recommend it enthusiastically and feel it has educational and personal therapeutic benefits, as well as providing an excellent basis for future group psychotherapy training. Astrachan and Redlich[19] found "it most useful in helping the residents learn the more unconscious aspects of group interaction, and while the group interaction caused some emotional disturbances in the members, it did not cause any excessive or psychotic reactions."

On the educational side of the program, participation in group psychotherapy can be seen as differing from therapeutic involvement in a group in that the focus is on educational goals rather than therapeutic ones. This educational involvement in group therapy should be part of the training program in which educational groups are held under the auspices of the training program itself. The members of the group are fellow trainees, and the leader is a member of the faculty of the training facility. Yalom states:

Groups of mental health professionals, especially psychiatric residents who will continue to work together, are extremely difficult groups to lead. The pace is slow, intellectualization is common, and self-disclosure and risk-taking minimal. The neophyte therapist generally is highly threatened by requests for self-disclosure; not only his personal, but his professional competence is at stake. In training programs the group leader is often placed in a double role in the student group: he is both teacher-evaluator, and T-group leader. Generally, this compounds the problem and forces undue attention to authority issues. Eventually the group's problem with the leader must be resolved around the issue of trust.[20]

This kind of group experience is greatly affected by the special transference to a leader who is both a teacher and a therapist to the group.

Also the behavior of members in the group will be affected by their outside relationships with one another. Strong attachments and antagonisms may develop. The group leader should limit the intensity and depth of exploration so as not to disrupt the fabric of the learner's daily working patterns. The leader should focus his attention on learning about group therapy by first guiding the group in *experiencing* and then *studying* the phenomena that occur. The group leader should limit the amount of self-revelation that is likely to occur. Members bring into the group observations about and reactions to one another, feelings of rivalry and competitiveness, all of which can give the experience a dimension lacking in a treatment. Group members can then see how the leader handles these matters. Early intervention to prevent acting out is necessary. Failure to intervene in a timely fashion may result in emotional reactions that interfere with members' daily work together. Indeed, one negative result sometimes is that the members behave inappropriately, as if all of life is like the group therapy situation. In one such group, there was such a highly emotional confrontation between two colleagues, who were in the same clinic, that their working together was jeopardized. This conflict was later resolved satisfactorily in the group, but there had been a temporary disruption in their relationship.

Yalom[5] points out that in a therapy group there should be a kind of rhythmic alternation between periods of free, uncensored, unintellectualized expression of emotion, and periods of calm, thoughtful examination of the reactions and interactions that have taken place. In the training group, it is especially important that the leader attend to this alternation and control it appropriately.

Supervision. Supervision constitutes an important component in the training process. After the trainee has gained sufficient insight into the different aspects of group therapy, he is ready to lead a group under supervision. In this part of his training, he will have the opportunity to reflect on his work in supervisory sessions with an experienced group therapist.

The trainee should meet with a supervisor before forming a group to plan selection criteria for patients, anticipate problems, and learn how to prepare patients for group therapy. The supervisor should teach the trainee to have realistic expectations in forming groups, and not to be discouraged by the rate of drop-outs.

Trainees should be made aware that there are great complexities to be encountered in group therapy (due to character and group dynamics), and that the choice of therapist interventions are varied. Supervision is necessary to aid the trainee in focusing on group processes and interactions, rather than details of patient history. Special stress should be given to how ways of relating interfere with the gradual unfolding of each member's self and with the development of group cohesion. The supervisor should help the group leaders examine these patterns of interaction and relate them to the member's current extragroup life, and, when possible, to childhood experience with parents, siblings, and others. Since leadership of the group provokes great anxiety, it becomes essential that the supervisor deal with the therapist's feelings and reactions early in supervision.

For this part of the training, the trainees should have regular meetings with their supervisor and other trainees. These may take the form of workshops or case study reviews.

Perls[10] emphasizes the importance of the supervisor's observing the group either through a one-way screen or by videotape. In the 75 residency programs he surveyed, 42 used participation as co-therapist with a senior group therapist, 26 used videotape in supervision, and 16 used one-way mirror observation. We agree; there is great value in the supervisor's viewing of the group because it is important to get a feel for the patients and, even more important, to see and hear the participation of the supervisee.

The supervisor should focus on the feelings provoked in the leader during group sessions. He should see how the group or its members trigger the leader's reactions, and help the leader to identify his reactions. These feelings can then be used to understand the group and perhaps show the group something about itself. In addition, the supervisor may point out the parts of the leader's reactions that are idiosyncratic and may have irrational, unconscious sources.

Brody[21] illustrates the dynamics of the supervisor-trainee relationship through a hypothetical dialogue between a neophyte and his supervisor in a dyadic model of training. He reveals the trainee's feelings of responsibility for the patient group (the need to "make it work"), concern about being technically adept (doing the right thing), and conflicts over therapeutic transparency (how much should I reveal about myself?).

The trainee should take notes on group sessions and focus on recording interaction as clearly as possible. He should also note the response of the group to interventions. The supervisor should point out the trainee's resistances, and assist the trainee in understanding his resistance on an emotional as well as intellectual level.

One useful supervision method in group therapy is for an experienced group therapist to act as co-therapist with the trainee. While this method may not provide the trainee with sufficient responsibility for conducting the group, the teacher should become less active as time goes on, allowing the trainee to participate more actively in the leadership role. Conducting a group with a trainee co-therapist is a very interesting and satisfying experience for the senior therapist. Teacher and learner collaborate and learn together. The senior member contributes from his special experience and knowledge and the learner contributes freshness of observation. For instance, in a recent group led by an experienced faculty member and a psychiatric resident, a man and a woman member began going out with each other, fell in love, and became engaged. The faculty member pointed out that the woman in this pair had become quite inhibited in the group. In post-group conferences, it was decided that having both of them in the same group was interfering with their full participation. The question of having one of them join another group was raised. The separation was accomplished and the female member who remained resumed her full participation. The inexperienced resident was doubtful about this direct intervention, concerned that the results would be deleterious. Having observed the more experienced co-leader deal satisfactorily with this group problem, he agreed that the result was good and that he would be able to take such action as a group leader in the future.

Another usefulness of the co-therapy teaching model is the opportunity for the trainee to see and hear the experienced person express his countertransference feelings in the post-group sessions. The teacher can show the trainees how he recognizes, expresses, and uses these reactions as guides to what is going on.

Miscellaneous. Some of these categories are inextricably interwoven. For example, some aspects of the didactic training merge with aspects of the experiential program. Thus, there are no clear-cut distinctions among the training components.

The psychoanalytic concept of countertransference has been described for individual analysis by Greenson,[22] who says that the therapist should use his spontaneous emotional reactions to aid his understanding of the patient. Understanding of this aspect of *group* leadership should be a focus in all segments of a training program. The group leader should monitor his reactions to see whether some are exaggerated by his own transferences. He should learn to use his transference; for instance, when he is bored or irritated or overly sympathetic, he can ask himself if the group or some member is unconsciously doing something to provoke just such a reaction. If this is the case, then it is a clue to the member's impact on others and may indicate one of the rigid socially "maladaptive behaviors" that group therapy strives to uncover and change.

When co-therapists are used, then each may aid the other in monitoring countertransference. The group members may sometimes identify a countertransference reaction in the leader and point it out. For instance, they may see him giving one patient undue attention.

Beyond countertransference lies the individual style of each therapist. The trainee should learn to be comfortable with his own style. Some group leaders tend to be pouncing and active, while others go about things more quietly. There is room for variation and for different ways of using the principles of analytic therapy.

NECESSARY CLINICAL SKILLS

Group psychotherapy training is for those mental health practitioners who have prerequisite or concomitant education in personality development, psychopathology, individual psychotherapy, and sociology.

Through the use of didactic seminars, group observation, co-therapy, practical experience, supervision, and personal group experience, the trainee should develop the following clinical skills. He should be able to do all of the following.

1. *Determine the appropriateness of any given patient for group psychotherapy.*

   The trainee should be able to spot patients who are not appropriate for the usual outpatient therapy group. Inappropriate patients may include those diagnosed as having antisocial personality disorders, being in paraniod states, being alcoholics or being in acute manic states. Some of these patients may be appropriate for special, goal-orientated, homogeneous groups, such as Alcoholics Anonymous.

He should also be able to select those patients who can benefit from insight group therapy; i.e., those with mild to moderate personality disorders. He should be able to distinguish patients who can benefit from a primarily supportive approach from those who can use a more confrontational, insight-oriented approach.

In forming a therapy group, he should be able to judge the "fit" of various patients with one another. For instance, he should not place in the same group one member who differs radically from all the others in educational level, cultural values, severity of psychiatric illness, or other crucial dimensions. Groups should also be formed of patients with a variety of coping styles, but similar levels of coping capacity (i.e., ego strength).

2. *Prepare the patient for group psychotherapy.*

Trainees should be able to explain the principles of group therapy, describe the kinds of experiences the patient may expect, and deal with the patient's specific fears regarding group therapy. This is a fundamental skill, since every therapist will have occasion to refer patients for group, even if he does not conduct group therapy himself.

3. *Conduct in the opening phase of a group.*

In the opening phase, the leader must deal with mistrust, fears of self-revelation, and a wish for exaggerated dependence on the leader. The leader's interventions, at this stage, are aimed at fostering group cohesion.

A skill that at this time is very important is the capacity to reduce initial paralyzing anxiety to workable levels. A leader should learn to do this without becoming so overly supportive that he fosters the group's wish to be totally dependent.

4. *Conduct in the middle phase of a group.*

In the middle phase, the therapist must deal with anger at the leader, hostile conflicts between group members and, later, strong positive feelings between members. He should use these various interactions to show individual members their particular "socially maladaptive behaviors." This requires intellectual understanding of pathological character traits, mechanisms of defense, and various patterns of pathological interpersonal relations (e.g., sadomasochistic relationships or interpersonal "games," as described by Eric Berne[23]). It also requires the emotional capacity to withstand an onslaught of subtle and not so subtle hostility from the group as a whole or from individual members.

5. *Conduct in the terminal phase of a group.*

Here the leader must deal with feelings of separation and loss by confronting group members' resistances to facing and expressing such feelings.

6. *Use a co-therapist and/or supervision constructively.*

It is most important for the trainee to be able to expose his personal emotional reactions in nondefensive ways. In supervision, the group leader should be able to explore his personal reactions to the group as a whole, to individual group members and to the co-therapist. When thus examined, these feelings can be valuable guides to understanding the group and its individual members.

REFERENCES

1. Dies, R. R. Attitudes toward the training of group therapists. *In:* Kaslow, F. W. (Ed.), *Supervision, Consultation and Staff Training in the Helping Professions.* San Francisco: Jossey-Bass (1974).
2. Stein, A. The training of the group psychotherapist. *In:* Rosenbaum, M. and Berger, M. M. (Eds.), *Group Psychotherapy and Group Function.* New York: Basic Books (1975), pp. 684-702.
3. Roman, M. and Porter, K. Combining experiential and didactic aspects in a a new group therapy training approach. *Int. J. Group Psychother.* 28 (3):373 (July 1978).
4. American Group Psychotherapy Association. *Guidelines for the Training of Group Psychotherapists,* Rev. Ed. (1978).
5. Yalom, I. D. *The Theory and Practice of Group Psychotherapy.* New York: Basic Books (1975), p. 504.

6. Parloff, M. B. Analytic group psychotherapy. *In:* Marmor, J. (Ed.), *Modern Psychoanalysis.* New York: Basic Books (1968), pp. 492-527.

7. Berger, M. M. *The Use of Videotape with Psychotherapy Groups in a Community Mental Health Program.* American Group Psychotherapy Conference, Chicago (January 1968).

8. Appley, D. G. and Winder, A. E. *T-groups and Therapy Groups in a Changing Society.* San Francisco: Jossey-Bass (1973).

9. Berman, A. L. Group psychotherapy training. *Small Group Behavior* **6**:325-344 (1975).

10. Perls, S. R. Personal communication (July 1980).

11. Haden, S. B. Training. *In:* Slavson, S. R. (Ed.), *The Field of Group Psychotherapy.* New York: International Universities Press (1956), pp. 302-316.

12. Ganzarian, R. et al. Study of the effectiveness of group psychotherapy in the training of medical students. *Int. J. Group Psychother.* **9**:475-487 (1959).

13. Semrad, E. V. and Arsenian, J. The use of group processes in teaching group dynamics. *Am. J. Psychiatry* **108**:358-363 (1951).

14. Berman, L. A group psychotherapeutic technique for training in clinical psychology. *Am. J. Orthopsychiatry* **23**:322-327 (1953).

15. Berman, L. Mental hygiene for educators: report on an experiment using a combined seminar and group psychotherapy approach. *Psychoanal. Rev.* **40**:319-332 (1953).

16. Berger, M. M. Experiential and didactic aspects of training in therapeutic group approaches, *Am. J. Psychiatry* **126**:845-850 (1969).

17. Sadock, B. and Friedman, A. Integrated group psychotherapy training and psychiatric residency. *Arch. Gen. Psychiatry* **18**:276-279 (1968).

18. Sadock, B. and Kaplan, H. J. Group psychotherapy with psychiatric residents. *Int. J. Group Psychother.* **19**:475-486 (1969).

19. Astrachan, B. M. and Redlich, F. C. Leadership ambiguity and its effect on residents' study groups. *Int. J. Group Psychother.* **19**:487-494 (1969).

20. Yalom, I. D. Concluding remarks: training and research. *In:* Yalom, J. D. (Ed.), *The Theory and Practice of Group Psychotherapy.* New York: Basic Books (1970), pp. 374-379.

21. Brody, L. S. Harassed! A dialogue. *Int. J. Group Psychother.* (1980).

22. Greenson, R. Loving, hating, and indifference toward the patient. *Int. Rev. Psychoanal.* **I** (3):259-265 (1974).

23. Berne, E. *Principles of Group Treatment.* New York: Oxford University Press (1966).

16
Group Therapy Training: The Ex-student's Point of View

Walter Heuler, M.D.

This chapter represents a personal statement of what I found most useful in my group therapy training. From my experience, I have concluded that the following, in descending order, helped me to become a competent group therapist.

1. A wide diversity of experience as a group leader and co-therapist.
2. Experience as a group therapist under supervision with many different supervisors.
3. Experience as a patient in group.
4. Experience as leader of an observed and closely supervised inpatient group.
5. Videotaping groups in which I was co-leader; using the videotape for supervision.
6. Observation of an ongoing group conducted by other therapists.
7. Supervision from notes and/or memory without direct observation by supervisors.
8. Observing videotapes of a group with supervisory commentary.
9. Reading group textbooks and journals.
10. Didactic teaching.

A wide and extensive variety of practical experience as leader or co-therapist with subsequent supervision seems, in retrospect, to be the most important factor in my group therapy training. Various other factors were also important and contributed different perspectives of group dynamics and therapeutic techniques. No one method could have replaced the educational spectrum. Even though there was redundancy, each experience led to some specific and unique understanding and skill.

The overall rank order of educational experiences is important, but it changed over time. Reading, lectures, and seminars, earlier in my training, were more important. They provided a basis for understanding and organizing practical experience. Didactic teaching and reading were less valuable later in my training, even though my grasp of the didactic material improved with time and experience (although rereading is still valuable today). Supervision seemed more valuable as experience and knowledge increased and I better understood how groups operated and how to use the supervision.

An important experiential aspect was the diversity of patients. I trained at a County Hospital with a wealth of patients. I was able to select and work with groups at all levels, from the most severe and chronic psychotics to highly functional neurotics. This required a diversity of techniques. The need to adapt to different and changing groups was stressful, but expanded my approach.

EARLY EXPERIENCES

There were some specific difficulties when I began to learn. Specific factors that inhibited learning were fear and lack of perception. One of my fears was that I was ignorant while there were patients who were relying on me. I had fears about my ignorance damaging patients and fears that the patients would damage me. Preoccupation with these fears is common to most new therapists. I found that early and frequent exposure to groups, when all was new and could be embraced with the enthusiasm of new knowledge, helped me through those initial fears. I got a message of confidence from supervisors and this was always reassuring. Another experience that helped was working with more experienced co-therapists. The co-therapists served, I felt, as a symbolic safety net protecting me and the patients from each other's well-intentioned accidents. Lack of a trained perception means not understanding group process, not grasping the complex interweaving of spoken and unspoken messages, expectations, transferences, countertransferences, and projective identifications that comprise the substance of any group. In order to feel that I had any idea what was happening in group, aside from obvious messages, I had to experience a fair amount of different groups over a period of at least two to three years, as well as have an extended exposure to group theory. After a critical mass of information had been incorporated, groups became self-teaching and self-rewarding.

The experience as a member of a group was different from all other parts of group training. I found it was invaluable. Even though the therapist is always a member of his group, he has a special place and is never quite a full member. The therapist is a participant but never a patient. A different perspective comes from the time spent as a patient.

I preferred being a patient in a private therapy group to groups made up solely of professionals. I cannot say the latter are of no value, but in my own experience they were less useful. During the first year of my residency I was assigned, as were all first-year residents in my program, to a teaching group. A staff psychiatrist with no administrative responsibility for the members was the leader. The group was required of first-year residents, and after that it was optional.

This group failed to accomplish very much for several reasons. One of these was ambiguity of objectives. There was a constant dispute over whether the group was a treatment group in which members would reveal personal secrets, problems, etc., or was a classroom in which professional decorum must be maintained. This issue became a point of repeatedly used resistance whenever any member was uncomfortable. Since the group was mandatory, the group's progress toward trust and communication skills was kept at the level of the least committed, most highly defended member. Such resistance is not unusual in groups, but a group of unwilling participants did not provide a climate in which this could be worked through.

In contrast, being a patient provided for me an unobstructed view of the group as an emotional experience uniquely different from that of the therapist. Though I was never fully able to shed my identity as a learning therapist, the skill of my group leader, combined with the lack of ambiguity in my role, prevented this from interfering with the full patient experience.

OBSERVED GROUPS

One of my first exposures to group therapy as a psychiatric resident was one of the most helpful. I have returned to this model several times in my training and my post-training experience, and I have found it always offered valuable advantages over most others. In my first year of residency on an inpatient ward, an ongoing group of four to ten nonpsychotic patients met three or four times per week for 30 to 45 minutes. The stated goal was exploration of problems both in and out of the hospital. This group served as preparation for later psychotherapy and seemed to help patients reintegrate themselves personally and socially before being discharged. The group was co-led by two first-year residents. Each pair led the group for three or four weeks and had the option of continuing for an additional three to four weeks. The group meeting was observed from behind a one-way viewing mirror and heard by strategically placed microphones. The observers consisted of the residents, nurses, psychologists, social workers, and the supervising physician. The observers were able to discuss and try to understand the group as it progressed without disturbing the group. Immediately following the group, a half-hour to 45-minute discussion was held, with the therapists and observers as participants. There was an attempt to arrive at some understanding of what had occurred. My experience in this group was probably not different from most new therapists in their first group. I was terrified and self-conscious, and I felt myself floundering. Although this experience was frightening, the experience behind the mirror caused greater concern. I spent several months hearing observations and implied meanings and intentions which were incomprehensible to me being ascribed to patients.

It was only after prolonged exposure that I began to understand that more was taking place than casually met the eye. It was especially unnerving when predictions of response and reactions seemed mysteriously correct. Yet I could not understand how or why the more experienced staff could see this. After many months of observation, I began to believe there was such a thing as group process and that an understanding of it could lead to the same knowledge the staff mysteriously displayed. I found this particular experience to be most valuable as an early key to following process. Participating as a group therapist, in this type of group, was a better learning experience than most, especially early in training. In the beginning, as a group therapist, I felt naked and unprepared and this feeling was only slightly tempered by the didactic training I received. Experiencing group process and understanding it is a social experience for which explanation alone cannot prepare us, just as explanations cannot prepare us for transferences. What this particular type of group offers that helps the new group therapist trainee pick up the feeling of how groups function is directly related to the one-way mirror observation. My anxiety was reduced by seeing peers and staff floundering helplessly without serious consequences. In addition, sharing the responsibility for learning helped, as did observing peers' comments and mistakes and hearing the supervisor's and other peers' feedback. Each of us who participated in this group was able to learn from his own mistakes and from the mistakes of others. Specific to the observed group was the advantage of immediate feedback, observations, suggested changes, and intervention. This was particularly helpful, since it occurred during the group and the observers' predictions could be compared with real events. The more the senior observers said about the group process, the more valuable the experience became. This particular group allowed a high degree of participation and observation by the supervisors and peers, and this was highly valuable.

Another specific quality of this group was a tendency for the group to remain a young, or early, group. Early group issues, such as trust, the place of each member in the group, and who is in charge of the group, constantly repeated themselves. This was due to rapid patient turnover, since most patients did not stay in the group after discharge.

Although rapid turnover might be a disadvantage for many inexperienced therapists, it was helpful to me. It provided me with several chances to master this most difficult part of group therapy. Also related to early group is the instability in group membership by members and therapists. This instability was more a disadvantage than an advantage. Painful separation and vulnerability to constant change were ever-present issues and preoccupied the group members.

There were also some advantages in that other therapists in training could come from behind the mirror and change from observer to therapist with less disruption than is usually the case when the new therapist must rely only on the report of the old therapist. The ability of another therapist, familiar with the ongoing group from actual regular observation, to walk from behind the mirror and take over is a marked advantage of this method. This also allowed the supervisors to occasionally substitute as co-therapists in order to model an intervention or demonstrate a specific technique for a difficult patient or problem.

The mirror and microphones provided their own input into the formation of the group. The mirror acted as a silent group member. It was noticed, but was rarely intrusive. Each patient was aware the group was observed before he joined. The mirror often stimulated useful projected material which could readily be incorporated into the workings of the group, although fearful patients required some reassurance about the purpose of the mirror. Discussion of how patients felt about this was usually encouraged and occasionally a quick visit behind the mirror after group was needed to calm a particularly edgy patient.

For the most part, I found that groups functioned with less inhibition in a room with a mirror that was consistent from group to group than in settings where they were directly observed. Videotape equipment, even on a consistent basis, seemed much more intrusive than a silent mirror. The camera was more inhibiting in the long run. I found having observers sit silently in the group room much more intrusive than cameras or mirrors. Observers in the room cannot detach themselves from the group and inevitably become part of the group process, as group members go to great lengths to either ignore them or draw them actively into the group.

Using videotape in psychotherapy has become a less controversial part of psychiatric training and research. Part of the group work I had in psychiatric training included the opportunity to observe videotape examples of groups. I found this a worthwhile didactic experience even though it had limitations. Specific interactions were selected, shown, and discussed. This was helpful because it allowed me to see live examples of reading and seminar topics. The examples helped me to understand and remember specific issues. Most of the examples were seen out of context rather than as part of an ongoing development in the life of a group, but I occasionally had the opportunity to observe groups in their entirety on videotape. Watching the entire group on videotape proved to be boring, however. I suspect that boredom resulted from the videotape providing too much emotional distance for the observer, who did not emotionally become involved in the group; it was rather like watching a videotape of a football game after the event and when you know the score and outcome.

In conclusion, I found it helpful to see excerpts of groups specifically tailored to reading or seminars, although seeing excerpts out of context limited my understanding of their place in the development of the group. Nevertheless, this was more helpful than watching an entire group on videotape, which was too emotionally distant to keep my interest. Direct observation was the more helpful and was best done through the one-way mirror.

Videotape was useful in another way, and ranks in that way just slightly lower in value to observing groups behind a mirror. I was able to have videotapes made of ongoing insight groups in which I was co-therapist. These tapes were available to the group and for supervision. I found videotape supervision more pointed and useful about the specifics of group dynamics than supervision from notes. This also provided more helpful information about my own behavior as a therapist. I have already commented that cameras are noticed by a group and do inhibit the group to some degree. However, my already functioning groups were able to overcome the intrusion of a camera and, after an initial 15- or 20-minute period of unsettled concern, the groups were able to have a relatively productive session. The supervisor was able to go over the group point by point and see the group as a totality. Feedback from this was in greater depth than had previously been possible from notes or from memory recitations. Supervisors who were able to use this technique expressed considerable pleasure at being able to supervise from videotape and seemed to feel it was helpful to them. The patients were able to observe the videotape in later sessions. This was used to encourage observation and discussion of themselves and others in the group process. Tapes seemed to provide emotional distance for patients, just as they did for trainees. The tapes may have allowed patients to more objectively study themselves. In one instance, a significant breakthrough occurred when a highly obsessive-compulsive individual was able to see his aggressive intrusiveness for the first time. His observation of "I look like a very formidable fellow" led to an increase in his comfort in the group and considerable progress in his ability to integrate and work with the other group members. This insight into oneself is apt to happen with therapists as well as patients. I found it was less likely to happen in supervision from notes.

MODELING BY EXPERIENCED THERAPISTS

As part of my training, I had an opportunity to observe through a one-way mirror ongoing group psychotherapy conducted by experienced therapists, while another experienced therapist watched, too, and commented during each session. This was a helpful adjunct to learning about group work. Learning from role models taught me how to pace sessions and how to approach specific problem patients. It also provided the opportunity to understand various appropriate and inappropriate therapist behavior. I later found myself using postures and interventions I had seen used by the experienced therapists. Having a model to fall back on gave me additional confidence and allowed me to develop my own style.

One pitfall I noticed in myself and other trainees was a tendency to over-identify with one particular therapeutic style and exclude other approaches. This limits the ability to develop one's own style. Until excessive identification could be overcome, the problem was reduced by the training program deliberately including several observational experiences with several different therapists. I feel that the greater the diversity of the experience, the more valuable it is.

Observation of ongoing therapy led by an experienced therapist was one of those experiences that I found had different (greater or less) value at different points in my training. Specifically, I found observation of experienced therapists was more helpful later in my training. At that time observation of my peers became less helpful.

As my skills sharpened, I began to question how to deal with specific problems. As my perception became more acute and my understanding of what was happening in group became better organized, I was better able to use the skills demonstrated by an experienced therapist to answer specific problems and questions. One additional value in observing several experienced group therapists in action was the powerful counterbalance it provided to the persuasive role modeling of the leader in my personal group therapy experience. As a role model, he was seductive in style and technique. If I had not seen other effective styles during my training and personal group therapy, I might have found this model to be overwhelmingly persuasive.

DIDACTIC TEACHING

Formally presented aspects in my group training and residency were based on the reading of one textbook, Yalom's *Theory and Practice of Group Psychotherapy*.[1] Supplementary readings were suggested, but were not emphasized. Yalom's basic text was an essential part of my development and understanding. At the time I started reading it,

I had had six months of experience observing and being observed with inpatient groups. The focus was on trying to understand what the patients were doing from moment to moment. Based on this experience, I was able to use the material presented in the book as a framework on which to assemble and further understand what I had seen and done. I could see its value as I read other books and articles, and saw how their observations and thoughts and my continuing clinical experience pointed the way to further necessary experience. The reading served as an outline, not a complete statement, on which I could hang and organize my understanding of group therapy. Why, then, do I not list this framework higher on my priority list? For me the substance of understanding came from experience. All those factors that I rated higher than the reading are experiential.

The center pin of my formal group therapy training consisted of a year-long course in the second year of training. It was built around multiple experiences as group leader and co-therapist, lectures combined with videotape presentations, and discussion of topics from the reading. I found the lectures were not particularly helpful except as supplements to the reading and as a formal way to bring me into contact with group concepts. At the time I was drowning in an excess of ideas and prone to avoid new concepts. Because of this, it may have been essential to my developing a good group style and may have prevented my avoiding some uncomfortable ideas. It also contributed to diversity in experience and in that way was important. I would not omit formal didactic teaching from a training program, but I would not overestimate its value. In conclusion, the following points seem to me to stand out.

1. The value of diversified experience. This was the most valuable aspect of my training. No one single factor could have contributed all of the benefits that a wide range of experiences provided.
2. At every stage of training, experiential learning was more valuable than the didactic.
3. Didactic learning was important as a framework for understanding experience. The two worked hand in hand.
4. Experience as a group member was almost as valuable an experience as leading groups, having my group work supervised, and having the chance to observe experienced therapists at work.

REFERENCES

1. Yalom, I. *The Theory and Practice of Group Psychotherapy.* New York: Basic Books (1975).

17
Training and Continuous Education in Group Therapy

Martin Grotjahn, M.D.

It is difficult to say anything specific about the qualifications of a group therapist, other than that he has to be much more active than the individual therapist. The ability to respond to a group spontaneously, honestly, and frankly takes courage and trust. Therapeutic mistakes eventually must be honestly examined, usually in the group. There is no "analytic blank screen" to hide behind in a group.

Foulkes[1] states that the therapist should trust the group; he must be able to listen, since he does not have the authority to control, discipline, or even lead the group process. The therapist must also trust his intuition, which is not a magic-mystic quality but the use of subliminal, unconscious clues that the group therapist perceives in the periphery of his awareness. The therapist must be a specialist in communication. To develop that, he needs personal therapeutic experience. He must learn to analyze himself as if he were another person, and must learn to analyze another person as if the patient were the therapist. In the group, he must be the central figure and also relate to himself as if he were a member of the group.

To be well trained, disciplined, and controlled, and still remain human is the great dilemma of the therapist.

In therapeutic work with therapists, it becomes clearly visible that therapists suffer from a "Mother Superior complex."[2] They show this complex at work, with their colleagues, in their societies, and often at home with their families. Sigmund Freud was not an exception, as Ernest Jones[3] in his biography describes so beautifully.

The therapist's marriage deserves special attention, since it is there that the therapist gets the strength to continue his "impossible profession."[4] The therapist's spouse must understand the therapist's profession in order to understand him and his needs. From the beginning, the spouse must realize that the therapist is a specialist and an authority only in his office and not at home. At home he should react, not analyze. The psychotherapist is often a great disappointment to a spouse.

The husband or wife of a therapist should be aware that it is usually easier for a therapist to get a divorce than to change professions.

Therapy of the therapist's spouse should also take place in groups, if at all possible. It should be a heterogeneous group, even if a considerable part of such a group consists of other therapists' partners. While my experience with husbands of therapists is limited, it is my experience that therapists' wives do better in groups than in individual therapy because they frequently (and secretly) want to simultaneously defeat their therapist and their spouse. Neither task is beyond them, but it is almost impossible to defeat a group.

When one looks at younger colleagues who want to study group therapy, one gets the impression that they all should be analyzed. When one then looks at the analysts who are supposed to do the analyzing, it seems they *too* could use further analysis. The question of the need for analytic training of group therapists is not yet decided. During this period of doubt, the analytic training of group therapists is considered necessary.[5] The answer probably lies in a combination of analytic and group experience. Therapists who specialize in the technique of standard analysis should also have a group experience, since in analysis the therapist in training remains an only child of his training analyst, while in the group he becomes a member of a family and then can analyze his interaction with people.[6]

Alexander Wolf makes a very valid point when he insists that the therapist should not be treated in homogeneous groups with other colleagues only. Therapists do need a group experience in heterogeneous groups (in groups with patients not from the healing profession). They should accept their own patienthood.[7]

Experience with groups of resident psychiatrists and with groups of senior analysts has shown that a combined analysis and group experience is highly advisable.[6,8,9,10]

After work as a co-therapist, the group therapist needs supervision. It is not possible to supervise without participating at least occasionally, if not regularly, in the group.

During the first part of supervision, the attention of the supervisors is group-directed. Soon the attention shifts and supervision becomes therapist-directed.

It is advisable to write a short report after all group sessions. During the session, note-taking is not possible for most therapists; however, the therapist should, within 24 hours after the session, take the time to write a one-page summary of what has happened during the group session. This is a most important "consultation with oneself," and offers continuous learning.

Another form of continuing education is the "leaderless group" for therapists.[9]

The aim of all training and all supervision is the development of free, responsive, spontaneous, honest communication between the therapist and his group. Only in his ability to communicate must the therapist be superior to his patients.

CONDUCT OF GROUP THERAPY AS A MATURING EXPERIENCE

Continuous education is an urgent need in medicine. Psychiatry and psychotherapy are no exceptions. How can the well-experienced therapist continue his training and in this way protect himself from becoming depressed, isolated, cynical, indifferent, narcissistic, and conceited?

A therapist with an open mind will continue to learn; he may develop the feeling that every year he becomes a better therapist than he was the year before.

The group therapist is not, and should not be, a patient among patients. He must not become a responsibility or a burden to his group. He occasionally has the right to explain himself like a father or a mother who at times wishes to be understood and therefore makes explanations to the family. A family who understands father or mother will have cleared the way to further growth.

The therapist must remain willing to learn and to express himself openly, honestly, and directly, without fear or anxiety. If he does that, he need not worry about keeping in touch with the literature or with new research or changing techniques. He will be able to do his duty with his patients.

One satisfaction the therapist gets from individual therapy is the feeling that he has lived many lives. The satisfaction from group work is different, but nevertheless deep. Groups are the psychiatrist's beloved families; to see them grow and mature helps the therapist to mature.

REFERENCES

1. Foulkes, S. H. *Group-analytic Psychotherapy: Methods and Principles.* London: Gordon & Breach (1975).
2. Morgan, D. A note on analytic group psychotherapy for therapists and their wives, *Int. J. Group Psychother.* 21:244-247 (1971).
3. Jones, E. *The Life and Work of Sigmund Freud* (three volumes). New York: Basic Books (1953-1957).
4. Greenson, R. R. The working alliance and the transference neurosis. *Psychoanal. Q.* 34:155-181 (1965).
5. Grotjahn, M. *Art and Technique of Analytic Group Therapy.* New York: Aronson (1977).
6. Kline, F. Personal group therapy and psychiatric training. *In:* Wolberg, L. R. and Aronson, M. L. (Eds.), *Group Therapy 1975: An Overview.* New York: Stratton Intercontinental Medical Book Corp. (1975), pp. 211-216.
7. Grotjahn, M. *Art and Technique of Analytic Group Therapy.* New York: Aronson (1977).
8. Kline, F. M. Dynamics of a leaderless group. *Int. J. Group Psychother.* 22:234-242 (1972).
9. Kline, F. M. Terminating a leaderless group. *Int. J. Group Psychother.* 24:452-459 (1974).

18

The Analytic Group Experience In the Training of Therapists: Report on Three Years with a Group of Staff Members

Martin Grotjahn, M.D.

In November 1968, the staff of a university psychiatric clinic invited me to conduct weekly group sessions, each lasting for 90 minutes, with the entire medical staff of the department. Resident physicians were not invited.

At that time the hospital was in transition. The director had left and the staff was waiting for the appointment of a new one. In charge were two acting directors, one in charge of the hospital administration and a second in charge of training and clinical work. The second of these two senior staff members was a friend and was my counterpart in the group. Due to the role he played opposite me, he shall be one of the two persons mentioned by name. He will be called "Max." Otherwise, this presentation will describe the group without giving the details of individual life histories.

In addition to the two acting directors or senior staff members, there were seven department chiefs and their seven assistants, a group that averaged twelve to sixteen members per meeting.

NOVEMBER 1968

We had a splendid start in the first meeting. I was the first one to arrive and then the group grew from three to finally thirteen staff members. We all sat in a tight circle in a basement room without windows.

I explained the aims of this experiment as I had described it in my paper about the analytic group experience with therapists.[1] We would aim at a spontaneous, honest, responsive, free communication and interaction among the group members. We would have to deal with the fear of intimacy, and of expressing hostility in the presence of superiors. It was made clear that everybody on the staff was—and should feel—invited, but should attend only voluntarily. Whoever started was to promise himself and us to give the experiment a three-month honest try. After three months, we would make a decision whether to proceed or to abandon the project.

A lengthy discussion started, with a rebellious and paranoid undercurrent, on whether attendance was really on a voluntary basis. The chief of staff mentioned that everybody was expected to attend these sessions. All wanted to come but all wanted to do so only voluntarily.

Three men in analytic training planned to participate.

I referred to the chief of staff in this session as "the boss" and to the second in command as "the slave driver." In later sessions I called everybody by his first name.

Everybody in the group had some experience with group work and was well versed in the use of dynamic and analytic terms. Everybody reacted more freely and spontaneously than I expected, since I come from a German academic background, where such freedom would have been unthinkable.

I singled out "the boss" for interaction with me and asked him: "Have you lost weight?" "Are you sick?" "Are you depressed?" "Is it true that you are getting divorced? What about your children?"

The group members reacted as if I had asked the right questions. They all had always wanted to know the truth about the many rumors that made the rounds in the hospital. Some expressed jealousy about my friendship with "the boss."

At another point in the session I turned to the only black doctor, asking him: "How are you?" He responded with loud irritation: "I resent this special attention." I felt misunderstood, but I understood his point and said nothing further.

Somebody asked me how much I was getting paid for the session; I said truthfully that I did not know, but that I hoped it would be between $75 and $100.

After the session everybody seemed enthusiastic, and has the feeling: "We got started. We got acquainted." This seemed to be important in a hospital in transition. Everybody disappeared quickly after the session as if everybody was defending himself against the collective suspicion that he was trying to "polish teacher's apple" by hanging back for some personal contact. Partly the rush was explained by the demands of hospital realities.

In the second half of this—our first—month, the group proceeded better and faster than I expected.

I was always ready to listen to any discussion of the reality of the hospital, as, for instance, changes in the situation of the staff of the hospital. Since I was an outsider, I sometimes asked questions and was heatedly rebuffed with the words: "Let us be in charge of what to choose as topics." I had to learn that I should not do things I never would have done in any other group. I had to learn that lesson repeatedly.

Once I stated my personal reasons for conducting groups. I too hoped to benefit. I like to be able to look people straight in the eyes, which I have avoided since childhood. I would like to be able to break somebody's neck without putting on kid gloves first. I would like to dissolve my rage and ambivalence and stop hiding the deprived baby in me.

At this point I wanted to tell a dream of mine, but I was interrupted with a question: "Are you being honest now?" The group actually doubted that the dream to be reported was an honest dream and felt I was "playing games" with the group. I was shocked by this suspicion and said so. Then I told the group my dream.

In the dream, I watched my newly born grandson rock in a basket. He fell out and hurt his head. I thought he had died and I was horrified. The dream was terrifyingly real and I woke up.

I explained that I often felt like a deprived baby, which led me to assume that I have the right to expect special favors and privileges—a habit that has led to many complications in my life.

Again I was asked whether I was being "honest." I had a double answer: "This is a real dream I dreamed last night in this form. I also am aware that I want to start group interaction by not hiding myself and by not holding back."

One doctor said that I reminded him of the boys he used to beat up because they wanted to be models for the class. Another doctor said that I was like one of the boys who used to beat *him* up in school. A third man interrupted and broke into a wild accusation about a colleague and his stupidity and unethical behavior (he had abandoned a patient by dumping him in the hospital). I suspected that the doctor was actually talking about me dumping myself into the group. I felt accused and simultaneously rescued: The speaker had turned the group's attention from me to an outsider.

It turned out that the speaker split himself between being the aggressor and the defender of the accused doctor at the same time. I realized, but did not say so at that time, that he, being a twin, tried to be two people at the same time: Bad and good, aggressor and defender, himself and his brother.

The entire group complained that I did not remember all their first names and wanted me to make a special effort to remember their names.

During this first month of our group sessions, a memorandum was circulated with which I could not agree—and I told the group about it. The memorandum stated:

The aim of the group is to understand the resistance of staff members against necessary and progressive changes in the administration of the hospital and in the diagnosis, evaluation, disposition, and treatment of hospitalized patients. We will try to understand this resistance and to develop more open-minded attitudes toward changes in the staff members and Department Chiefs, to deepen their responsiveness to changes in administration and treatment, and to help the development of a positive team spirit for further progress in the hospital and the teamwork of the staff. We will try to accomplish this assignment by a group experience which intends to sharpen sensitivity for oneself, other people, their ideas, motivation, feelings, and means of expression. Tolerance should be developed by the group experience for interaction with special regard to the expression and tolerance for intimacy, and also for freer expression of hostility in order to dissolve conflicts and free the development of human responsiveness in the individual and the group spirit in the entire staff. It is the aim of the group experience to develop freely responding individuals in an open-minded group . . . .

I expected a lengthy discussion, but it seemed as if my younger colleagues took this memorandum of the administration less seriously than I was accustomed to do.

At the end of the month, the group was, however, quite upset about three members of the staff having resigned from their jobs. Somebody else resigned from attending the sessions because his training analyst advised him that these group meetings would interfere with his analysis.

The group was caught in the crisis of being decimated while still trying to get started and acquainted. Now we had to say "goodbye" instead of "welcome" and had to wait for new members, of which the first two had already joined us. I started to worry about the future of the group after such early complications. The acting chief of staff announced that there would be no further changes in the staff. He added, however, that two staff members had been given warnings. They would have to perform their duties more effectively. Everybody but me seemed to know the details. I felt like an outsider. I did not do anything about it, since I assumed that such a position would have its advantages at other times.

In the last session of this month, I turned once more to the black colleague and invited his participation. He brusquely told me to wait and added: "I don't care." Later I learned that this doctor resigned in anger from his position.

There was a strongly rebellious and critical attitude focused on the acting director, "Max," who attended the meetings. It was clear that the conflicts about him were a part of the staff's reality and also a stimulus to express hostility to authority.

At the end of the first month, the group was torn and upset, but it was a group nevertheless.

December 1968

As expected, the session in the second month started slowly and was often interrupted by silence. As a rule, only the last half-hour showed interaction of more than minimal courage. Several of the doctors hung back, mostly watching me, and waiting. The majority of the group seemed to me to be newcomers. The question was: How far can we go? And do we continue after three months, since only twelve meetings were authorized?

I suggested that we postpone a decision until the end of the three-month period. I said clearly that I would be ready to continue indefinitely. I declared my eagerness to make this group "successful," meaning to achieve an interacting analytic group experience for everyone willing to participate.

I tried to get the group started once again and took my curiosity about my colleagues as a guideline.

I tried some remarks to the two new men and compared their ambitions: One was ambitious for himself, and the other ambitious for his job.

I then turned to a third doctor and the pencil that I was holding in my hand flew like an arrow at him as I asked him: "I hear you are my son's friend?" This started a short and pleasant exchange.

I turned to the man who had complained so loudly during the previous session and with whom I had been well acquainted for years. I told him he was a twin who tried to incorporate his twin brother. I was aggressive and interpretive, but careful and not invasive.

Several of the men were experienced therapists with astonishing insight into me. The discussion about me and my "technique" or "style" always unified the group and stimulated interaction. They were always ready to analyze me.

My opinion about the group after the first half of the second month was: "Everybody knows everybody a little bit better—and all begin to know me well." I tried to move more into the background but the group always watched me closely. I felt like a member of the group, but I remained aware of my primary duty as a communicator.

Another time, somebody opened the session by saying that on the way to the clinic he had seen some buildings on fire. This I interpreted as meaning that he wanted to burn down something. I wanted to know what. The doctor's office? The city of Los Angeles? Me? After a short startled reaction, the speaker confessed his rage against Max and the wish to see him burn. Somebody else defended Max, calling him a Prussian. Then there was silence again.

I interrupted the silence by saying that I was always willing to start the proceedings again but it was not always good to do so. It would put me too much into the focus of the group and would turn the group to me instead of to itself. I added that I was slightly depressed about the death of a colleague. I had been sick myself. Finally I asked myself whether I was getting old. It appeared to me that I did not want to let the clash between the doctors get out of hand so early in the life of the group. Today I would act differently.

One of the senior colleagues joined the depressive atmosphere. He missed the four men who had resigned. In terms of interaction it was clear what happened: One of the doctors wanted to burn down Max, who in turn apologized for having fired some members of the group.

At the session before the Christmas interruption, someone reported about the recent death of his father, another man spoke about "the two times I died," when he suffered a heart arrest and his heart had to be shocked into action again. Another doctor reported on his coronary two years before, and finally we wondered about the range of age difference in the group.

I turned to one of the men and asked him whether he wanted everybody to die, especially the older men. He did not reply but his thoughtful face showed me that he probably would come back to this topic at another time.

One of the experienced therapists complained that we did not talk to one another but that we seemed to address the empty space in the middle of the circle. The entire group slowed down after this remark and spoke only haltingly about the wish to kill and the fear of death. After the Christmas sadness, the hope for the coming New Year concluded the second month of our work together.

During the last session of the year, interaction began in different ways. It started between the two senior colleagues, and it was followed by the junior members. The new men were still searching for a place in the structure of the group. I tried to communicate with all different levels of the hierarchy.

January 1969

Again the group started slowly, probably due to two new members, with whom new relationships had to be established. One of the senior men did not attend, which annoyed me.

The two new men were experienced in group psychotherapy and one of them announced as a kind of introduction that his wife had delivered "the most marvelous baby in the world." The other man reported on his sickness and I warned him to go slow with further revelations because "you may feel badly about your astonishing openness in your first meeting with us."

I wondered aloud whether we should ask Max to resign from the group, since he seemed to provoke and inhibit everybody. My question was greeted with noncommittal silence. As much as he was disliked, the group also realized his value as a target.

During this month the group increased to fifteen men, which was the entire staff of the hospital. Attacks against the bosses became frequent. It seemed that we attacked them because they provoked everybody in the course of their duties, but at the same time we were aware that we were talking about our attitudes toward authority. Somebody reacted by telling a dream of the previous night: "An airplane crashed. I stepped aside not to be burned or crushed." The dreamer felt a strong temptation to leave the group whenever Max entered the room. The dreamer just could not stand him.

The group took up the debate about Max and criticized me for having invited him in the first place. The group furthermore criticized me for always greeting Max as a guest of honor (which I denied). It was my intention to show how to conduct groups and I felt that I could use his help. He was, I claimed, a good member of the group; he quickly learned what we were trying to establish with these sessions. However, I began to realize that Max succeeded in antagonizing everybody, including me. Max seemed to enjoy his position as a controversial figure. We were beginning to waste time by discussing him too often.

In response to the dream of the airplane, I told a dream of my own: "I was on a road in Germany, passing a farmhouse, and a 'Hitler dog' shot out and threatened me. I thought: 'That dog means business.' I tried to kick him hard and discovered that I was barefoot. I hollered for help but nobody heard me and I woke up." The group named the Hitler dog "Max," who is of German origin. According to the group, Max and I personify two of the "worst German character traits." Max responded to the group's interpretation of my dream by offering a peculiarly tangential interpretation: The "mad dog" existed in reality but was never his dog but the dog of somebody else. Then Max said loudly and clearly that he would not mind being a dictator. The group agreed with him, adding that I too wanted to be a leader—a beloved one, a Christ-like figure. I silently accepted this interpretation as astonishingly accurate.

I interpreted my dream: I am not afraid of Max or his dog—I am afraid of being a brother to Max in spirit—a dictatorial leader at heart.

The last hour of the month was split in two parts: The first half was slow and silent, while the second half was active and interpretive. Most of the time was spent in protest against the director of the hospital, who had dismissed a colleague.

The group included three impatient and rebellious young men who were also the most ambivalent ones. They started a discussion which sounded more like combat between the chief and his younger colleagues. I interpreted the proceedings by saying that the group seemed to be occupied with the question: "How can we be expected to talk freely in a group with men who can fire us?" The question was unanswerable.

There were complaints at the end of the month that we were stuck on the surface of reality. I thought that the reality in which the group existed could not and should not be excluded since we may proceed only from there to deeper levels of communication. I was then accused of not giving an example of how to get underneath the surface. I did not defend myself, but explained how I went further than anybody else—for instance, in telling my dreams. I added that it may be easier for me to behave in this free manner because the reality of the group was not the same as the reality in which I live.

In spite of all the realistic complications, the group felt more closely bound at the end of this month and seemed willing to risk more than before.

Max promptly provoked everybody again to wild outbursts of anger when he haughtily proclaimed: "Nobody can help me here. I do not give a damn." There was not much doubt that he meant what he said. We discussed inviting him out of the group.

I too was angry and worried about the future of the group, especially when the group was about to call the meetings "a waste of time." Somebody noticed my concern and rushed to help me, calling me "fragile." He wanted the group to be more careful in their attacks against me. The group reacted to this as if a long-awaited opportunity had arrived and somebody said: "I know the secret of Grotjahn's fragility! It is as if he says to us: Do not hurt me, I am so fragile, but if you do hurt me you will see that I change from Jesus to Satan to Hitler. Grotjahn's so-called fragility makes me laugh!" I felt that the group began to know me, and hope for the future returned to me. I remained silent about my thoughts.

At the end of the last hour in January, the group's response was summarized with the words: "We all like you better—we all have learned."

February 1969

The month started under a dark cloud: One of the junior doctors reported that his young wife was ill with a malignancy. The group responded with helpless silence.

Somebody else told a dream: "I was playing a violin with a friend in an orchestra. The conductor was my friend's mother." The dreamer interpreted the dream as symbolizing the group, the hospital, and the therapist, of whom he was extraordinarily fond.

Some doubts came up about the group, which I interpreted as resistance, perhaps against intimacy. There is no doubt in my mind that the two senior men were blamed like sacrificial lambs for every ill of the hospital. Everybody felt, to my surprise, that every group member had become a better teammate on the hospital team.

Max interpreted all hostility as defense against intimacy. This provoked the predictable protest, which I joined. There was repeated criticism of the large size of the group, which now numbered fourteen. It was suggested to divide the group into two groups of seven, but then everybody wanted to remain in both groups.

There was a general demand for definition of the group process, a clear announcement about ground rules, and the aims of the meeting. I responded with a brief summary of what I had said previously, for the benefit of the new members: I wanted to develop enough group courage to permit free communication. To work on such honesty is the analytic experience. "If you sit here for two hours expressing yourself freely, you are not quite the same as you were when you came in. You have proceeded an inch on the way to the moon." I used such allegory in order to prohibit further intellectualization.

While I was awaiting opposition to such an unscientific definition, I heard instead acceptance and reluctant recognition.

Max continued his line of arguing that nobody was afraid of hostility, but everyone was afraid of intimacy. He never said this was especially true of him. There was doubt about this, and a discussion followed. Somebody started the group by asking whether there was anybody among us who had ever killed somebody. There was silence and then one of the World War II veterans said quietly: "I have." I wanted to turn to the man who had asked this provocative question, but our time was up and, as usual, everybody left the room in a rush.

At the end of the month, it seemed as if everybody understood what these meetings were about—an exercise in analytic honesty, meaning an honesty that includes the unconscious.

The last meeting of the month was taken up with the analysis of somebody's dream. He was at a beach; the Americans and the Germans were fighting. He was caught between the lines. He grabbed two hand grenades, which would explode in four seconds. He threw them at two Germans (or at Max and me). An American (pointing at the other senior colleague) came to help with a bazooka. "I tried to hide between two trees, and woke up in terror." He told the dream with anxiety and embarrassment. His associations, together with the response of the group, dealt with changes of the personnel of the hospital, and the group did not know how to deal with that. "The Germans" seemed to endanger the entire hospital—one with his power, the other with his group.

The second part of this session was taken up with a complaint by one of the younger men: He had invited the entire group, including the therapist, to a party in his house, and only one of us had come. The discussion turned to the speaker's greedy demands to incorporate the whole group.

March 1969

Most of the time in the beginning of the month was taken up with work on resistance in the form of inhibited communication. Only the last 20 minutes of the first meeting progressed more freely. The question was raised again: Is the group too big? (To which I responded with the question: Whom do you want out?)

I tried to analyze my feelings: I did not feel hostility, nor did I feel a special need for intimacy. I did not feel defensive and felt that we were forming a cohesive group. That satisfied me for the time being.

Somebody wanted to know whether we would continue and everybody agreed to let me make the decision. Somebody felt bored when I tried to get him to help us back into action. I did not get anywhere with my invitation.

Later in the month the resistant talk was repeated, culminating in the question: Would we attend if we would not be paid for our time anyhow? Half of the men said they would come on their own time.

How far do we go? One doctor was quite upset about an analyst in town, whom he repeatedly called "Grotjahn." He was shocked when he was made aware of his slip of the tongue by the group. Only at the end of this hour was free, responsive interaction established. One man concluded the meeting with the words: "I have found relief from tension only in my little sailboat and now here too."

Everybody with some clinical experience agreed that nobody could think of a more difficult group than this one: Fourteen physicians, all psychiatrists, working together in the same hospital, representing the entire hierarchy and structure of the hospital, and using rationalization and intellectualization as effective defenses.

At the end of the month, everybody was present and there was a reliable group cohesion. The majority of the group was annoyed about a minority who never talked but attended, attentively listening. There were critical comments repeated: This is a waste of time, it is boring, or only mildly entertaining at best, and nothing is happening.

Max took the lead by saying: "I am an existential man, I am in charge of my destiny. I live like an analyst, with extended ears and eyes. I may change my entire existence, and may go into politics or business. I have lived long enough to start a second career."

Due to the needs of the hospital and the division of the group into men of power and men in subordinate positions, we remained careful and suspicious. We trusted one another only to a certain degree, and this resistance could not be changed by insight only.

I tried to give a "comparative interpretation" by relating the different men to the structure of the group. In my mind's eye, one of the senior men seemed to repeatedly say: "I am the only one who knows how to run this outfit and I will show you what to do." The other senior member, Max, put himself outside the group in a class by himself, calling himself a "genius." We also had a "mad man" among us who seemed to say: "I am a Christian and you should learn from me." Somebody else seemed to proclaim loudly to all of us: "I am a loser. Let me alone. I don't want to know it."

In this way, I made the rounds of most of the men and described my image of them. The group agreed, corrected, disagreed, and deepened their understanding of one another. The group accused me of not focusing the discussion upon one man or one topic. I explained that I did not want one of us to remain in the center of the discussion or in the "hot seat." I considered such a technique forced, artificial and detrimental to our primary aim of spontaneous interaction.

I was accused of being a narcissistic therapist who always wanted to get the group to turn back to him. I listened to this criticism and tried to find a realistic justification for it. I intended to learn and change my style if the criticism was valid. Only after that did I give a transference interpretation. Somebody had the last word and said: "Fuck the transference!"

April 1969

One of the ward chiefs was called "killer" because he drove his colleagues to exhaustion. He in turn called his colleagues "lazy."

Somebody else talked about his fears and his provocative masochism, which were expressed in his attempts to "bully the bully." Later homosexuality was brought up and was heatedly discussed, but it remained in the abstract.

Again the discussion changed to whether or not it was good or dangerous to be free with one another and then to work together. Everybody agreed—to my surprise—that it made work easier to know about one man's temper and another man's dependency needs. I added that we so far had not seen one single example of abuse. In fact, the group seemed to help form a spirit of cooperation in the hospital team.

We had left the door to the meeting room open and a secretary walked in and gave papers to one of the men to sign. The doctor reached for his pen to sign, whereupon Max got up and in a rage took the papers, ripped them into pieces, and threw them on the floor. He hollered: "You are not signing papers here. You always do things like that!" The three men sitting between the colleague and Max laughed and so did the colleague. Whether this was really how he felt was not clear, but he said that he himself felt like throwing the papers down but did not have the courage to do so. I remarked that I would have slugged Max.

At the end of the month, Max loudly declared: "It does not work—it cannot be done." I took a somewhat modified position: I could see how the group could work, how it could help the hospital team, but I realized that we were far from our goal. The group's reply: "Grotjahn avoids intimacy, which keeps us from going further. We have seen it hundreds of times." However, the group grudgingly admitted: "Grotjahn is doing all right. We all have secrets none of us is willing to talk about." Nevertheless, there were always between twelve and fourteen staff members present.

The group told me that I did everything right, that I did everything wrong, that I destroyed intimacy, that I was afraid of emotions, that I was an outsider, that I betrayed confidence and disappointed people, that I was not a leader, that I was too much in the foreground, and that I should be quieter and interpret more. Then the group decided: "Let us not talk all the time about Grotjahn."

Somebody raised the question of homosexuality again and asked one of the doctors: "Did you ever have a homosexual experience?" The doctor answered in the negative.

I offered a dream. "I was in a state hospital. I was my present age but still a newcomer. Nobody knew me. I felt terribly handicapped because I was on the closed ward and had no key of my own."

The dream was self-evident and somebody asked whether it was really possible that it could "cause me anxiety." I answered that it certainly could. I did not feel "in charge."

Then the revolt was continued: "This damned hospital is run by passive, hostile cowards who have given the hospital a bad name. They hand it over to a bunch of lesbians whom we should sue." Max presented his interpretation: "You defend yourselves against your need for intimacy." Whereupon the revolting men turned against him: "We have no time for that kind of nonsense. We need every minute for fighting." I asked if this is not something the group should discuss in the staff meeting. The group loudly declared that this kind of difficulty belonged here, and the railing against the "matriarchy" continued.

The group was at all times fully represented, with nobody missing. My notes contain the frequent notation: "Good interaction, free and spontaneous communication." Besides the criticism here reported, there was also an occasional expression of appreciation.

There were complaints that the group was still not free enough and my answer was: "Perhaps that is as far as we can go. We certainly can try to develop a team that works well together."

At the end of the month, the most outspoken rebel and Max, the representative of the establishment, were missing. I summarized the situation with the words: "With these two opponents present we were struggling for a free expression of hostility. Without them we are trying to express our friendship for one another.

The group did not consider hostility and intimacy to be a central conflict. The question really was how to trust me and one another.

June 1969

During this last month before the summer vacation, the discussion started on racial integration and the lowering of standards in order to accept minorities for training and for staff jobs. Everybody was emotional and deeply involved.

One of the last hours was very moving. It started with me being five minutes late, which nobody noticed, but somebody asked: "How many more sessions do we have? What do we do after the vacation?" Two new staff members would be eligible. I considered this as a group decision, whereupon everybody got angry and critical of me for not taking proper leadership. I answered that this was not "my group" but the "group's group." By now I was more sure of myself and began to feel quite comfortable with a group of sons I was not going to adopt.

One man, at this point, associated to his dying brother and began to cry. Four other men began to talk about the death of their fathers. My interpretive response was: "I do not intend to die, no matter how ambivalent you are about that. I will return to these meetings in the fall. Then you may try to kill me."

I added that I could not think of anybody who could conduct this group any better than I did. The criticism of the group then changed to a declaration of love, affection, and even trust. Finally it was time to adjourn.

October 1969

The first meeting after the long vacation of three months was like a funeral. Only one of the senior men joined me in my determination to continue. There was no team spirit. "We all come to the hospital to do our duty, get our checks, and go home. That's it."

Then, suddenly, at the end of the session, they all agreed we should meet again and not yet invite four new staff members. Max raised a completely new question: The time the staff members spent in these meetings cost the city $800 to $1,000 each time we met.

In the middle of October, only four men were left and I felt like the captain of the Titanic, who did not leave the ship—the ship left him. Most of the men had left the group and the hospital simultaneously.

I told the new men: "I am disillusioned, almost ready to give up. I have a new project waiting to start."

At the end of the month, the new members were in the majority, but the group developed much faster now than at the beginning of this experiment. The new men took to the group with cautious enthusiasm. It seemed to make them feel easier in their jobs, welcome, and well placed. It was a most peculiar sensation to see this largely new group continue almost exactly where the old group had terminated.

November 1969

The many new people continued the work as if they were all old timers. The criticism against me continued. Somebody called me: "A sneak with a bazooka." One of the men was my sharpest critic, another my best defender. Somebody claimed that he had always thought I was a horrible narcissist but he now thought better of me.

At one point I said to a man who always wanted to love and be loved, and who thought we could forget hostility: "Love less and mean it more." He later claimed that this slogan had changed his life.

The giant of the group (6' 8") considered me too fragile to fight with. He looked for an analyst who could stand up against him. Somebody else told him: "Don't kid yourself. Grotjahn can take care of himself."

I interpreted the behavior of a depressive man, who was very critical and easily bored, by saying: "You want to say, 'I am not good but you are worse.'"

At the end of the month, it was quite clear that the group continued to work better than it ever had—certainly better than these incomplete reports indicate.

The month of December was taken off by general agreement.

January 1970

In the first meeting of the new year a small group tried to get acquainted with one another again. One of the doctors had been delivered of a kidney stone and somebody else became the father of a little boy.

One of the doctors remained impatient in his need for "instant intimacy." At other times the group was called a "ridiculous experiment." One of the doctors was on his way to New York to live with a friend's family, while the friend came to Los Angeles to live with the doctor's family. This was planned because both families wanted to write their wills and wanted to see whether in case of death their families could live together. I reacted with alarm to this announcement and called this arrangement grotesque and bizarre. It turned out that both families had suffered early parental death and wanted to protect their children against possible repetition of such traumatization.

During the last hour of January I gave a comparative interpretation. (What I said will be repeated here only in general terms.) "We are all trying to be good mothers to each other. One of us is the Mother Superior who plays the role of protector. Another one is the perfect screen for everybody's projection and we use him for that. The 'lover boy' wants to love everybody instantly and wants to be loved by everybody. The 'giant' of the group is Cain, who slew his brother and is now afraid of himself as if he were a public menace. We have a parcifal among us who wants to find the grail in psychoanalysis." About one of the doctors I had nothing to say.

I realized that I had addressed myself to each individual of the group, not to the group as such. It was an expression of my experience that group interpretations remained ineffective because everyone has the feeling that the interpretation was not meant for him but for everybody else.

February 1970

At the first meeting in February, the group consisted of ten men. I was discouraged, partly because nobody was on time. The first doctor arrived ten minutes after we should have started. I began the meeting with saying: "I am discouraged and ready to give up. Shall we quit?" Unanimously, the group raised up in protest, with a loud "No!"

One of the men could hardly wait to tell his story: He had been caught in a hold-up. Two juveniles had ripped the handbag from a woman. He, crippled by a broken leg and in a cast, drove after them in his car, leaning against the horn, pinning the boys against a wall. They returned the purse. A dream of glory came true. The group did not really respond. I warned him that he could get away with one such heroic deed but not with the next one. The man himself could not explain his rage and his action. His further associations led to complicated, partly unconscious motivation of this acting out. Afterwards many men told dreams of glory—and of shame.

When I turned away from one man who was near tears the group protested and accused me of being afraid of emotion. Another man confessed that he was very glad when I had once let him alone when he was near tears.

Once more the session threatened to become one of those "hate Grotjahn" affairs—but somebody turned the discussion by talking about his bitter resentment against the hospital. The accusations were directed against the highest ranking staff member of the group, who did not react. I had a hard time following the discussion, since I was not familiar with administrative details.

March 1970

My notes about these meetings began with the words: "Emotional, deeply experienced, and well interpreted by the group." Somebody wanted to quit and everybody turned against him. He then tried to get into an argument with everybody, which I tried to stop since we were here not to argue but to understand. Only then the reason for the dissatisfaction of this doctor became clear.

Somebody's wife had fractured her leg, and another doctor told a horrible story of his wife's operation, during which she almost died, as she had predicted. She appeared to be all right again.

The group turned out to be a good and reliable mother and without doing or saying much, the sad and confused man felt relieved and reassured. It was as if the group had said: "We can give you what you need, but we will not put it into words."

All through the month, the meetings were on deeper emotional levels than ever before. One time, for instance, one of the doctors talked about his suffering when as a boy he had to go to a strictly orthodox school. The sickness and death of his brother gave him the courage to start a new and more meaningful life. Everybody in the group felt for him.

During this month the group had moved to a new room, the empty office of the former director of the hospital. Everybody felt comfortable and quietly triumphant to meet here "after the departure of the father." It helped that Max had left the group quietly and without announcing it.

Everybody knew everybody else by now. I still had the feeling that the group cohesion was not as reliable as in other groups in my experience. Once again I began to feel that this group was difficult to take.

In the second half of March, the interaction deepened and we talked about our inner rage, the lust to murder, and the fear of death.

April 1970

The group turned against itself. Everybody was angry and fought with everybody else—and avoided me. At one time I tried to explain something and was told: "We do not need your commercials any-more."

At the end of the month, I told one of my dreams. I was on a free-way going to the hospital and a wild, free black horse was coming head on. A big truck on my right side had to pass so I turned to the left and the horse was hit in the middle and ripped open by the truck, doubled up, and fell. We stopped and walked back. There were many people and the police. The torn and bleeding horse was carried off to die.

I gave some associations, mostly revealing my preoccupation with this, my most difficult, group; my wish to terminate—which was an-swered with cries of "treason" and "betrayal", etc.; and my hope to master all difficulties here. The wild horse was the group, which I killed. However, the truck that had passed me was also the group.

The group reacted with astounding understanding. There was a quiet double triumph. "The office of the departed director is our meet-ing place and Martin Grotjahn has given up his place as the 'leader' and joined us as a member of the group with his dream. The horse is dead; the group lives."

Simultaneously, the group felt sad, as if after the death of a father. There was much talk about sickness, death, and dying, and everybody felt old.

May 1970

In the first meeting of May, it was decided to close in June, whereupon everybody discussed continuation without me, but no decision was made. The last meeting of the month was called "a truly great meet-ing." I had expected to be the only one present and was glad to see everybody coming in, in spite of the holidays. There was talk about plans for the future, where to meet, whether or not to go into analytic training, or to take the board examinations.

June 1970

The first meeting of the month took an unexpected turn. Somebody said that "pornographic movies" were being shown as part of medical education. We all decided immediately to go and see whether we could learn something new.

A week later the movies were discussed. Somebody arrived late and protested loudly against this kind of "locker room" talk.

I was more explanatory than interpretive: We needed this kind of "locker room" conversation so that we may start to talk freely about sex. Whereupon someone answered: "What do you want to know?" I gave him some loaded questions and it was as if a silent bomb had exploded. Then somebody else made a beginning and talked about his love affair, which had lasted for two years now. Somebody else confessed several one-night stands, and almost everybody had a similar experience, or at least fantasies.

Saying goodbye before vacation brought the group closer together than ever. Much affection was shown to everybody who departed from the hospital, but also to the ones who stayed, including me. Somebody called me a man who loved and was kind to his own family and his group-family.

September 1970

The group assembled again after a two-month vacation and besides me there were seven members of the staff. The intention was to continue where we had left off. There was some trouble with the administration's claim that "the group is not in the interest of the hospital—only in the interest of the individual doctor." Eight new doctors had joined the staff and were eligible. It was decided to wait with invitations. Nobody cherished the idea of accepting too many new people and starting all over again forming the group.

At the end of the month, the group had grown to ten members. One of the new men loudly proclaimed that he did not come here in order to be bored; he clashed immediately with everybody. After that, the new members were quickly integrated into the group. Everybody was loudly interacting, and I retreated to my observation point.

October 1970

Soon the group turned to the only black doctor, who had talked about his bitter life in the South. The turning point in his life was reached when he was in uniform. He spoke about his rage and finally the triumph to being admitted to medical school and being here now. The attention given to the black man made me wonder whether a new road-block was in the making, but I said nothing.

It turned out that two of the new staff members were experienced group therapists and they helped immediately with the group process. For instance, when people criticized me again, one of the new men said: "It is always fun to analyze Martin Grotjahn, but it is a waste of time." The group then talked about hidden hostility and competition in the hospital and here in the group. I asked whether it would be in the interest of the group if I were not always present. The group un-animously decided: "No, but don't always push yourself in front."

Somebody dreamed that the group was conducted by his former analyst: A bathtub was brought in and it was explained to him that to take a bath was a way to get started.

I interpreted the resistance symbolized in this dream: Taking a bath and cleaning up what one wants to say before one says it. In this case, the cleaning seemed to relate to something concerning the former an-alyst. It turned out that three other members of the group were, or had been, in analysis with the same training analyst. Under these con-ditions the group could not be used to resolve any residuals of the first speaker's transference neurosis.

November 1970

Due to rain I was 30 minutes late. Everybody else was there and a friend of mine, who had joined the group recently, conducted the ses-sion from my chair—which I did not claim for this session. There was heated discussion between one white and one black doctor, and it seemed to me as if one of the doctors represented the silent majority in confrontation with the black minority.

At some point the friend of mine got into a hassle with a young man, who finally told him: "You do not deserve to be a friend of Martin's." My friend reacted by becoming deadly pale: He felt like throwing up, got up from his chair to leave, but sat down again. The group con-cluded that my friend's strong reaction was a defense against confessing feelings of intimacy. This impressed me as a typical patterned response of a group of intellectualizing therapists. The man did not need any defenses against love or tenderness—but he was deadly afraid that he might be found to be not good enough as a friend.

December 1970

The same man, who shall be called "Mark," was startled by a dream: After some happy days visiting his father, Mark dreamed that he was in jail. He could not explain this dream. Somebody else followed by telling his own dream: He was visiting his old university and was seeking friends there. It seemed to the group that Mark was trying to deal with his fear of being an unworthy friend and son; something similar was expressed in the dream of the second dreamer.

During this month I had a knee injury, which gave everybody a chance to talk about my knee first and about their own sicknesses and fears of sickness later. Somebody had discovered his diabetes recently, and had tried to keep it as a secret so far. Now he talked about it. Two more doctors talked about their own diabetes. It was as if the group wanted to reassure me: "We did not wish the injury on you—and you are not the only invalid here."

One of the doctors had a Mongoloid son, and said: "That is a real tragedy." The mood of the group became depressed, the talk slowed down, and we all started the collective Christmas depression.

January 1971

I felt out of contact with the group and felt that "nobody invited me in." Mark tried to get things started and so did others, but not much happened.

The meetings were now always from 8:30 to 10:00 AM, and we were as a rule ten men. I missed two sessions because of my knee injury, and Mark had taken over. He told me that at first there was a long period of small talk, then everybody was loud in their praise of the absent Grotjahn. Mark confessed that these meetings were becoming important to him and he lashed out at somebody who did not participate enough.

February 1971

Some time was taken to discuss my knee and then sick fathers in general. I did not feel like a father but much more like a brother to the group. I was criticized for "sidestepping the transference—talking about it, not interpreting it."

At the end of the month, the acting director announced his resignation from the hospital and the group immediately attacked him because of his passivity, his inadequacy, and his inability to lead or to deserve trust. I interpreted the hostility as our reaction to the desertion by the father. I also made some remarks that this kind of criticism could only help him in his new job. I was viciously accused of avoiding hostility and of lacking courage.

March 1971

Like after the departure of the arrogant and dictatorial Max a year before, so again after the departure of another father figure, the group settled down in the peaceful and quiet atmosphere of the surviving brothers. I learned that good friendships between some of the men had developed.

I interpreted the remarks of somebody in analysis: "You try to announce to all of us that you are not dangerous, but a coward, like all of us." This prompted two other people to talk about their analysts more openly and directly than before. After that a number of people made highly critical remarks about their analysts.

April 1971

There was a depressing atmosphere spreading over the group. Mark was angry and depressed, and everybody turned against him and his irritation. Questions were asked: "Is M.G. quitting the group?" Mark answered: "Grotjahn is right. He is getting old and should retire. It's high time." I must have said that when we go into the summer vacation we will close the group.

The entire group was upset, and said: "You quit us just after we got started. You wanted to show that it could be done, that you could make a group like this work. Now the group works, your job is done, and you leave us." Mark, my friend, seemed ready to bury me in a collective "group-grave."

The next meeting was short and deeply felt. Mark reported his rage, breaking several bones of his right hand. I wondered whether his "rage" was actual guilt about his readiness to bury me.

At this time we were locked out of our meeting room, which I took as a sign of disrespect by the hospital. I was angry and hurt, all out of proportion. It must have been my grief over the threat to the life of "my" group-family.

All through the month, sadness and anger were in the foreground, but we always were a full group of ten.

Then there came a period of mourning. At times the group asked: "Did M.G. do it right, or did he do it wrong?" There was an outspoken ambivalence, which was all much easier for me to take since Mark now had started, unofficially, to function as my co-therapist. Mark repeated: "M.G. is an old man, and he should retire." I felt as if he could hardly wait.

The last hour of the month was spent in mourning and grief about the end of the group. There was an astonishingly free, emotional discussion: Now everything could be said.

Somebody brought a dream: "I was screwing a pretty girl. I was much aroused while penetrating her. M.G. was standing by, cheering." Our interpretation: The end of the group gives you a chance to do a "penetrating job" in the hospital, the institute, and in the planned board examination. I intentionally avoided giving an obvious and quite different interpretation.

Everybody came out with fantasies about having affairs. After the death of the group-family, everybody went out for himself and looked for love on the outside, no longer here in the group-family.

At almost the last minute I turned to a timid, shy, mostly silent colleague and asked him: "Where have you been? Why are you always quiet?" He responded with a confession: He too had been having a happy love affair for the last two years. There was great surprise and laughter in the group. Somebody turned to me and said: "What about your divine intuition? Even you did not suspect that." My response was: "I have my doubts whether we are told the truth." I felt immediately sorry for having said that, whereupon the colleague topped his remarks with a new surprise: "You are right, I was joking." There was more laughter—why, I don't know. If this had not been so close to the group's final session, this "joke" on us would probably not have occurred, otherwise I would have protested seriously about it. The group process is nothing to joke about, as far as I am concerned.

May 1971

A small but well-functioning group continued. Mark reported on his visit to his father, somebody else on the pregnancy of his wife. The talk vacillated between birth and death, inside and outside of the group.

Mark's presence activated the anger of the group: "He does not come to the group; he comes to Grotjahn."

June 1971

The last sessions were spent trying to deal with the loss of the family. Mark said to me, with his usual ambivalence: "You can turn things on and off without much emotion." The group decided not to continue with anybody else. Everybody realized that it was easier to deal with an outsider, like me, as a therapist, than with any insider, like Mark or Max. It was feared that the group would end up in frightening fights with either of them.

I talked briefly about things I had learned here in the group. It was for me another lesson in learning to express myself freely and spontaneously, and regardless of fears about intimacy or hostility. The group experience was another step in my lifelong self-analysis, an experience of hard work on my inner self. This must have been clear to everybody and may have helped to create the group atmosphere.

I explained that if I were invited to conduct a group with staff members again, I would be more selective and not accept the entire hierarchy of the hospital structure. In other words, I would not have invited the two acting directors; they were too inhibiting to the free development of the group process.

One of the members complained that the group was dissolving at the same time his wife had left him. He felt sick, defeated, and depressed. I invited him to talk with me individually after the termination of the group. I felt he should not be without support.

Then we said goodbye.

Part VI:
Special Issues

19

An Example of Clinical Group Research: Insight Patients Assigned to Group Compared with Those Assigned to Individual Therapy

Frank M. Kline, M.D., Martin Grotjahn, M.D., Joe Yamamoto, M.D.,
Fred Staples, Ph.D., George Wolkon, Ph.D. and Rodney Burgoyne, M.D.

This is not presented as a definitive study of group psychotherapy, but rather as an example of the type of clinical study that can and should be carried out by group therapists.

Case reports, opinions, literature surveys, and theory are helpful but we need a higher percentage of nose count research. The results of such research always contain a few surprises—surprises that more than 20 years of clinical experience do not reveal or suggest.

The overly precise and even precisely precise statistician will be critical of this study, but it was useful to me and to the clinic. It helped me to feel more confident about the value of group therapy and suggested that there may be better ways to select patients for group than just the clinician's opinion. It laid to rest my concern that group patients prematurely drop out of therapy more frequently than do patients in individual therapy. It helped the clinic ask why group was under-utilized and to begin to correct a situation that wasted our resources.

Finally, our modest results may help others in their practice or research. Other work may suggest our results are relevant or only a fluke. Either way there will be more research, more data, and eventually statistically convincing results. Mostly we hope group therapists will be a little more convinced of the value of their work and note what seems to us to be an overemphasis on individual therapy.

Any therapist, in his work with groups, is painfully aware of many unanswered questions. Any teacher of group therapy is even more aware of these problems, since unanswered questions make a systematic approach to teaching exceedingly difficult.

The situation is further complicated by the practically unlimited variety of clinical material with which the therapist and teacher must deal in a large metropolitan medical center. In private practice, a certain selective process helps the therapist develop highly specialized forms of treatment for the groups of patients that he selects, or, based on his reputation and predilections, that the community selects for him. In the big institutions, little selection occurs and every admitted patient widens the challenge of therapeutic need and the variations of technique.

With these problems in mind, we tried to investigate the following basic questions: In our clinic, which patients are referred to group therapy? Is it possible to more carefully select patients for individual and/or group therapy? Are there rational reasons for patient selection? Is group or individual therapy more effective? Are the drop-out rates for group and individual patients different? Which therapeutic mode is more successful at keeping patients in treatment? Which treatment is the more economical in terms of cost to the patient and to the health care system?

In an effort to gain information to help find rational answers to these questions and provide a basis for further research, we followed 354 consecutive patients from their initial contact with the Adult Psychiatric Outpatient Clinic at the Los Angeles County/University of Southern California Medical Center until they unilaterally stopped coming, were discharged by the treating physician, or had been in treatment for nine months.

METHOD

A total of 354 consecutive patients who came to the clinic were asked to complete a Minnesota Multiphasic Personality Inventory (MMPI), a Fundamental Interpersonal Orientation Inventory (FIRO),[1] and a form to assess what the patients specifically hoped to accomplish at the clinic (WHY-1) (Fig. 19-1). This last form was based on Lazare's[2]

REASONS	THIS REASON IS:			
	VERY IMPORTANT	IMPORTANT	SLIGHTLY IMPORTANT	NOT IMPORTANT
1. To get help to put things into perspective—to clarify things.	□	□	□	□
2. To get someone to help me with my problems with the law, social service agencies, school, or other agency.	□	□	□	□
3. To get help in controlling my feelings, and/or what I wish to do.	□	□	□	□
4. To have a place where I can discuss things of which I feel ashamed and guilty and can tell no one else.	□	□	□	□
5. To help me know whether or not I am having a nervous breakdown.	□	□	□	□
6. To gain some understanding and some care from someone.	□	□	□	□
7. To have a place where I can get it all off my chest.	□	□	□	□
8. To find a place I can count on for help.	□	□	□	□
9. To get advice on what I should do.	□	□	□	□
10. To understand better my motives and thinking patterns—why I think and feel as I do.	□	□	□	□
11. To get medication, tranquilizers, or nerve pills.	□	□	□	□
12. To get someone to help me with a particular person (wife, husband, boss, friend, parent, etc.).	□	□	□	□
13. To find out where I can get the help I need—if you can't provide it, you can direct me.	□	□	□	□
14. I came because someone sent me.	□	□	□	□
15. I came for some other reason. (Please state why.)	□	□	□	□

OF ALL THOSE REASONS YOU MARKED AS "VERY IMPORTANT," CIRCLE THE ONE REASON THAT IS THE MOST IMPORTANT.

Fig. 19-1. WHY-1.

14 categories of patient requests. It began with the question, "Why did you come to the clinic?" Each category was slightly reformulated to facilitate understanding by our specific patient population. The patients were asked to check how important each reason was in their decision to come to the clinic. Answers were given on a four-point scale. All these forms were completed by the patient prior to his initial interview with the resident therapist.

At the end of the initial interview, the resident physician also filled out a form, which was identical to the patient's questionnaire except it was headed "Why did this patient come to the clinic?" (WHY-2), and a Client Episode Outcome Summary (CEOS). The CEOS is a list of 30 defined problem psychiatric areas adapted from Spitzer,[3] in which the rater indicates the absence or presence of each psychiatric problem area.

At the end of the initial interview, the resident physician decided on a disposition. The patient could be discharged or referred to other agencies, to insight groups, to large supportive medication groups, or to individual psychotherapy. Later, after the patient had been discharged from the clinic, had unilaterally discontinued treatment, or had completed nine months of therapy, each therapist ranked the patient's improvement on a five-point scale. A rating of 1 indicated that the patient was markedly improved, 5 that he was worse, 2 that he was moderately improved, 3 that he was slightly improved, and 4 that there was no change.

RESULTS

After the initial interview, 14% of the 354 patients were referred to insight groups, 42% were referred to individual therapy, 32% were seen only for evaluation, and 12% were referred to large supportive medi-

Table 19-1.

	#	%
Evaluation only	115	32
Insight group therapy	49	14
Large supportive medication group	42	12
Individual psychotherapy	148	42
Total	354	100

Table 19-2. Mode of Termination (N.S.)

	Individual	Group
Mutual agreement	50	53
Patient initiated without doctor's agreement	50	47

cation groups (Table 19-1). This study compares only the patients that were referred to insight groups and to individual psychotherapy. Other patients, those seen only for evaluation and those referred to large supportive medication groups, were considered by definition unsuitable for insight therapy.

The data were examined to see if patients referred to group therapy were significantly different from those referred to individual therapy. The MMPI's of patients referred to group had significantly lower L scores (49 versus 46), lower hypochondriasis (68 versus 61), and lower hysteria (71 versus 60). They had significantly higher ego strength (46 versus 40) and higher dominance (52 versus 45). The therapists, after the initial interview, ranked the patients referred to group as having less interest in obtaining specific advice. Otherwise there were no significant differences between group and individual patients' stated reasons for coming to the clinic (WHY), FIRO, CEOS, or the demographic data.

These data suggest that patients assigned to group may be slightly healthier and more socially adept than those assigned to individual therapy. However, since only 6 of 89 comparisons reached statistical significance at the 0.05 level and 5 in 100 would be expected by chance alone, it seems reasonable to interpret these differences as suggestive.

There were no differences in the drop-out rate between group and individual patients (Table 19-2). Thus, in our clinic at the time the study was done, patients were no more apt to unilaterally discontinue group therapy than to unilaterally discontinue individual therapy. This was our second most significant finding.

When we compared the number of visits and the length of treatment, we found that group patients came for significantly more visits and for a longer period of time than did individual patients (Table 19-3).

Table 19-3. Length of Attendance

Number of Visits	Individual	Group
2-6	40%	25%
7-20	37%	35%
25+	24%	43%

Table 19-4. Improvement as Rated by the Therapist (N.S.)

	Individual	Group
	2.74	2.71

Outcome, as ranked by the therapist, yielded no significant differences in improvement between group and individual therapy (Table 19-4). However, improvement in both types was modest, since 2.7 indicates something between modestly and moderately improved.

When the pretreatment patient data were compared to outcome, we found there were significant differences ($p < 0.05$) between the patients who were actually helped by group and those who were referred to group. Group therapy was generally more helpful with patients who stated before their individual evaluation (on the WHY-1) that they wanted a place they could count on for help, a place to get things off their chest, and a place to learn to control their feelings. Patients did not do as well in group if they said they wanted to put things in perspective and if the doctor indicated on the CEOS that they had somatic concerns and grandiosity.

Individual therapy patients were more likely to improve if, at the end of the initial evaluation, the therapist thought the patient had a strong desire to understand his motives (insight). A patient did not improve as much if, prior to the initial interview, the patient indicated that he wanted medication and help in learning how to deal with public agencies. He also did not do as well in individual therapy if he was trying to find additional sources of economic support. It was also noted that patients with obvious disorientation and grandiosity (on the CEOS) did not do as well in individual therapy.

Finally, we examined cost efficiency, by assuming that individual therapy cost twice as much per session per patient as group therapy. This gives the economic edge to individual therapy, since group probably cost only one-fourth as much per session as individual. Nonetheless, based on the first assumption, an equal degree of improvement costs only 60% as much in group as it would in individual therapy (Table 19-5).

Table 19-5. Relative Cost of Therapy

	Individual	Group
	$7,900	$4,768

DISCUSSION

There has been considerable discussion and some experimental work designed to ferret out the patients most suitable for group therapy.[4,5] In spite of prior work, however, there is as yet no consensus as to which patients should be referred to group therapy. It could be claimed that in a public clinic like ours, an attempt should be made to include almost every patient in group therapy. It would then be up to observational research to decide who from such "holding groups" would ultimately be referred to insight group therapy and who would go to individual insight therapy. Probably the wisest course would be to refer to individual therapy only those who are obviously unfit for group, those with a marked preference for individual therapy, or those with a vigorous objection to group. "Private" patients should also have the economic benefit of group therapy.

The data suggest that in our clinic, the patients our residents referred to group therapy were somewhat more adept and forceful in social situations that those referred to individual therapy. Five scales on the MMPI seemed to best predict who the residents would refer to group.

However, of the patients who are referred to group therapy, those who will improve are best predicted by their own stated reasons for coming to the clinic and by the absence of grandiosity and somatic concerns as judged by the physician. These patients want a reliable social setting where they can express themselves; they are not necessarily looking for insight. This suggests that our current referral criteria are not entirely reasonable. Perhaps a short questionnaire filled out by patients, combined with the physicians' estimate of grandiosity and somatic concerns, may be a more reliable guide to treatment than the clinicians' judgment. It certainly seems to be worth further investigation.

The drop-out rate for group patients is no higher than it is for individual patients and is smaller than clinical experience led us to expect. We would have doubted these results if Hart[6] in 1967 had not obtained the same results. It does not seem necessary to put patients in individual therapy in order to keep them from dropping out of treatment. In addition, group patients clearly come to more sessions for a longer period of time than do individual patients. For advocates of group treatment, this finding is most important and most encouraging, since one reason mental health professionals may hesitate to put patients in group is their concern that the patients will drop group treatment sooner than they would individual therapy.

The problem of evaluating therapeutic efficacy remains unsolved. Even though this has been explored and thoroughly discussed, there are no definitive answers (see Eysenck,[7] Frank,[8] Strupp,[9] Sloane,[10] Hardy,[11] and Glass[12]). We are aware that the therapists' estimation of improvement is open to question. However, it is, we think, reasonable and reliable in our study. There is additional evidence of group therapy's effectiveness provided by Luborsky.[13] Other additional evidence suggests group may be as effective[14] or even more effective than individual psychotherapy.[15]

It can also be argued that group therapy is not as effective as individual therapy because patients are seen in group for a longer period of time, with only equal improvement. Stone et al.[16] and Luborsky[17] noted that improvement correlates with length of treatment.

SUMMARY

In a large sample of psychiatric patients evaluated and treated in a teaching clinic, group therapy seems to be as effective as individual treatment. The patients were not randomly assigned to treatment. Treatment decisions were made by the physician who evaluated them. However, our pretreatment data indicate only minor differences between the patients assigned to group and those assigned to individual therapy. We think it is reasonable to conclude that the patient samples were comparable. Patients who are referred to group after the initial evaluation will stay in treatment for a longer period of time than those referred to individual therapy, and they show at least equal improvement. If these findings are confirmed in further clinical or experimental investigation, then the conclusion is justified that group therapy is under-utilized in our clinic, since only 14% of patients are assigned to groups and 42% are assigned to individual psychotherapy.

It seems possible to identify patients who will profit more from group than from individual therapy.

Finally, group seems to provide equal improvement with less therapist time and at less cost, even though the duration of treatment is longer.

REFERENCES

1. Schutz, W. C. *FIRO: A Three-dimensional Theory of Interpersonal Behavior.* New York: Holt, Rinehart & Winston (1958).
2. Lazare, a., Eisenthal, S., Wasserman, L., and Hartford, T. C. Patient requests in a walk-in clinic. *Comp. Psychiatry* **16**:467-477 (1975).
3. Spitzer, R. L., Endicott, J., Fleiss, J. L., and Cohen, J. The psychiatric status schedule. *Arch. Gen. Psychiatry* **23**:41-55 (1970).
4. Yalom, I. D., Houts, P. S., Zimerberg, S. M., and Rand, K. H. Prediction of improvement in group therapy. *Arch. Gen. Psychiatry* **17**:159-168 (1967).
5. Grunebaum, H. and Kates, W. Whom to refer for group psychotherapy. *Am. J. Psychiatry* **134**:130-133 (1977).
6. Hart, W. T. and Bassett, L. Measuring consumer satisfaction in a mental health center. *Hosp. Community Psychiatry* **26**:512-515 (1975).
7. Eysenck, H. The effects of psychotherapy: an evaluation. *J. Consult. Psychol.* **16**:319-324 (1952).
8. Frank, J., Gliedman, L., Imber, S., Stone, A., and Nash, E. Patients' expectancies and relearning as factors determining improvement in psychotherapy. *Am. J. Psychiatry* **115**:961-968 (1959).
9. Strupp, H. Psychotherapy. *Ann. Rev. Psychol.* **13**:445-478 (1962).
10. Sloane, R. B., Staples, F., Cristol, A., Yorkston, N., and Whipple, K. *Psychotherapy versus Behavior Therapy.* Cambridge, Mass.: Harvard University Press (1975).
11. Hardy, M. and Horwitz, L. Therapeutic outcome as rated by patients, therapists, and judges. *Arch. Gen. Psychiatry* **33**:957-961 (1976).
12. Glass, G. Primary, secondary and meta-analysis of research. Presented at the 7th Annual Meeting of the Society for Psychotherapy Research. San Diego, Calif. (1976).
13. Luborsky, L., Singer, B., and Luborsky, L. Comparative studies of psychotherapies. *Arch. Gen. Psychiatry* **32**:995-1008 (1975).
14. Herz, M. I., Spitzer, R. L., Gibbon, M., Greenspan, K., and Reibel, S. Individual versus group aftercare treatment. *Am. J. Psychiatry* **131**:808-812 (1974).
15. Prince, R. M., Ackerman, R. E., Carter, N. C., and Hamison, A. Group aftercare — impact on a statewide program. *Dis. Nerv. Syst.* **38**:793-796 (1977).
16. Stone, A., Parloff, M., and Frank, J. The use of "diagnostic" groups in a group therapy program. *Int. J. Group Psychother.* **4**:274-284 (1954).
17. Luborsky, L., Chandler, M., Auerbach, A. H., Cohen, J., and Backrach, M. Factors influencing the outcome of psychotherapy: a review of quantitative research. *Psychol. Bull.* **74**:145-185 (1971).

20
Group Psychotherapy in China

Zhong-Yi Liu, M.D.

FOREWORD

To carry out a revolution a leader must be able to instill and maintain hope. Hope is crucial to all successful revolutions. It is also hope that keeps patients in therapy long enough for curative factors to take hold. Indeed, the psychotherapeutic process ultimately demands an inner revolution.

Mao instilled faith and hope on a political and psychotherapeutic level and brought to life one of the major revolutions in the history of civilization. Whatever faults or failures Mao may be criticized for, his utilization of group process and its institutionalization into Chinese culture will leave its mark—even if it is eventually altered or destroyed.

Early in Mao's political development, he evolved a form of group process that made the revolution possible. Historians describe the "turning point" as Mao's belief that the Chinese revolution must come from the peasants and the countryside. From the beginning of his work with the peasants, he used intuitive understanding and group psychotherapeutic process to produce an effective revolution.

Bernard Teitel, M.D.

GROUPS IN CHINA

As I read the books on psychiatry in the library at the Veterans Administration Medical Center in Long Beach, California, I was surprised to see so many books and journals on group psychotherapy. When I was editor of the psychiatry section of the *Journal of Foreign Medicine*, a nationwide quarterly in China, I never accepted any articles on group psychotherapy. To the best of my memory, not a single article on this topic was published in the journal since its beginning in 1974.

Why do Chinese psychiatrists pay so little attention to group psychotherapy while American psychiatrists devote so much time to it?

After living, observing, and working in this country for three months, I received an answer. Rosenbaum and Berger[1] say: "Philosophic tradition in the United States stresses the ethic of individual responsibility, with, historically, little emphasis on the group and its relationship to the individual. Nevertheless, the country is in fact group oriented. . . . Today the student of human behavior, however deeply concerned with the individual, must also be concerned with the individual within the group." What the authors advise is especially important in America; thus people are gradually paying more attention to group psychotherapy. Paradoxically in China, everyone is *first* a member of a group, and *second* an individual. Chinese people have been organized into groups since the foundation of the People's Republic, whether they behave normally or not. It seems that psychiatrists in China do not have to pay attention to group process, since the group process is part of everyday life.

How the group process works in China is an interesting question and requires more consideration. But before examining the group process as it exists in China, I would like to give a brief introduction to China's basic social structure.

Except for those in the Army, all the people of China fall into one or more of the following three units.

Those who work or study in a unit, such as a factory, a school, or an administrative organization. They are grouped with 15 to 20 colleagues. My hospital, for example, is a teaching hospital of a medical college. In psychiatry, there are 25 doctors, 30 nurses, 7 orderlies, and a few technicians. The psychiatrists and technicians are divided into smaller groups, as are the nurses and orderlies. In other words, those working together are grouped according to whether they work in a ward or an outpatient clinic. Group activity takes place twice a week. Usually it occupies two afternoons and is called political study. Once a month the group meets for trade union activity. Actually, political study is group process and not necessarily related to politics. It might more precisely be called public affairs, and includes political study, academic activity, or anything that requires everyone's attention. It often involves discussion of the personal problems of one or more members.

Peasants, who are grouped into production teams of approximately 15 to 20 families. The adults, including housewives and the aged capable of walking, meet one evening a week for political study, cultural activities, and discussion of personal problems such as aging, children, and marriage.

Those without a definite professional identification and who live in cities, such as retired people, young people waiting for a job, and housewives. These people are organized into Neighborhood Committees around common interests and capacities.

Of course, all students from kindergarten to college are organized into groups. Not everyone belongs to a unit, but everyone belongs to a group. The relationship between an individual and his group does not change until his job changes or, for the jobless, his residence changes. Some people belong to the same group for life. People usually get to know one another very well, since they work and live together.

In the group meeting, people will follow the authorities' suggestion to study political documents and important articles in the party newspapers. Sometimes, however, people chat just to pass time since they must remain until the scheduled time is over. It is interesting that what people chat about is usually personal and concerned with their everyday life. This affords an opportunity for people to exchange ideas and opinions about family problems, or share their common pleasures, disappointments, or resentments about current events.

Thus, Chinese people become used to group activities, as they are exposed to them from early childhood. When people with current or potential psychiatric problems are taken into a group for treatment or prevention, few show any resistance. They expect to be in a group, are used to it, and have a positive attitude toward groups. They expect to, and will, receive emotional support from their group.

GROUP THERAPY ON A PSYCHIATRIC WARD

Most psychiatric inpatients are schizophrenics. In local mental hospitals, they make up about 90% of all patients. In teaching hospitals, they constitute 60% of all patients. Group therapy mainly involves schizophrenics. As soon as the patient is cooperative, he will be taken to a group where the ward staff teaches him how to take care of himself and how to deal with mental illnesses. The staff will explain how to take medicines, and discuss the possible side effects and how to manage these. In the group, patients are encouraged to tell their life histories and to talk about their illnesses and their reactions to past and current treatment. A convalescent patient usually is better behaved and more cooperative in the group than when he is alone. Sometimes if a patient refuses treatment, whether medicines or electroconvulsive therapy, he may accept it after attending a group, where the other patients explain the benefits they gained from treatment.

After the psychotic symptoms of delusions, hallucinations, and ideas of reference disappear, patients are encouraged to write a reminiscence of their illness and, if appropriate, talk about it with the group. In this way, the patient's positive accomplishments are reinforced.

In the late 1960s, during the Cultural Revolution, Mao Zedong's Thought was supposed to be universally effective in dealing with the ideological problems of the normal and the mentally ill. Mental illness was seen as nothing but an ideological conflict between the bourgeois and the proletarian world outlooks. In most mental hospitals, all sorts of therapy, from psychotropic medicines to electroconvulsive therapy and insulin shock treatment, were denounced and forbidden. Patients were organized into groups and spent the day studying Mao's works. Some patients were encouraged to do self-criticism to enhance the "proletarian world outlook" and weaken or eliminate the "bourgeois world outlook." This was supposed to purify the mind. The wards were decorated with a variety of revolutionary slogans and with Mao's portraits and quotations. It was thought that this would help the patients become mentally revolutionized, purified, and cured. This period afforded a rare opportunity to carry on a strong, serious, and rather pure group psychotherapy. My feeling is that in this period most patients who were well enough to think reasonably behaved more cooperatively, were more concerned with, and more actively helped others, and were willing to criticize anyone who behaved badly. Patients, like everyone else, were encouraged to recite Mao's *Three Articles:* "Serve the People," "In Memory of Norman Bethune," and "The Old Fool Moves a Mountain." Most patients would identify themselves with Zhang Side's, Norman Bethune's, and the Old Fool's desire to take care of others and "be utterly devoted to others without any thought of self."[2] To some extent, though temporarily, this group process was helpful to those inpatients who were well enough to benefit from the group process. In the long run, however, it could not take the place of physical treatment for most patients, nor could it disprove the belief that mental illness was something more profound than a conflict between proletarian and bourgeois world outlooks. This period could be seen as a Chinese version of the worldwide 1960s antipsychiatry movement. During this time, there was turmoil due to anarchy in Chinese society. On the psychiatric wards, there was also turmoil due to patients that could not be treated by modern means but who were too ill to benefit from Mao's teachings. Since Mao's death and the downfall of the "Gang of Four," no one stresses ideological conflicts as the cause of mental illness anymore. Group psychotherapy remains as an adjunct measure for inpatients and is most useful when used with other modern treatment.

GROUP THERAPY FOR OUTPATIENTS

In China, there are not enough hospital beds to meet the needs of society. A large number of patients live in the community and are treated in various ways as outpatients. There are two ways for a patient to see a psychiatrist. One is for the patient, alone, or, more often, escorted by his family, to come to an outpatient clinic or hospital. The other is when the Prevention and Treatment Network (PTN) arranges for a medical worker, psychiatric nurse, or general practitioner to see the patient regularly. In both cases, group psychotherapy is used.

In the outpatient clinic, patients are usually assigned to groups by diagnosis. Most groups are for chronic schizophrenics and psychoneurotics. The incidence of depressive disorders, hysteria, and obsessive-compulsive neurosis is too low to provide separate groups for these diagnoses.

In the group for schizophrenics, the medical worker encourages the patients to talk about themselves, how they get ill, and how they feel about their psychiatrist, their medicines, and their group.

In recent years, a broad network of prevention and treatment for mental illnesses was established in many cities. Shanghai was first and became the pacesetter for all the other cities. It deserves further detailed description.[3] The PTN in Shanghai organized people who worked in health, civil affairs, and public security into groups for the prevention and treatment of mental disorders. These groups drew up a grassroots overall program for collaboration between medical workers, the units where the patients worked, their families, and other social agencies. In Shanghai, up to ten thousand people have some sort of mental disorder. Not all of them want to be hospitalized, nor is this always necessary. But since there are more patients than beds, there is still the problem of providing treatment for them. Shanghai adopted several programs to suit local social conditions and medical facilities.

First are treatment groups sponsored by neighborhood organizations (grassroot units in urban areas). A patient who has been stabilized and discharged from the hospital is admitted to one of these groups. The patients do manual labor within their capabilities and receive some remuneration. The group sees that the patients take the medicines prescribed and receive psychiatric treatment and ideological education. The patients in these groups may read books and journals, sometimes see movies or watch television, occasionally go on an outing, or attend their own sports meets. Today there are 105 such groups in the city. They take care of about 2,300 patients.

Secondly, there is a nursing network. A nursing group is composed of the patient's family members and neighbors, plus some retired workers living in the vicinity. This network sees to it that the patients take their medicines, observes the patients, and make timely reports to the medical workers concerned. They help by giving the patients advice, information, and education. They solve the social and psychological problems that may contribute to mental disorders. There are more than 350 such nursing groups in the city, taking care of over 5,000 patients. More than 10,000 people work to provide this care and do so without remuneration.

In case of emergency, a patient can go to the neighborhood hospital for treatment. Medical personnel there also visit patients at home, give patients advice on how to take care of themselves, and provide necessary medical treatment. They also give advice to the nursing network and help educate the masses.

In the countryside, the network is not yet developed, but there is a model. Barefoot doctors play an important role in mental health. "Barefoot doctor" is a pet name given to peasant—doctors in China.[4] This comes from the peasants in South China, who farm paddy-fields in their bare feet. At first, barefoot doctors received only brief medical training before working as part-time doctors and part-time peasants.

Now they have developed into the main force for prevention and cure in rural areas. They are still essentially ordinary peasants, but are deeply appreciated by the people. They are paramedics who dispense prompt and inexpensive medical treatment. Each rural commune has set up a health center to train health workers recruited from the peasants. After training, they serve the production brigades. After three months of study, the trainee returns to his brigade with a small medical kit to treat minor illnesses of fellow peasants.

Since barefoot doctors usually were born and grew up with their brigades, they know the people and the natural conditions very well. They may have many uncles, aunts, grand uncles, grand aunts, nephews, nieces, or even grandchildren. There are usually one or two barefoot doctors for a brigade of 500 to 1,000 (100 to 200 families). No acute group of mental patients, however, could be found in a brigade. It is important to point out that the barefoot doctor works only with chronic or convalescent mental patients who can be helped at this level. This program prevents further social withdrawal and isolation. People are educated by the barefoot doctors to take the mentally ill to group activities whenever possible. This group activity is even more important to the patients in the countryside than in town. Peasants work more and are busier than people in town. They get up early in the morning and work near home until they breakfast late in the morning. Then they take a packed lunch, return to work, and only return home late in the evening. As the mental patients do not work, and are supervised by a few older comrades, they have less social contact than patients in town. Thus, group activity affords a cherished opportunity for human contacts. This is very important for mental health.

GROUP THERAPY IN THE PREVENTION OF MENTAL ILLNESSES

As mentioned before, all the Chinese people have been organized into groups. Everyone attends a group activity at least once a week. These activities are usually called "political study," though the implication is broader and not limited to political study but will include items of general public interest. This is especially true of trade union meetings, where the once-a-week meeting may serve as a form of psychological consultation. Personal troubles may be presented and help or consultation requested. For example, if a member or his family has an accident that results in expense beyond his income, or if interpersonal relationships between family members or with others concern a worker, he may discuss this at the trade union meeting. Such things are commonly explored and usually the members help with good suggestions on how to cope with the issue within the current social values and within the standards and policy of the government. Sometimes, if substantial measures are required, the group leader makes a suggestion to authorities on behalf of the group. For example, the financial troubles of a member might be solved by relief from an organization, usually the trade union itself. In interpersonal problems, the authorities will try to improve relationships and avoid conflict by providing an opportunity for antagonistic marital partners to reconcile or, in impossible cases, change jobs or residences.

If someone behaves badly, for example, a young orderly "goofs off" and neglects his job, the group meetings will criticize and educate or, in Chinese, "help him improve." If he fights or quarrels with someone, or does a bad job, he must confess and pledge not to do it any more. A simple confession is not enough. He has to find out why he did it the wrong way; i.e., "touch the root" of the misbehavior. If he cannot do this, the members of the group will help him to do so. Sometimes this produces resistance. Usually the group will do its best to resolve the resistance. For example, if the young person refuses to confess or realize his problem, he would be taken to visit a model worker who has the same job to see how he does the work, or he may be taken to visit a retired worker who could compare the difference in life and work before and after liberation. The young person is expected to become enlightened through the good examples of others.

In China, promiscuous sexual union is regarded as a very serious error. When people commit it, they must be criticized or, if they broke the law, tried. It is illegal to have sex with a girl under 18 or with a serviceman's wife. This misbehavior sometimes causes quite an awkward situation and makes public criticism or discussion difficult. Then a carefully selected member of the group will first meet with the person. On this occasion, the individual is asked what was done and asked to "touch the root" of the misbehavior. To help the person overcome the awkwardness of the situation, the group will appoint a woman to talk to a woman and a man to talk to a man. This reduces the risk of misunderstandings, hurt feelings, and suicide.

Sometimes if there is a conflict between a husband and wife on how to spend money and they cannot reconcile it with each other, they may quarrel and shout. The neighbors, and certainly their group, will know. The group will try to find out what the trouble is and what the essence of the conflict is. They try to help the family with this problem, and most of the time they succeed. At first the family might not like the intrusion, but eventually they are glad to have the problem resolved. People get used to this kind of help from the group in their personal lives and appreciate it.

As a matter of fact, the group meeting affords an excellent chance for human contact and plays a part in the prevention of mental illnesses, particularly depression.

According to the psychiatric epidemiological surveys recently published in China, the prevalence of manic-depressive psychosis is low, ranging from 0.03% (Shandong province) to 0.24% (Shanghai city). My personal impression is that depressive psychosis is also rare. When I was in charge of a psychiatric ward at a teaching hospital, I always presented every case of depressive psychosis to young residents as soon as the patient was admitted. From October 1979 to April 1980, I only gave one presentation. So, from statistical studies and personal clinical impressions, I conclude that depression in China is rare, much rarer than in Western countries.[5] Why it is so rare cannot yet be explained to my satisfaction, but I believe it has much to do with the active group process built into the everyday life of the people. The group process described above is a strong psychological supportive system to normal people and helps them avoid loneliness and stress. Hence, it plays a preventive role for affective disorders such as depression. The positive effects of group therapy on depressed patients have been noted by Grotjahn in his chapter on group therapy for the aging, in this book.

From statistical surveys, the incidence and prevalence of schizophrenia in China is nearly the same as in Western countries. This observation seems to support the view that schizophrenia is mainly caused by biological mistakes in the brain, although environmental factors may play important roles.

GROUP PROCESS EVALUATED SOCIOLOGICALLY

Man is a social animal who is born into a group and lives with a group. He eventually dies alone, but until the last moment he is part of a group. The first group a man faces is his family. The importance of a family to normal mental development cannot be overestimated.

In China, to date, the family is stable and strong, although there are evidences that it is not as strong as it used to be.

Since the foundation of the People's Republic, there have been a series of political campaigns to gaurantee the success of sociopolitical reformations. Most of these political campaigns have been carried out in a massive way. They actually use group process. The campaigns are, at the core, aimed toward reforming or changing minds and thoughts. Judged by the aim of the deviser of these campaigns, they were successes; people did genuinely change their minds, thoughts and politics.

In group meetings, discussions, and criticisms, one is less apt to resist and more willing to accept a new idea, especially if it seems to be accepted by the majority of the people. In the group meeting, someone was appointed to tell how he had thought previously and why he had changed his mind. In most cases, it sounded reasonable to the audience, and they changed their minds. This could explain why there have been so many group meetings in the People's Republic. At the peak of a political campaign, there might be group meetings every evening, including weekends.

To enhance the effect of a group process, something like psychodrama might be used.

I studied and worked at Hunan Medical College from 1948 to 1980 (except 1968–1978 when I was sent to the countryside to 'receive a re-education from the peasants'). Before the revolution, it was called Hunan-Yale Medical College. It was founded in 1916 by graduates of Yale University. Until 1949, it was supported, managed and guided by the Yale-in-China Association. The attitudes and values were borrowed from the United States. In 1949, the Communist revolution took place. In 1952, there was a political campaign at the college. The campaign's intention was to reform the people's political stance from pro-American to pro-Communist. The campaign lasted almost one year, and was called "Reformation of Hunan-Yale Three Units." The medical college, the hospital, and the nursing school were included in the campaign. I was studying at the college and was one of the leaders of "Hunan-Yale Drama Club." We took an active part to help promote the campaign and follow the guidelines suggested by the party leader of the college. I was the one who wrote, directed, and played a role in the production of a play entitled "Revival."[6] The story of the play took place in early spring in a big hospital at Changsha. On a Sunday night in 1952, Dr. Wu and a nurse, Ms. Zheng, were chatting in the nurse's office about a dance that was taking place in the hospital, Dr. Yang came in the office after night rounds and took part in the chat. All of them resented the conditions that developed after the liberation. One of their major and shared resentments was that patients now criticized doctors and nurses. On this occasion, a patient suffering from dysentery was to be transferred from a surgical ward to a medical ward. Dr. Yang was on duty. He refused to accept the patient because he thought that this case had no research interest and it was too late at night. But Dr. Ding, a League member, disagreed with him, holding the view that the staff had to pay attention to the patient's interests and needs before they considered their own. Dr. Yang, who was on duty, got very angry at Dr. Ding's intrusion and angrily left his job. Dr. Yang was portrayed as typical of the doctors, raised in the American-Yale spirit, who treated patients without regard for the patients' needs. These doctors and the Yale spirit had to be reformed. With this as background, a political study campaign was launched and scheduled to begin under the leadership of comrade Tien, the new Chief of Medical Serivce. Most people looked forward to it as the only way to get the hospital and its personnel reformed. Contrary to the mainstream, Dr. Yang showed great resistance to the campaign. He did as he always had and became more and more unkind to patients. He kindled even greater criticism from the patients. Dr. Yang was unhappy about his situation. He contemplated leaving the hospital. He became even more resentful when his father was arrested by the government. Dr. Yang showed hostility to society, the government, and the Communist Party. He could barely perform his duty and take part in political study. Through comrade Tien and Dr. Wang's patient explanation, persuasion, and psychological help, Dr. Yang gradually realized that he was wrong. Fortunately, his father was released, without conviction, after a thorough probe. He began to feel that the government was reasonable and not vicious. He was so deeply touched, educated, and persuaded that he made up his mind to follow the present government and its policies. Eventually, in August, he voluntarily responded to the Nation's call and went to a new post, where a doctor was urgently needed.

The essence of the play was: Bad as Dr. Yang was, he could be reformed. If he could reform, then anyone could.

To the best of my memory, the campaign and the psychodrama was successful and a new value system was established.

During the Cultural Revolution, there was a strong group process among the ordinary Chinese. In late 1966, people gathered together as they started work to learn the latest instructions from Chairman Mao. Strangely enough, this soon became a definite ritual all over the country. What they were actually doing was planning their daily work in a group. First, as directed by the leader, they read Chairman Mao's *Little Red Book*. The sentences selected applied to work needs as seen by the leader of the group. If they were trying an especially hard task, they would read such sentences as: "Be resolute, fear no sacrifice and surmount every difficulty to win victory."[2]   If they were sharply criticizing someone, they would read' "A revolution is not a dinner party, or writing an essay, or painting a picture, or doing embroidery; it cannot be so refined, so leisurely and gentle, so temperate, kind, courteous, restrained and magnanimous. A revolution is an insurrection, an act of violence by which one class overthrows another."[2] Following the reading, the leader would allocate work for everyone. Of course, most of the people had some idea what work needed to be done that day from what they had already done. But through this group process, people would show less resistance to the leader's assignment of work. Someone even might change his or her mind from a negative to a positive attitude. For example, one spring day, in my hospital, every group had to select someone to form a team to plant small trees outside the hospital. A nurse, who was inconvenienced by this, did not intend to apply for the job. Through group process in "To Learn Instructions from Chairman Mao" in the morning, she changed her mind when she was asked if she would like to take the job. Her response surprised her. I asked why she had changed her mind and she said "Everyone tries to learn from Zhang Side, why should I be an exception?"

On september 9, 1976, Chairman Mao died. This was an occasion for people to pay their last respects and express their loyalty to the late Chairman. The authorities provided a good opportunity for people to do so. It was a very emotional group process. In the Hall of the County Government of Longshan, *where I had lived and worked during the ten years of the Cultural Revolution,* they set up a mourning hall for Chairman Mao. This provided an opportunity for people to offer one another condolences. The hall was well decorated and had a solemn and respectful atmosphere. There was a large portrait of the late

Chairman with black cloth surrounding it. There were many wreaths and similar objects to set the tone. As chance would have it, before everyone went to the hall to offer condolences, I passed by with two female students of mine and dropped in to take a look. We all felt that the hall was well decorated. That was all. There was not much emotion or affect. The next day, as arranged by the authorities, I led the students to the ceremony in the mourning hall. We lined up in the hall. There was funeral music. The atmosphere was so sad that almost everyone was touched to tears, including the two girls I had been with the day before. The father of one of the girls used to work in a hospital in town and was sent to the countryside during the Cultural Revolution, just as I had been. I knew that all of her family was very unhappy about this situation and resented the government and even the Chairman personally. I did not think that she would cry over his death, but she did cry in the mourning hall.

Later when I chatted with her and pointed out that I had noticed whe had been touched and had cried in the hall, she said: "I was just crying for my grandmother who died last month. The atmosphere reminded me or her death." Consciously, she would not have cried for Chairman Mao's death and she did not cry when she was there accompanied by me and the other student the day before. But in a group she cried for the death of a man she disliked. Consciously, she denied the real cause and made a pretext for doing so.

This story shows the powerful impact of group procession psychology and its potential for good and ill. It may offer us our best hope and our greatest danger.

REFERENCES

1. Rosenbaum, M. and Berger, M. M. (Eds.). *Group Psychotherapy and Group Function,* 2nd Ed. New York: Basic Books (1975).
2. Mao Zedong. *Quotations from Chairman Mao Zedong.* Beijing: Foreign Languages Press (1971).
3. Report: mental patients. *Beijing Review* 25:24 (1980).
4. Special feature: countryside; barefoot doctors now "wear shoes." *Beijing Review* 25:25 (1980).
5. Zhong-yi Liu. Psychiatric epidemiological studies in China today. Lecture delivered at Grand Rounds, Veterans Administration Medical Center. Long Beach, Calif. (July 18, 1980).
6. Wei-lian Lan, Zhong-yi Liu, and Hua-yu Kong. "Revival" (four-act play). Hunan: Hunan-Yale Drama Club (1952).

21

The Group Therapist As A Person

Martin Grotjahn, M.D.

The personality of the therapist is of greater importance in group therapy than in almost any other modality of psychotherapy. This is due to the fact that group therapy is a relationship therapy. A group therapist does well when he gives full credit to the group at times when the therapeutic process proceeds well, and takes full blame when the process slows down or stops altogether.

Any therapist should know himself well, but the group therapist must not only know himself but also use himself as his most reliable and effective tool of treatment.

The best group therapists are people of great spontaneity who are frank, free, and honest in their relationship to people and to themselves. The group therapist does not need to be superior to his patients in intelligence or knowledge, but in the urge to understand nobody should be superior to him. He must be a master of honest communication. This mastery must not only extend to consciousness but must penetrate into parts of the unconscious.

This honesty demands that whatever he says or feels must be truly felt and cannot be pretended. He may be a good performer—which implies he makes whatever he does visible to the group—but he should not act like an actor, meaning he should not pretend "as if."

The group therapist should have confidence in his group, because only then will the group have confidence in him. He should be—or he should be on the way to becoming—"a man for all seasons." This means that he must know how it feels to be alive. He must have known

275

fear and anxiety, mastery and dependency. Most of all, he must not be afraid to love, and does not need to be a stranger to hate. He must have known one woman in love and through her he may know them all.

He should consider himself as his own favorite patient, and as a person who has to learn as long as he lives. He should learn how to treat himself as his favorite patient—and how to treat his patient as if he were himself.[1]

He does not really need to be "a knower of men," meaning that he does not need to know men in the practical sense of this word—because that would imply that he is always aware of the baseness of man. It helps to be a good therapist when he can hold on to a certain faith in the essential good will of all men.

The true psychologist must be driven by the wish to understand, and in that way he is a scientist. At the same time he must be able to stand the tension of not understanding his patients. As Theodor Reik said, it is better not to understand than to misunderstand.

The therapist ought to have a central, firm, constant ego identity,[2] which he should combine with a "peripheral looseness" in the form of an open mind. He must accept a certain degree of motherliness in himself. He must be tolerant and able to proceed in the face of contradiction, as he must be able, for instance, to be patient and impatient, loving and fighting at the same time, and toward the same person.

The therapist must also know the difference between an unconscious need (to which he should respond) and a conscious wish (which he ought to recognize but not to fulfill).

The group therapist must not be afraid to show his own true self to the group. However, he should reveal this only when it is in the interest of the group process. Under no circumstances should he become a patient in his own group, which means a burden and a responsibility to the group. This would make a free communication and interaction between therapist and group impossible. A parent is allowed to appeal for understanding of himself in his family and the family may see the weakness or the doubts and respect the parent's strength to proceed in spite of these difficulties. He must not be dependent to the degree to which the sick members of the group or the family depend on him.

To have a sense of humor is advantageous for the group therapist. No therapist can remain a blank screen within his group. He should not pretend to be, or even try to remain, in reserve. At the same time the therapist has to be somewhat on guard against his ready wit and his fondness for the wisecrack or sharply pointed and often painfully penetrating remarks. He has to combine therapeutic carefulness with communicative freedom and spontaneity.

The therapist's office is not a wailing wall; neither is therapy a laughing matter. Most therapists do not cry with their patients, but all of them laugh—and remain aware that the telling of jokes and a hilarious atmosphere may easily grow into a resistance that prohibits true communication, which is the essence of the group process.

The therapist is allowed to make mistakes—but when he realizes that he has committed a mistake he must not try to hide it, and must learn from it with the group.

THE GROUP THERAPIST IN TRAINING AND AS A PATIENT

Training is not limited in time. A therapist should consider himself a student of human motivation who will never finish studying. Formal training is the beginning: It should open the doors wider so that the therapist can continue to learn from experience, from reading, from his own sickness, his marriage, his family life, and his patients.

Many therapists still believe that psychoanalytic training or at least the training analysis should be a part of the group therapist's training. The therapist, however, should never forget that psychoanalysis offers insight; group therapy offers therapy to the therapist. In psychoanalysis, the therapist is an only child; in group therapy, be becomes a member of a family and has a chance to analyze his family romance, which is essential for the group therapist.

As a rule, a therapist is a poor patient—and that is nothing to be proud of. The problem of the therapist is how to become a patient—how to accept his patienthood.[3] The physician in medical treatment and the therapist in training have each to learn how to split themselves into two parts. One part remains a therapist and joins his colleagues as co-therapist; the other part becomes a patient in therapy (or training). This splitting makes the working alliance in training different and difficult.

The analytic group experience is of equal importance to the analyst and the group therapist. Without analysis of the peer transference relationship, no therapist fits well into the therapeutic community, which includes his colleagues and his patients.

There is a second, important feature in the analytic experience for any therapist, whether he specializes in group analysis or any other form of treatment. Standard analysis leaves a great part of negative transference neurosis unanalyzed. Most experienced training analysts agree on this point. The analytic group experience is the best available situation in which this defect of psychoanalytic training can be corrected.

Psychotherapists in training frequently use intellectualization as a form of resistance. An often-heard phrase in a didactic group is: "We all talk like a bunch of smart professionals." This is insight and resistance at the same time.

The avoidance of intellectualization, after it has been repeatedly called by that name, may lead to a new form of resistance: All insights are resolutely rejected because they may sound too intellectual to a board of experts. There are sometimes episodes of resistance in a group of therapists where every interpretation is labeled as "rationalization" and only emotions are considered therapeutically valid. The therapist in charge has to deal with this through interpretations of the resistance.

THE THERAPIST'S WIFE

I used to separate couples and place the partners in different groups, since I assumed it would be advisable for them to develop the courage for free communication with others before I let them try it on each other. But I soon came to agree with David Morgan,[4] who had treated therapists and their spouses simultaneously and concomitantly, that a great deal of a therapist's future depends on his attitude toward his spouse and children. The analyst should never be a therapist in his own family; there he should act and react, not analyze or treat. It is more meaningful for therapists to gain insight into their "Mother Superior complexes" (Morgan) while working with their spouses in the same group than when working alone.

Group therapy seems especially suited to satisfy the specific needs of therapists and their spouses because it offers them an extended family. The spouses of therapists have to learn that nobody can be a therapist in his own family, even if he is considered an expert and "The Professor" by his wife and his community. In the extended family of the group, a learning experience is offered to him—how to be helpful and understanding without abusing the tools of his trade.

The therapist's fateful need to be "Mother Superior" can be best analyzed in a couples group. This need is frequently neglected in individual analyses, since it is often conflict-free—it belongs to the attitude of the healer. Many male analysts, and perhaps all male physicians, have an unconscious need to show their wives that women are bad mothers and that doctors would be much better mothers if given a free hand. The male doctor's Mother Superior complex leads him to unfair competition at home, causing heartbreaking trouble and frequently leading to a sadomasochistic, malignant acting out, which can be aggravated by quick and unannounced role reversals. Frequently, the children pay the price for their parents' competitiveness.

Any woman so foolish as to marry a therapist, assuming that he may be an ideal husband, must gain insight into her husband's tendency not to project his own femininity onto her but to keep it jealously embedded in his own person. In this respect, the therapist strays specifically from the normal course of heterosexual development. The therapist's wife has to learn how to invite her husband to trust her with his femininity and to love it not exclusively in himself but also in her. The other wives of therapists in the group of therapists and spouses often restore a woman's confidence in her femininity, which has been endangered by her therapist-husband's competitiveness in mothering the children. As a therapist, he may use his professional skill to win his fight, never being aware of what he is doing.

One of the many things the therapist's wife has to learn in the beginning of her marriage is that her husband, supposedly an expert in the art of loving understanding of people, may not be a model of loving care at home. Often enough he leaves his understanding at the office and acts out at home. The love of wives must stand that disappointment.

A therapist works as a rule in utter isolation and therefore may lose the benefits of feedback from his colleagues. This line of communication can be reestablished in group work. With increased freedom, the therapist's dialogue with his group, his family, and, finally, with his patients becomes less defensive, freer, deeper, and more spontaneous and fulfilling. He even may learn how to overcome his isolation and how to be more trusting, open, and, ultimately, more loving.

THE THERAPIST'S MENTAL HEALTH

The therapist does not need to be a paragon of mental health. He can proceed efficiently with all kinds of psychosomatic symptoms, such as high blood pressure, migraines, or even a gastric ulcer. It is preferable for a therapist to overcome his symptoms, and he sometimes does. The analysis and correction of conflict-free areas takes time, and the therapist may work well before his own therapy is completed. As a matter of fact, the therapist should remain his own favorite patient for the rest of his life.

A therapist is mature when he has learned how to deal with the inner and outer reality of himself and his patients. He also must learn how to deal with his ever-present guilt of not being "good enough." One has to accept—reluctantly—one's limitations.

REFERENCES

1. Reik, T. *Listening With the Third Ear.* New York: Farrar, Straus and Giroux 1948.
2. Kohut, H. The evaluation of applicants for psychoanalytic training. *Int. J. Psychoanal.* **49**:548 1968.
3. Krikson, E. H. *Childhood and Society.* New York: W.W. Norton 1950.
4. Morgan, D. Psychoanalytic group psychotherapy for therapists and their wives. *Int. J. Group Psychother.* **21**:107 1971.

Index

Index